W9-ADR-864

PRAISE FOR "ON THE BALL"

"Don't be fooled by the fun and games approach. This book takes its examples from the sports world—from NASCAR to the Dallas Cowboys—but it's serious business. David Carter and Darren Rovell use sports to teach some important lessons about branding, crisis management and a host of other everyday business issues."

Rick Alm
sports business reporter
Dallas Morning News

"Carter and Rovell have written a manual for teaching people how things have been and could be done in the sports business which is clearly transferable to the private sector. Nothing is better from which to learn than actual, real-time experiences and the authors have captured them perfectly. The Leadership chapter should be mandatory in all business schools."

Tony Attanasio
sports agent, Ichiro Suzuki

"As entertaining as it is informational. True tales of infamous sports personalities and the way they do business. Puts the spotlight on many fascinating and unbelievable inside sports stories that affect the way we all do business today. Enjoyable reading."

Peter J. Barnett
Producer, HBO's *ArliSS,*
The Art of the Sports SuperAgent

"Carter and Rovell deliver the goods! In a concise, entertaining and informative manner, *On the Ball* melds the multibillion dollar sports industry into lessons that everyone can benefit from."

Howard Bloom
Publisher,
SportsBusinessNews.com

"David Carter and Darren Rovell have combined to show how the business world really works through the prism of something we all love: sports. The sports business provides us with all the examples we need to fully comprehend business done well and business done poorly. David and Darren have written a compelling and exciting book."

Fred Claire
former Executive Vice-President
and GM of the Los Angeles Dodgers

"Business people looking for enterprise tips from the world of sports will find a lot to like in *On the Ball*. The authors have assembled a treasure chest of eye-opening anecdotes, and presented them clearly and forcefully. Highly recommended."

John Dempsey
TV sports reporter,
Variety

"*On the Ball* provides those aspiring for career success with noteworthy case studies from the sports industry that will no doubt help them to achieve their career goals and aspirations. A must read for all those who turn first to the sports pages, but understand that their success will be determined in the business field, not on the athletic field."

Darryl Dunn
General Manager,
The Rose Bowl

"Don't miss out on reading this one! A highly successful sports marketer and one of the best sports business investigative reporters around present a lively collection of object lessons for all interested in the sports business. For those watching the sports business from the periphery or for those involved in the day-to-day business, Carter and Rovell pull no punches and lay out invaluable lessons for all. For my money, their presentation of Jerry Jones' turnaround of the Dallas Cowboys alone is worth the price of admission."

Rodney Fort
Professor of Economics,
Washington State University
author of *Sports Economics*

"As Carter and Rovell so skillfully convey, continual learning is an important part of the essence of leadership. There is much to be learned from the complex business of sports that is applicable to all businesses. *On the Ball* is an interesting and well-written account of many of these lessons."

Bob Graziano
President & COO,
Los Angeles Dodgers

"Carter and Rovell have successfully and creatively used the sports world to provide invaluable lessons about the trials and tribulations associated with running businesses of all sizes. *On the Ball* is a compelling playbook for businesspeople."

Pat Haden
former USC quarterback
and 1975 Rose Bowl co-MVP,
Partner,
Riordan, Lewis & Haden

"If you read the sports and business pages with equal passion, *On the Ball* is definitely for you. You'll not only have a great time reading this book but will actually learn about key business practices and principles along the way."

Ted Leonsis, majority owner,
Washington Capitals
minority owner, Washington Wizards
and MCI Center
Vice Chairman, AOL

"*On the Ball* takes you where you want to go—behind the scenes, where the sports reporter does not take you, to learn the best moves off the field, in the broadcast booth, and in the front office. A great book both for the sports fan and for the businessman looking for lessons from true sports insiders."

Mark Levinstein
Partner, Williams & Connolly LLP
Adjunct Professor of Law,
Georgetown University Law Center
and Acting Executive Director,
U.S. National Soccer Team
Players Association

"From managing the George O'Leary/ Notre Dame résumé flap, to placing a smiling Barry Bonds in TV commercials, the high-profile challenges and success in sports invoke the same business principles as any thriving company. Carter and Rovell capture this with imagination, in an insightful treatment any executive will find essential."

Bob Ley
Host, ESPN's *Outside the Lines*

"David Carter and Darren Rovell have taken a unique approach—showing how savvy business leaders can learn from the successes and failures in the sports industry. *On the Ball* provides specific ideas and strategies for today's sophisticated and enlightened business executive."

Abraham Madkour
Editor-in-Chief,
The Sports Business Daily

"I might have paid $3 million for Mark McGwire's 70th home run ball, but I still know a value when I see one. If you want to learn about business without being bored to death, you're not going to find many books more entertaining and informative than *On the Ball*."

Todd McFarlane, Spawn creator
owner of McFarlane Toys
and part owner of Edmonton Oilers

"In *On the Ball*, David Carter and Darren Rovell have devised a novel way to impart important management lessons—wrap them into a tome rich with anecdotes that span the world of sports. The result is a touchdown of a business book."

Ciro Scotti
Senior Editor, *BusinessWeek*

"*On the Ball* takes a unique look at sports and recognizes it for what it has become: A complex and dynamic business and not just fun and games. It is an essential read for those who want a successful career in business."

Jeff Shell, CEO,
Gemstar-TV Guide International

"*On the Ball* is just that. The perfect combination for the business person who is also a sports fan. A side benefit of reading about the business lessons that come from sports business leaders is the opportunity to read a rich sports business history. As the authors make clear, the lessons from sports business leaders transcend the field of play."

Kenneth L. Shropshire
Professor and Chairman of Legal
Studies Department,
Wharton School,
University of Pennsylvania
co-author of *The Business of
Sports Agents*

"You hear people use sports analogies all the time, but *On the Ball* isn't about that. This is an idea book on how to run a business better. Sure, the teachers may be guys like Jerry Jones or Jerry Colangelo, but they aren't talking about tackling or jump shots, they're talking about different strategies that propelled their businesses."

Jon Spoelstra
author, *Marketing Outrageously*,
a *Wall Street Journal* best-seller

"The sports marketing industry has been screaming for someone to chronicle how this young industry has made the transition from pure entertainment to business. David Carter and Darren Rovell have done this in great detail but in a very readable and usable format great for any business executive who wants to advance his or her career—a must read!"

Bob Williams, President,
Burns Sports & Celebrity Services

On the Ball

ISBN 0-13-100963-X

9 780131 009639

In an increasingly competitive world, it is quality
of thinking that gives an edge—an idea that opens new
doors, a technique that solves a problem, or an insight
that simply helps make sense of it all.

We work with leading authors in the various arenas
of business and finance to bring cutting-edge thinking
and best learning practice to a global market.

It is our goal to create world-class print publications
and electronic products that give readers
knowledge and understanding which can then be
applied, whether studying or at work.

To find out more about our business
products, you can visit us at www.ft-ph.com

On the Ball

What You Can Learn About Business from America's Sports Leaders

David Carter
Darren Rovell

FT Prentice Hall

FINANCIAL TIMES

An Imprint of PEARSON EDUCATION
Upper Saddle River, NJ • New York • London • San Francisco • Toronto • Sydney
Tokyo • Singapore • Hong Kong • Cape Town • Madrid
Paris • Milan • Munich • Amsterdam

www.ft-ph.com

Library of Congress Cataloging-in-Publication Data

A catalog record for this book can be obtained from
the Library of Congress.

Editorial/production supervision: *Nick Radhuber*
Executive editor: *Tim Moore*
Editorial assistant: *Rick Winkler*
Marketing manager: *Alexis R. Heydt-Long*
Manufacturing buyer: *Maura Zaldivar*
Cover design director: *Jerry Votta*
Cover design: *Nina Scuderi*
Art director: *Gail Cocker-Bogusz*
Interior design: *Meg Van Arsdale*

 © 2003 Pearson Education, Inc.
Publishing as Financial Times Prentice Hall
Upper Saddle River, New Jersey 07458

Financial Times Prentice Hall books are widely used by corporations and
government agencies for training, marketing, and resale.

For information regarding corporate and government bulk discounts
please contact: Corporate and Government Sales (800) 382-3419 or
corpsales@pearsontechgroup.com

Company and product names mentioned herein are the trademarks
or registered trademarks of their respective owners.

All rights reserved. No part of this book may be reproduced, in any form or by any
means, without permission in writing from the publisher.

Printed in the United States of America

10   9   8   7   6   5   4   3   2   1

ISBN 0-13-100963-X

Pearson Education LTD.
Pearson Education Australia PTY, Limited
Pearson Education Singapore, Pte. Ltd.
Pearson Education North Asia Ltd.
Pearson Education Canada, Ltd.
Pearson Educación de Mexico, S.A. de C.V.
Pearson Education—Japan
Pearson Education Malaysia, Pte. Ltd.

To Paige, whose infectious smile and endearing personality provided all the motivation (and, on occasion, insight) necessary to complete this book.

–David M. Carter

To Mom, Dad, and Brian, for letting me immerse myself in sports and business, but always reminding me that family comes first.

–Darren Rovell

Financial Times Prentice Hall Books

For more information, please go to www.ft-ph.com

CONTENTS

CHAPTER 10   REPOSITIONING A BUSINESS 231

CHAPTER 11   LEADERSHIP V8.1.PH. FINAL 259

ACKNOWLEDGMENTS

Naturally, dozens of people contributed their valuable time and resources to ensure that our rough literary concept became a reality. While we will no doubt fail to recognize everyone that assisted along the way, the following (extremely patient) individuals deserve our deepest thanks.

A sincere debt of gratitude goes out to those industry pros who provided us with the endorsements and testimonials that enabled us to piggyback on their extraordinary industry success. We truly appreciate the unwavering willingness of the following who supported our work: Rick Alm, Tony Attanasio, Peter J. Barnett, Howard Bloom, Fred Claire, John Dempsey, Darryl Dunn, Rod Fort, Bob Graziano, Pat Haden, Ted Leonsis, Mark Levinstein, Bob Ley, Abraham Madkour, Todd McFarlane, Ciro Scotti, Jeff Shell, Kenneth L. Shropshire, Jon Spoelstra, and Bob Williams.

In addition to the sports business industry leaders who endorsed this book, we would like to recognize the noteworthy contributions from those at Financial Times Prentice Hall. We begin with Stephen H. Soucy, whose serendipitous email resulted in our working with the great professionals at FTPH, particularly our acquisitions editor, the insufferable Yankee fan, Tim Moore, whose stewardship was not only welcomed, but also required at virtually every turn. Others from FTPH who were crucial to the completion of this book were content editor Russ Hall, whose 24/7 commitment to this project was apparent from the hundreds (if not more) of emails sent out at all hours of the day and night, as well as Alan Bower, Laura Bulcher, Laura Burgess, Bryan Gambrel, Anthony Gemmellaro, Kate Hargett, Teresa Horton, Allyson Kloss, John Pierce, Nicholas Radhuber, and Gardi Wilks.

Those who reviewed the manuscript, namely Allen Sanderson, Fred Claire, and Louis Columbus, provided the invaluable insight required to improve it and have earned our profound respect along the way.

Our student researchers and graduate assistants Alexander Allper, Bernard Ford, and Charles Green were vitally important contributors, as were those that helped frame our initial concept, especially Howard Steinberg, Greg Dinkin, and Frank Scatoni.

Finally, there are a handful of family, friends, and associates that allowed us to carve out the time and energy necessary to complete *On the Ball*, particularly:

From Carter...

My wife Vickie, who not only didn't mind the early morning hours—even on weekends—but grew to encourage them. She continues to provide the support necessary for me to accomplish any and all things—whether personal or professional.

From Rovell...

The ESPN.com bosses John Skipper, John Marvel, and Neal Scarbrough for realizing how important this project was to my career and allowing me to follow through with it. And to Mike Lowe, Mark Gordon, and Lauren Lipson for proving that youth should never serve as an excuse to achieving excellence.

Finally, to Jack Gordon, a great sports fan who was an even better grandfather.

Introduction:
On Deck

Legendary sportscaster Howard Cosell referred to sports as "the sandbox of life." An escape from the demands and frustrations of everyday activities, sports continue to serve as a refuge for millions of fans wanting a break from their daily grinds. A walk-off home run, a half-court buzzer-beater, or a successful Hail Mary touchdown pass as time expires all make us momentarily forget tomorrow's all-day sales meeting or time-wasting video conference call with headquarters.

This "refuge" has become a massive industry all its own, one estimated to generate spending approaching $200 billion annually. The sports business not only continues to expand, but it seems to do so against an increasingly intriguing backdrop, occasionally highlighted by seemingly unorthodox and questionable decision making from many of the industry's top executives.

The sports business has become an extremely involved industry that now includes the same elements and applies the same business principles seen throughout the rest of big business. As it grows, the industry provides compelling examples of business building, strategic marketing, brand management, customer service, and leadership, among other business tenets. There is much to be learned about everyday business from the way sports handles its own operations and there is also a lot of fun to be had in the process.

In the following pages, *On the Ball: What You Can Learn about Business from America's Sports Leaders* delves deeply into the sports business, examining traditional business practices as they have been applied in the sports industry. *On the Ball* provides relevant and important examples that readers can immediately apply to their own business environment. Along the way, *On the Ball* also answers the following questions:

What can I learn from...

- How sports franchises and leagues, including National Association for Stock Car Auto Racing (NASCAR), have established and built their businesses?

- The major corporations that sponsor sports, such as Master-Card, and how they effectively and efficiently reach customers?

- The way sports teams and leagues, especially those throughout Minor League Baseball, handle customer service?

- The manner in which athletes like Tiger Woods and Andre Agassi have developed, extended, and in some cases harmed, their own personal brands?

- How professional sports leagues, such as the National Hockey League (NHL) and Major League Baseball (MLB), have handled employee relations?

- How and why major sports organizations, including the New York Yankees, form strategic alliances?

- How sports power brokers, such as National Football League (NFL) Commissioner Paul Tagliabue, handle crises?

- Sports marketing-minded corporations, including Nike, that have successfully penetrated new markets?

- Examining the way sports leagues, such as the National Basketball Association (NBA), have established themselves as brands?

- The strategies employed by sports executives, like Dallas Cowboys owner Jerry Jones, to turn their businesses around?

- Sports business industry executives, including Branch Rickey and the Maloof brothers, about leadership styles and traits?

On the Ball chronicles many of the sports industry's largest developments and provides specific lessons that can be learned from the actions and, in some cases, inaction, of industry leaders. *On the Ball* provides businesspeople with an inside look at how the sports business game is played and, in the process, unveils business tactics and strategies that apply to companies large and small, public and private.

These questions, along with industry developments and outrageous anecdotes, are discussed throughout the book and addressed in the following chapters.

CHAPTER 1: BUILDING A BUSINESS

This chapter reviews how to build a business from scratch and includes, among other examples, how the France family has taken NASCAR from a regional sport with a "redneck" reputation to one of America's most prominent sports leagues. Its relatively recent and rapid growth, which has resulted in a multibillion-dollar broadcast TV contract, has not been without its challenges.

Chapter 1 examines the issues and growing pains experienced by entrepreneurs as they navigate their business's life cycle while protecting the organization's fledgling brand name at every turn. This chapter also includes a discussion of leadership, overcoming shareholder concerns, litigation, and personnel and management issues.

CHAPTER 2: REACHING CUSTOMERS

Chapter 2 looks at how companies, including MasterCard, Coca-Cola, and Miller Brewing, use sports to reach intended target markets. It contains a framework for how best to segment markets and conduct target marketing, and incorporates a discussion of MLB, the Olympics, and soccer's World Cup.

This chapter answers the following questions: How do companies know they're reaching the intended audiences? How does the company measure the return on investment related to marketing initiatives?

CHAPTER 3: CUSTOMER SERVICE

This chapter considers the increasingly important role of customer service. By reviewing the eight principles of customer service, it examines how small businesses have mastered—and botched—the art of customer service.

Minor League Baseball, as well as amateur sports leagues, has thrived because it has not lost touch with families and the affordable, nostalgic entertainment they seek. With a focus and dedication to making their organizations important community assets, hands-on local team owners and universities have customized the game-day experience. Paying keen attention to the likes and dislikes of fans has allowed amateur athletics to become among sports' most appreciated and sought after properties.

Not surprisingly, this commitment to customer service easily translates to other businesses, providing businesspeople with the insight necessary to provide great customer service.

CHAPTER 4: PERSONAL BRANDING

Chapter 4 considers issues of how athletes, including Lance Armstrong, Barry Bonds, and Anna Kournikova, like other sports properties, seek to make money from their brands. Today, corporations and charities have become risk averse when selecting sports personalities to endorse or promote products and services. Some corporations now purchase image insurance to protect against the foibles of the modern-day athlete.

This chapter discusses what it takes to profit from a personal brand whether you are an athlete or a corporate executive. It includes the decision-making process of companies considering the use of athletes and focuses on such criteria as the ability to convey a message, charisma, and believability, the same issues that contribute to success in the traditional workplace.

CHAPTER 5: EMPLOYEE RELATIONS

This chapter analyzes employee relations in sports and reveals what other companies can learn from these relationships. Most major sports leagues and properties have created significant ill will by failing to adequately, and in a timely fashion, determine how best to divvy up the billions of dollars flowing into their industry.

It examines how labor strife has tarnished sports marketing and branding initiatives and discusses what lessons have been learned by big-time sports as they continue to alienate fan bases and jeopardize their relationships with the next generation of customers. Specifically, what measures have they taken to build a reservoir of goodwill? How do these experiences translate to other businesses and industries?

CHAPTER 6: BUILDING ALLIANCES

Chapter 6 reveals the tenets required to establish profitable strategic alliances. Included is a discussion of the elements needed to build both horizontal and vertical alliances.

Incorporated in this chapter are examples of NBC's strategic alliance with the ill-fated XFL, as well as Nike Golf's alliance with Bridgestone.

As *On the Ball* chronicles, such alliances provide great insight to any organization that is considering entering into a strategic alliance.

CHAPTER 7: CRISIS MANAGEMENT

This chapter analyzes the decision-making processes of those involved in high-profile sports crises, specifically the fallout from the Salt Lake City Olympics bribery scandal, the handling of the death of NASCAR icon Dale Earnhardt, and the sports world's reaction to the terrorist attacks of September 11, 2001.

From natural disasters like the earthquake that rocked the 1989 World Series to Magic Johnson's 1992 HIV disclosure, sports has always had to rapidly—and in a highly public fashion—respond to issues threatening its viability and cash flow. The 10 steps to handling a business crisis frame this chapter's discussion.

CHAPTER 8: PENETRATING NEW MARKETS

Chapter 8 reveals the process by which organizations penetrate new markets, whether they are international or merely a neighboring town or county. Specifically addressed in this chapter are issues dealing with cultural and political nuances, as well as distribution and marketing challenges.

An examination of how Nike has continually tapped into America's consciousness by attaching its brand to world-class athletes that have dynamic personalities and the talent to match is undertaken. Athletes such as Bo Jackson and Michael Jordan have been among Nike's biggest stars, allowing Nike the foot in the door necessary to enter and successfully compete in foreign markets. Today, Nike is utilizing its extensive endorsement deal with Tiger Woods to not only increase revenue from an expanding golf market, but also to leverage Woods' global appeal to enhance the company's brand.

This chapter uncovers what initiatives companies must undertake if they hope to penetrate and eventually dominate new markets.

CHAPTER 9: BUILDING A BRAND

This chapter examines how organizations position themselves as global brands. In doing so, it highlights the six stages of branding and reveals how sports entities, such as the NBA, have successfully branded themselves both at home and abroad by integrating their assets. The NBA, as an example, has masterfully extended its brand by controlling all aspects of its content, from what happens on and around the court on game days to the customization of its international marketing efforts.

Chapter 9 examines the seamless cross-promotion and branding opportunities required if a company is to emerge as a stellar, well-regarded brand.

CHAPTER 10: TURNING AROUND A STRUGGLING BUSINESS

Chapter 10 analyzes the steps necessary to resurrect a struggling business and how best to reposition one in the eyes of disenfranchised customers. This chapter takes into account the important role played by senior management and marketing executives as they navigate tough times.

Because Dallas Cowboys owner Jerry Jones took over a 1–15 team (a dormant brand) and turned it into one of sport's top brands—one worth more than $700 million—this chapter examines, among other examples, how Jones has increased his franchise's value by leveraging his clout and maverick business style to excel at sports marketing.

Taking a page or two out of Jones' playbook provides guidance to those organizations that face the daunting task of turning their business around. It also demonstrates why turning a business around once isn't enough to stay on top.

CHAPTER 11: LEADERSHIP

The final chapter provides readers with the important lessons to be taken away from the book, and does so by blending them with an examination of 10 important leadership attributes. How sports business leaders have leveraged their passion, integrity, and intuition, among other traits, to lead their organizations is chronicled.

The role leadership plays in establishing and managing personal and corporate brands, addressing strategic developments both at home and abroad, dealing with crises, and rebuilding faltering businesses are all examined.

It must be noted that the intent of *On the Ball* is to provide a fresh perspective to readers with key elements of important business tenets and to explore these tenets using representative, rather than exhaustive, examples along the way.

1 BUILDING A BUSINESS

The Point: The sports world, like much of the mainstream business world, has its stories of organizations and teams that seem destined for success, but fail, as well as those that seem to fail, and in fact succeed. Because the sports world has provided both sound and unreasonable approaches to business, it provides useful insight that should be considered by businesses of all sizes, especially when they are being established and built.

What business executive hasn't gotten the nudge from a marketing manager just before giving an important presentation and leaned close to hear a whispered, "Try not to use any sports metaphors." Yet, sports provides a sound metaphors not only for life, but for business as well. Given the sporting world's ubiquitous nature throughout our culture, it is ideally suited to be used as a backdrop against which important business lessons can be enjoyably learned.

You might differentiate your experience as a sports fan from your career and your responsibilities as a decision maker, but by understanding precisely how and why sports and business have converged, you can improve your business acumen and become an even more valuable executive. In short, there is much to be learned—and applied—from understanding the structure of the sports business. Sports business industry leaders are continuously adapting to uncertainty, not only producing change, but also shaping the future of this lucrative and rapidly growing industry. Along the way, they consistently demonstrate just how varied the results can be when adhering to—or dismissing—important business tenets.

Like most business executives, sports industry leaders wrestle with how best to segment domestic markets and penetrate foreign ones. Can they just slap their logo on the team's jersey and get the entire country to believe in their brand?

They struggle to establish mutually beneficial strategic alliances that won't compromise their brands or hinder their ability to grow. Is this cable TV network merely the highest bidder for the team's broadcast rights or is it the highest bidder than can and will convey the quality of the team on the field?

These leaders worry about financial and human resource management. How many free agents can a team really bid for without leveraging the team's financial future?

They obsess over customer service and crisis management in an effort to stave off erosion in market share. If we run out of beer, how will our fans react?

Sports industry leaders also concern themselves with employee relations and improving their own corporate standing. Are sports agents happy at a particular sports management firm or are they likely to defect and start up their own agency as soon as they make a name for themselves?

They make it their business to understand government relations and regulatory issues. How much does the organization have to know about the country to employ a workforce to make its baseballs?

In essence, the sports industry mirrors most others and faces similar trials and tribulations, but with a few insightful and different approaches. As the sports business industry continues to evolve, it often does so strangely, drawing the attention of fans and business people alike.

DON'T TRY THIS AT HOME

Before reading about how to build successful sports business models, consider a couple of examples that, although they hardly hold up as sound models for business, are worth mentioning.

Long before we were intrigued by the NFL and MLB—and the antics of successful yet controversial team owners like the Oakland

Raiders' Al Davis and the New York Yankees' George Steinbrenner—there were the Silna brothers.

Ozzie and Dan Silna, arguably among the shrewdest and most opportune owners in the history of big-time sports, purchased the Carolina Cougars of the American Basketball Association (ABA) for $1.5 million in 1973. When the brothers bought the team, which they ultimately held for only three years, they surmised the league had a shaky future and a merger with the National Basketball Association (NBA) was, if not imminent, at least likely.

Hoping to be one of the teams that would successfully merge into the NBA, the Silnas moved their team to the largest city they could find that lacked a major sports team—St. Louis. The Silnas invested big bucks in players like Moses Malone, Marvin Barnes, Maurice Lucas, and Fly Williams. However, the team only averaged about 3,800 fans per game in its final year, after, according to Ozzie Silna, a promise by the St. Louis Blues owner to secure 5,000 season ticket holders never came to fruition.

When the NBA Board of Governors met in 1976 to broker the ABA–NBA merger, they only wanted four of the six ABA teams—the Denver Nuggets, Indiana Pacers, New Jersey Nets, the San Antonio Spurs. The NBA agreed to buy out the remaining two franchises. The Kentucky Colonels owner John Y. Brown, accepted a $3 million settlement. The Silnas, on the other hand, accepted far less—$2.2 million. However, the brothers also had the NBA agree that they would receive 1/7 of the national television revenue from each of the four accepted teams, *in perpetuity*.

At the time, it wasn't necessarily easy money. The NBA Finals were worth so little during the early 1970s that they were shown on tape delay in the wee hours of the morning. The Silnas had no idea that their share would grow to be as valuable as it is today.

It turned out to be one of the most brilliant—if not serendipitous—moves in sports business history. Thanks to the explosion of television rights, and the fact that they have not yet been bought out despite numerous offers, the Silnas have collected approximately $100 million over the past 25 years.

The Silnas made an estimated $8 million throughout the 1980s and, as broadcast rights fees swelled, so too did their share. They received checks annually totaling approximately $4.6 million from 1990 through 1994. The checks increased to $5.6 million per year until 1998. And the Silnas' portion of the NBA's recently expired four-year, $2.64 billion contract with NBC and Turner netted them $13.5 million annually.[1]

Thanks to the NBA's current six-year, $4.6 billion TV deal with ABC/ESPN and AOL Time Warner's Turner Network, which runs through the 2007–2008 season, the Silnas could receive more than $20 million a year from the four teams combined. Although the affected teams have spent more than $250,000 trying to find a way out of the deal, the brothers have no inclination to accept an offer.

Just because the Silnas weren't aware of the future impact of TV on the NBA, that doesn't discredit their business decision. Plenty of high-powered executive decision makers have found themselves in similar positions. Successful executives don't allow themselves to easily take these types of risks frequently, but when they are presented with an opportunity, they possess the vision necessary to accurately gauge the risks and potential returns.

If that example doesn't leave you shaking your head about the sports industry's decision-making ability, try this one.

In 1995, the city of San Diego, to ensure that the NFL's Chargers would remain in the city, agreed to an amazing deal that would eventually include $78 million in stadium renovations (at then-named Jack Murphy Stadium, now known as Qualcomm Stadium). Along with the 14,000 additional seats, new scoreboards, and additional luxury boxes, the city council agreed to guarantee that from 1997 through 2006, if the Chargers didn't sell a minimum of 60,000 tickets per game, it would cover any shortfall.

If attendance were healthy, the city would stand to make a nice profit off the team because of the sharing of parking and concession revenue, as well as proceeds from ticket taxes. However, if the attendance figures lagged, the city would be paying the Chargers more in compensation for unsold tickets than the team would pay in rent.

The Chargers' annual rent to the city, not including what the team generates from the ticket guarantee, is approximately $5.7 million. Under the guarantee, the Chargers have paid an average rent of $1.5 million when enjoying strong attendance. In the team's lean years, the city has actually paid the Chargers through the purchase of unsold tickets for using the stadium.

---

1. Rovell, Darren, "Spirit of ABA Deal Lives on for Silna Brothers," ESPN.com, January 22, 2002.

From 1992 to 1996, the Chargers were a competitive team, never posting a losing record. From the 1997 through the 2001 season, however, the Chargers won fewer than one in three of their games (23–57 for a .288 winning percentage). Not surprisingly, the city reportedly paid the Chargers $882,463 for 21,129 tickets for a game against the Chicago Bears in 1998. In the 2000 and 2001 seasons alone, the city paid for $14 million in tickets.

For the 2002–2003 season, ticket prices to Chargers games—whose six-year playoff drought was the second-longest in the league—increased $5 to $10. The taxpayers of San Diego remain understandably squeamish. Even though they had new coach Marty Schottenheimer at the helm and league newcomer Drew Brees calling the plays in 2002, enough damage was done from years of losing that the city had to buy over 30,000 tickets at a cost of $1.6 million for a preseason game against the Arizona Cardinals.

For the Chargers, however, the ticket guarantee is not unlike the tax breaks major corporations seek from cities in return for their commitment to the community and the scores of local residents they will employ. The guarantee also allowed the Chargers to use their local leverage to gain an important economic advantage.

BUILDING A BUSINESS

For centuries, families have taken great pride in starting their own businesses. The family businesses, many of which began as garage start-ups with small amounts of borrowed capital, have always been the backbone of the American economy. Over time, and as a right of passage, some of these businesses have been handed down through generations, with those inheriting the family business continuing to see that it thrives and, on occasion, transforming it into a large, publicly traded company.

The list of American families who have successfully participated in this process range from the Fords and the Disneys to the Rooney and McCaskey families in professional sports, who continue to own the NFL's Pittsburgh Steelers and Chicago Bears, respectively.

It matters not whether these family businesses have been linked to the industrial revolution, the development of the entertainment industry, or the growth of professional football. Each has addressed issues of growth and family succession. They've all encountered economic downturns and fundamental shifts in consumer attitudes and regulation. They've all survived and, for the most part, thrived, revered for their perseverance and tenacity.

It's not just small family businesses that have captured the imagination of American business. Small businesses of all origins and entrepreneurial makeup have established themselves brick by brick, business deal by business deal, until that fateful day—the day of their initial public offering (IPO).

The tenets for building a business are largely the same whether founded by a family patriarch like Sam Walton (Wal-Mart) or Vince McMahon (World Wrestling Federation [WWF], now called World Wrestling Entertainment [WWE]), or merely cobbled together by old college roommates or business associates, such as Yahoo! and Hewlett-Packard. The daunting challenges and stories of sacrifice are prevalent; so too is the commitment to tackling the long odds of being a successful entrepreneur.

When Vince McMahon Sr., a well-known wrestling promoter, handed the family business over to his son in 1982, Vince, Jr. had big dreams. McMahon Jr. wasn't afraid to take risks to expand the family business. He changed the company name from Capitol Wrestling Corporation to World Wrestling Federation, a name he strove to live up to. By developing compelling personalities such as Hulk Hogan and Randy "Macho Man" Savage, and by promoting wrestling on a national basis, dreams of an empire weren't hard to imagine.

McMahon didn't build the international brand, one marked by 300 full-time employees and more than 100 wrestlers under exclusive contract, without taking significant risks. In 1985, McMahon started the sport's major event, WrestleMania. Because the concept of pay-per-view TV had not yet gelled, McMahon believed enough in the product that he rented out more than 100 arenas to show the event on the big-screen TVs. According to the WWF, by fiscal year 2000, 2.3 million people attended 210 live wrestling events in 100 cities in North America, including 45 of the 50 largest metropolitan areas in the United States.

Today, with 5 million to 7 million paying for its content per year, the company has not only become among the top pay-per-view producers in the world, but its "free" programming has consistently attracted more viewers in the coveted 18- to 34-year-old demographic group than any other property airing in prime time.

After surviving a fiercely competitive ratings battle with Ted Turner's World Championship Wrestling (WCW) in the late 1990s, McMahon decided to buy the WCW in 2000. This acquisition became tougher for McMahon due to shareholder considerations that arose following his taking the company public in late 1999.

McMahon had far greater creative control and latitude when he owned 100% of the WWF. However, a reported $70 million loss in the first year of his new football league, the XFL, was enough for WWF and GE (which owned half the league) shareholders to pull the plug on the fledgling league.

And, as is often the case when companies become giants, McMahon had to deal with many lawsuits, including the one that changed the name of his brand forever. In May 2002, the WWF was forced to become WWE after losing a fight for the three-letter abbreviation with the World Wildlife Fund.

Despite its status as a publicly traded company, WWE and McMahon have still done their best to keep the business largely a family affair. His wife Linda serves as CEO and McMahon's son and daughter, Shane and Stephanie, have been worked in as WWE characters.

Long before the McMahons wrestled with shareholder issues, they focused on building their business methodically, exploiting their competitive advantages while carving out a unique niche within the sports and entertainment industry.

THE BUSINESS LIFE CYCLE

Those building businesses must recognize that every product and industry evolves in stages and that such life cycles require senior management to constantly assess, and then reassess, where their business is headed. Ian MacDougall, the founder and professional director of Corporate Lifecycles LLC, believes that the stages to any business can be boiled down to the following four:[2]

- *Infancy*: Period in which the business is founded and scrambles to survive. The focus during infancy is on achieving what needs to get done to ensure that early customers are satisfied.
- *Go-go*: Second stage in which the initial customer base allows the business to break even, and then grow rapidly through proactively exploiting new opportunities.

2. Adapted from TEC Worldwide, Inc., "Best Practices: Sustaining Growth."

■ *Adolescence*: As growth continues, lack of infrastructure can cause growing pains and forces organizations to focus on what needs to be done to sustain early success.

■ *Prime*: At the peak of the company's growth cycle, the organization is finally hitting on all cylinders, simultaneously enabling it to turn a profit and allowing the company's personality and culture to shine.

These stages of the business life cycle will be explored in greater detail later in this chapter by considering NASCAR, one of sport's best examples of how to build a small regional business into an international powerhouse. Prior to that analysis, however, it is necessary to consider what issues fledgling businesses must address if they are to hit the ground running.

Regardless of which stage a company finds itself in, impediments to starting and growing the business exist. How *exactly*—from both a financial and strategic perspective—will you go about getting started? What kind of leadership style do you prefer? Once a business gets going, understanding and acknowledging precisely where a particular organization is in its life cycle will allow it to accurately diagnose and then address issues that could stunt company growth.

For example, in the infancy stage, cash management issues and personality clashes among founders might persist. During the second stage, vulnerabilities could include a lack of human or financial resources necessary to meet demand. Inappropriate organizational structure and goal setting might mar the adolescence stage. Finally, and from MacDougall's perspective, the prime stage routinely brings with it the challenge of redefining what business (or businesses) the company should pursue.

Before obsessing over business stages, budding entrepreneurs must decide for themselves if they have what it takes, particularly in terms of vision, to get into the game.

GETTING STARTED

Imagine you were the owner of the newest expansion team in professional sports—or the CEO of any start-up business for that matter. What actions would you take to propel the business beyond the initial planning process toward that of market leader? Once obscure companies like Microsoft and ESPN began with a mere vision and plenty of skeptics, but grew to become the bellwethers by which other industry participants measure themselves in the software and sports media industries, respectively.

After being fired by the World Hockey Association's (WHA) New England Whalers, Bill Rasmussen, a public relations specialist, launched ESPN on September 7, 1979. The handful of people who noticed the network's launch undoubtedly dismissed the notion of a 24-hour cable sports station. How could the sporting world warrant that much nonstop coverage? Who would watch it? How could it be economically viable?

Compelling programming was thin for ESPN in its early days. ESPN's first live event was the 1979 Professional Slo-Pitch Softball World Series between the Milwaukee Schlitzes and the Kentucky Bourbons. But once *SportsCenter,* the network's flagship news program and highlight show, was supplemented by college basketball programming, the station managed to cobble together enough programming to fill each day. Nonetheless, few existing networks viewed the start-up cable network as a legitimate threat.

As the popularity of cable television grew, *SportsCenter* began to overshadow local sports broadcasts. Soon, as the concept gained support, *SportsCenter* junkies became acquainted with personalities like Chris Berman, Bob Ley, and Dan Patrick, each of whom became cult heroes who were just as famous as most of the athletes they covered. Today, *SportsCenter* airs in more than 80 percent of U.S. homes and ESPN is far and away, as its tagline suggests, "The Worldwide Leader in Sports" with ESPN, ESPN2, ESPN Classic, and ESPNEWS. The ESPN brand has also been attached to ESPN.com, ESPN The Magazine, ESPN Radio, and ESPN Zone restaurants. With the acquisition of the NBA's broadcast rights in 2002, the network became the first to broadcast games from all four major sports leagues at the same time.

Just like Rasmussen was able to get past the initial skepticism, so too was Frank Batten, who helped start the 24-hour, 7-days a week Weather Channel a couple of years after Rasmussen began ESPN. The initial response to the Weather Channel was just as bad. After all, who needed to watch anything but their local weather? Who cared if there was a massive storm in Oklahoma if you were soaking up rays in Malibu? Well, by 2000, the Weather Channel was generating $320 million in revenue and boasted a steady following of nearly 100 million weather watchers.

In addition to ownership believing in a business concept, most successful businesses, regardless of their industry, have adhered to the following process to achieve market leadership positions.

They must begin with a vision. An organization must be able to look at the future and determine its short-, medium-, and long-term strategic goals: How will the business adapt to inevitable change? What direction should the business take when faced with this change? Where should the business focus its human and financial resources? Creating a tight strategic plan answers these questions and provides a guide for growth and success.

Owners of expansion teams in professional sports must address these issues upon being granted their franchises. They must decide how they will stock their teams with players (employees). Will they do it economically and methodically over time through the draft and their newly established minor league affiliates? Or will the new owner choose to go the free agency route, electing to use checkbook diplomacy to rapidly—and expensively—establish a contending team? How will the primary stakeholders, namely the media, sponsors, and fans, react to the new owner's strategy for building a franchise?

In many respects the sports world has a lot in common with the dot-com frenzy, in which capital was easily raised and quickly spent to rapidly establish a brand. Financial returns were less important than establishing a strong Web presence. Throughout much of sports, success is measured not by operating incomes but by winning percentages. When sports teams fail to take into account the financial bottom line they face the same challenges encountered by online companies who invested heavily in establishing a brand name but lacked the business acumen to capitalize on it.

Business leaders are also measured by "winning percentages," such as stock price and other yardsticks, like profitability. However, unlike baseball players, corporate leaders need to bat well over .300 in their decision making to be considered successful in today's fiercely competitive business world.

Unlike Jerry Jones, who built the Dallas Cowboys over time while leveraging the rich tradition of the team, Arizona Diamondbacks owner Jerry Colangelo built his team rapidly and without the benefits of an established and committed fan base.

In 1995, Colangelo—long-time managing partner of the NBA Phoenix Suns—and numerous limited partners purchased the MLB expansion team, the Arizona Diamondbacks, for $130 million, $20 million more than the group anticipated it would cost.

Colangelo's primary goal was to field a competitive team that played in a great ballpark. He achieved this goal, as the Diamondbacks became the quickest expansion franchise to win the World Series, doing so in only the team's fourth season. However, the costs incurred by Colangelo and his partners were enormous.

Before taking the field in 1998, the costs associated with building Bank One Ballpark soared from $230 million to $368 million. Following the inaugural 1998 season the Diamondbacks increased the team's payroll to about $70 million, giving it one of baseball's top 10 highest payrolls. The signing of six free agents, including pitcher Randy Johnson and outfielder Steve Finley, whose combined contracts cost Colangelo $118 million, was primarily responsible for the rapid increase in player costs. Despite these changes in the lineup, season ticket sales declined. The number of season tickets fell from 36,000 in 1998 to 27,000 in 1999 and again to 24,000 in 2000. For the Diamondbacks championship year, the season ticket base fell to 22,000.

Due to this eroding season ticket fan base Colangelo sought— and received—financial relief in the form of a $10 million loan to provide the team with the necessary capital to sign additional free agents. But even this proved to be insufficient.

By 2001, Colangelo took the extraordinary measure of asking his top 10 players to defer a reported $150 million to $200 million in salaries over five years. By the end of 2001, Colangelo had existing partners invest another $160 million over a 10-year period to ensure a financially stable and competitive team in the years to come.

Despite much criticism throughout the process, Colangelo said it all paid off—that merchandising, postseason ticket revenue, and the rebounding season ticket base allowed the team to lose only $44.4 million in its championship year and that the team would eventually be debt-free thanks to the owners providing the necessary cash. In the process, however, Colangelo's ownership stake in the team was further diluted and the franchise faces ongoing financial problems arising from the deferrals on player salaries, as well as $150 million in stadium debt. This financial situation has been further exacerbated by the fact that, as part of the team's agreement with the league, it did not begin to share in the national television revenue monies until the 2003 season.

Amazon.com, the Internet's largest retailer, and the Diamondbacks of the dot-com world, lost $2.8 billion from 1995 through 2001 before announcing in January 2002 that it had made its first quarterly profit, a meager yet welcomed $5.1 million.

Given the game plans undertaken—and well communicated to important constituents—by both Colangelo and Amazon, each was able to avoid some of the scrutiny associated with such extraordinary investment spending. Based on shareholder input, senior management must decide if the industry that a company is in, and the circumstances in which it operates, will allow it the latitude to undertake a similar strategy. They also must decide what constitutes "winning." Might it be having the greatest market share in the industry (the championship) or could winning be defined as being the most profitable (highest franchise value)? Perhaps winning requires both.

In sports, expansion teams—much like any new business—must assemble a great, service-oriented sales staff to help sell everything from season tickets to luxury suites. Along the way, aggressive sales forecasts are made and in the competitive world of sales, marketing representatives who aren't putting the proverbial fannies in the seats typically find themselves scrambling to keep their jobs.

Some employees in the sports world are driven by the fear that many others would love to work in their field and they are therefore, in essence, more replaceable than employees in other businesses. However, employees who are lower on the team's totem pole are often driven to do well for a team and sell as many tickets as possible because of the commissions they earn in the process. Small businesses and organizations, like expansion teams in sports, must consider which aspects of their operations allow them to attract, and then motivate, their own employees.

Because management has to more personally acknowledge employees in a commission-based system, it tends to be more cognizant of who is doing extremely well. Those that are excelling are routinely identified as fast-trackers, employees with a work ethic and track record that warrant senior management's attention. However, these fast-trackers are but a single component of a comprehensive strategic plan.

The strategic plan, which must include dedicated employees, might be the framework for the organization, but it alone is not enough. A company must establish measurable performance benchmarks and hold its management accountable to meeting agreed-on targets. The business should develop a financial and operational reporting system that allows it to track all of the critical performance numbers. Periodically revisiting and refining performance standards will contribute to broader companywide goals. Markets don't wait for annual planning reviews, so the business shouldn't either.

Respected, revered, and dedicated leadership in the organization is also of paramount importance. Often a business owner is passionate about his or her product or service and knows the market well, but lacks sufficient expertise in management and leadership. Some of the best sports owners are those who admit to themselves that they can't manage or lead (or possibly even both), and thus delegate authority at the appropriate time and to the right people.

It is also critical that the owner of the business makes the personal transformation from technical expert to master strategist. The personification of this is Bill Gates. He is undoubtedly a computer genius, but he had to develop the key strategic and leadership skills needed to nurture and then lead a global organization.

It is equally necessary to assemble a competent, creative management team. A good manager will become a great one if he or she surrounds himself or herself with the best people possible. The key to manageable and sustainable growth is avoiding inconsistent or unpredictable leadership. By identifying all the key people who are driving the business and creating incentives for each of them to stay and help grow the business, the company will remain in a position to optimize its growth. This has been evidenced in both baseball and basketball, where the most successful active manager and head coach—New York Yankees manager Joe Torre and Phil Jackson of the Los Angeles Lakers—have spent many seasons discussing game strategies with their faithful assistants, Don Zimmer and Tex Winter, respectively.

Fear of inconsistent or unpredictable leadership is one of the reasons the founder of a family business might be hesitant to approve of his or her children's wishes to expand the business. The founder might think that the company would be compromised if one of them cannot possibly be in charge of every aspect of the business.

In the sports world, such issues prevail between university presidents and athletic directors who are required to relinquish a significant measure of control to the school's head football coach and pigskin patriarch.

Likewise, when an athletic director gets comfortable with a certain coach—even if he or she is no longer winning—he or she tends to keep that coach longer than he or she should.

Such was the case with college basketball coaching legend Denny Crum, who was forced to resign from the University of Louisville after the 2001 season. Crum coached the Cardinals for 30 years, during 23 of which the team went to the NCAA Tournament, including six Final Four appearances and two national championships (1980 and 1986).

However, midway through the 2000–2001 season, Crum was forced to say he would resign at the end of the season. At the time, the team was 11–18 and 61–61 over the last four years with two first-round losses in the NCAA Tournament.

After Crum's firing, ESPN basketball analyst Jay Bilas likened being the head coach at a traditional power to being the CEO of a major corporation. Bilas suggested that success and succession were always major issues and that it would be unimaginable for a corporate board of directors and the company's shareholders to allow an aging CEO to serve at his pleasure when the company's fortunes were sagging. This would particularly be the case if no credible evidence existed to indicate that the company's future would improve.

Louisville basketball's new CEO was former Kentucky coach Rick Pitino, a man not unlike former Louisville football coach Howard Schnellenberger, a coaching patriarch who enjoyed the challenge of turning around programs.

PATRIARCHAL LEADERSHIP

Most leaders, including those charged with bringing Florida Atlantic University (FAU) into prominence, aren't fortunate enough to always start at the top—they have to start from scratch, attempting to build an unbranded product into a well-known and revered competitor.

FAU had an ambitious, but responsible, plan when it decided to establish a football program. First, in May 1998, it hired Howard Schnellenberger, a man with tremendous credentials in the football world, to lead the way. He was offensive coordinator for Paul "Bear" Bryant's three national championship teams at Alabama in the early 1960s. He resurrected a University of Miami program that, in 1979, averaged fewer than 13,000 fans per game in the Orange Bowl, by leading the team to a national championship and thus capacity crowds in 1983. Schnellenberger then went on to Louisville where his success increased attendance by almost 40 percent, and filled the stadium with standing-room-only crowds.

Before long-term success could be achieved—defined as moving FAU to the "big-time" college football division, Division I-A—short-term successes had to be demonstrated. Thanks to Schnellenberger's hard work, FAU raised the necessary $10 million from more than 70,000 alumni to start the program and signed some quality recruits for the inaugural 2001 season.

Although Schnellenberger dreamed of 25,000 fans showing up per game, the team averaged a respectable 12,987 in Pro Player Stadium, playing the likes of Division I-AA teams including Slippery Rock, Jacksonville, and Gardner-Webb.

To be considered for the jump to Division I-A, the team has to average 15,000 fans at home games and play at least five home games against Division I-A opponents, which remains a significant obstacle for the school.

The Schnellenberger name means something throughout Florida, the state considered by many as the hotbed for college football recruits. Schnellenberger even suggested as much when he reminded people that 300 kids from Florida go to Division I schools and even if the Florida powerhouses (Miami, Florida State, and Florida) took their fair share of them, he believed there would still be plenty left for him to recruit.

Sure, Schnellenberger also has to compete with the likes of Central Florida and University of South Florida, the only two schools among the 122 Division 1-AA programs in 2000 that drew more than 24,000 fans to their games and have gained fame through alumni including Daunte Culpepper and Bill Gramatica, respectively. However, everyone knows FAU has a distinct advantage: Schnellenberger knows how to build a successful program. Whether that knowledge will translate into success for Schnellenberger—whose team endured a very unsuccessful season in 2002—might be another story.

As small or family businesses grow they occasionally outgrow their initial management model. The ownership and management structure that helped launch the company might not be ideally suited to expand the business. Consequently, the need to analyze the old model and perhaps create a new one exists.

In 1846, New England physician Dr. Austin Church and his brother-in-law John Dwight started the first American-made sodium bicarbonate (baking soda) plant in the Church's kitchen. The two went their own ways the following year and formed Church & Co. (which used the Arm & Hammer label) and John Dwight and Company. Fifty years later, the companies merged as Church & Dwight under the Arm & Hammer label.

Although the original use for baking soda was for cooking, flexibility and creativity became the product's key to long-term success when a decline in cooking before and after World War II caused sales to fall. Some organizations fail when they deviate from their core business or competency, but with a legitimate and authentic connection to other aspects of their consumers' lives, differentiation was the key to Arm & Hammer's success in the 20th century.

In the 1960s, Arm & Hammer ran advertisements that encouraged people to place a box of baking soda in their refrigerators to keep the contents fresh. Numerous other uses were detailed on an Arm & Hammer "versatility wheel" located on the box.

A carpet deodorizer entered the market in 1981 and a cat litter box version followed seven years later. Today, Arm & Hammer has spray room deodorizers, laundry detergents, toothpastes, and gum. In 2002, the company signed Yankees slugger Jason Giambi as a spokesperson for its body deodorant.

Had Church & Dwight management believed that baking soda was only good for cooking, Arm & Hammer would have never emerged as one of America's most recognizable brand names. The corollary here is that just because a company has reached the prime stage, it is not necessarily ideally positioned. Companies must continue to evolve, as did Arm & Hammer. Should a business not continue to evolve and refine itself, it could become the next Converse or Polaroid.

Before Nike sneakers and Air Jordan became ubiquitous with American sports and pop culture, Converse dominated the athletic shoe market. Wilt Chamberlain and Julius Erving wore them. Magic Johnson and Larry Bird also laced them up while leading their teams to NBA championships. Even Richie Cunningham appeared brand loyal to Converse on the hit show *Happy Days*.

College basketball coaches across America, including high-profile programs led by Crum at Louisville and Bobby Knight at Indiana, had contracts to outfit their teams in Converse shoes. However, the "Made in America" shoes took a hit as a result of the Nikes and Reeboks of the world emerging in the 1980s. Combine these competitors' strategic vision with Converse's messy series of corporate takeovers and it's easy to see why Converse had to file for Chapter 11 bankruptcy in 2001.

After Converse's logo was acquired in a bankruptcy sale, a new holding company led by former sales executive Jack Boys decided to reintroduce the brand. With new spokesmen including Cleveland Cavaliers guard Andre Miller and Minnesota Timberwolves forward Wally Szczerbiak, Converse hopes to make a comeback. The popularity of the retro craze could afford the brand the opportunity.

After being in business for roughly four decades, Polaroid cameras, which could produce a photo in less than a minute, were so popular in the 1970s that the company name came to mean a photograph in much the same way Kleenex means tissue and Xerox means photocopy. However, in the 1980s, less expensive cameras and one-hour photo shops threatened Polaroid's competitive advantages. By the late 1990s digital cameras entered the ever increasingly competitive market. Polaroid had made a concerted effort to evolve, but it wasn't enough. The company rested on its historic past and, in 2001, filed for Chapter 11 bankruptcy. In July 2002, 65 percent of Polaroid was sold to One Equity Partners, an investment unit managed by Bank One, for $255 million to help the company reorganize.

When industries evolve and expand, established businesses within those industries must revisit their ability to not just remain afloat, but to compete successfully. Sometimes, if the head of a private organization doesn't want to adapt with the times and conform to the new state of business, he can choose to sell his organization, as was the case with Calvin Griffith and the Minnesota Twins.

When Clark Griffith purchased the Washington Senators in 1919, his nephew Calvin Griffith was already eager to be involved. He started as a batboy in 1924 at the age of 12, made his way to concession manager, and eventually team president before taking over as majority owner (with his sister Thelma) when Clark died in 1955.

In the early 1960s, Griffith moved the team to Minneapolis, and thanks to hall-of-famer Harmon Killebrew and the great Tony Oliva, the Minnesota Twins found themselves in the 1965 World Series. However, in the late 1970s, as the Players Association gained more bargaining power and player salaries began to increase, Griffith didn't want to spend beyond his means to remain competitive.

Whatever he made, he would invest in the team. If the team wasn't doing well financially, he wasn't going to dish out large salaries to players, because—unlike some other owners—his income was coming solely from baseball.

Calvin's son Clark, who was an executive vice president along with his nephew Bruce, wanted to talk to him about the business, the broadcasting, and the finance, but Calvin was disinterested. The business he spent 72 years of his life building had become too much of a business. So, in 1984, Calvin Griffith, unable to deal with the behemoth the sport had become, sold the Twins to local banker Carl Pohlad for $37 million, of which $24 million went to the Griffiths.

Seventeen years later, history seemed to repeat itself as Pohlad who, after winning championships with the Twins in 1987 and 1991, with one of the lowest payrolls in baseball, said he wanted out of the business because it was unprofitable. Somewhat ironically, in 2002 Clark Griffith attempted to structure an ownership group to buy the team from Pohlad.

LOWER-PROFILE LEADERSHIP

Leadership issues are not limited to matters of succession; they often require the head of the business appreciating when to take a back seat in the decision-making process. This happens frequently in the sports world when neophyte owners purchase teams they do not have the expertise to run from a player personnel perspective. Instead, the owner surrounds himself or herself with management pros who have experience, and who understand what the owner's overall business goals are for the team. This helps the new owner deflect criticism about his or her knowledge of the game while adding credibility to the franchise. Significantly, it also provides the owner with his or her own personal set of consultants, savvy pros who can help acquaint the novice sports owner with the pressing issues of the day.

When Computer Associates Chairman Charles Wang bought the NHL's New York Islanders with his CEO Sanjay Kumar in April 2000 for $175 million, they both admitted they knew nothing about hockey. Wang said he had only seen two hockey games and was reading *Hockey for Dummies*. So Wang stayed behind the scenes, while he opened his checkbook for General Manager (GM) Mike Milbury, who was GM of the team since 1995. In the press, Milbury remained the voice of decision making on the ice, and Wang worried about servicing customers and getting to know the personalities and work habits of his personnel. Although Wang was not recognized by his own Islanders fans while sitting in a seat at the team's 2001 draft party, it was his investment that enabled the Islanders to reach the playoffs for the first time in seven years in only his second year of ownership. In response to the team's performance, the Islanders began the 2002–2003 season with their largest season-ticket-holder base since the 1988–1989 season.

Wang's nearby New York rival is the New York Rangers, run by Cablevision mogul Charles Dolan's son James. Dolan also provides a compelling example of this approach to management. As chairman of Madison Square Garden, Dolan, a second-generation Cablevision executive, oversees the Rangers and the NBA's Knicks and the Women's National Basketball Association's (WNBA) Liberty. Although the Rangers media guide says he's "an ardent fan of the three MSG teams," Dolan downplayed his in-depth sports knowledge at the 2001 press conference announcing that former Philadelphia Flyers star Eric Lindros had been acquired by the Rangers.

At the news conference Dolan indicated that he didn't know much about the specifics of the organizations that he runs. He then went on to add that he manages the teams by placing trust in those that he hires, such as Rangers president and GM Glen Sather.

Dolan has a similar perspective on the Knicks and his role in running the franchise. He says he believes that, in addition to delegating authority, it is important that the people in his organization know that the company is not a faceless, soul-less corporation, and that his presence is not merely limited to a signature on the bottom of a check.

These might not seem like comments you would expect to hear from a guy who, along with his father Charles and his uncle Larry (who owns MLB's Cleveland Indians) was named the third most powerful person in sports by *The Sporting News* in 1999. However, it is a managerial style that, at least in James Dolan's case, works for him.

Many frustrated Rangers and Knicks fans who have witnessed escalating payrolls without the corresponding victories to match over the last several seasons disagree with Dolan's style. In 2002, the Knicks and the Rangers—neither of which made the playoffs—paid their players more on a per-win basis than any other NHL or NBA team. Meanwhile, the nearby and former laughing stock New Jersey Nets played their way into the 2002 NBA Finals.

When growing a business it is necessary to have short-, medium-, and long-term game plans. These plans must include strategies for increasing human and financial resources, and must focus on the tactics that will enable the cash register to ring today and tomorrow, as well as a year or two from today or tomorrow. Unlike established Fortune 500 firms that might have thoroughly developed five- to seven-year business plans, most start-up businesses have difficulty projecting out further than about three years. Companies, regardless of size, that focus on growing their business in the short and medium term don't have to worry as much about growth over the long run.

A unique variation of this theme occurs throughout sports, especially within college athletics where athletic directors and coaches convince recruits and their parents into thinking the university has a five-year plan—when in fact it might really just be a year-to-year plan.

When a coach and his or her team are playing well, the coach's contract is generally automatically rolled over to give the appearance of long-term stability. Because many coaches have five-year contracts that are extended annually by a year or two, the coach can confidently say to a recruit, "I'm contractually obligated to be here for your entire playing career." Of course, he or she never says, "There's a buyout of $1.2 million, which I'm sure the school will pay if I'm not doing well or if I'm doing too well that another school is willing to pay it for me to take a better coaching position."

Two days after fourth-year head coach Bob Davie led the 2000 Notre Dame Fighting Irish football team to its first major bowl in five years, the school's athletic director Kevin White announced a five-year extension for Davie. Of course, after Davie's team was blown out by Oregon State in the Fiesta Bowl, 41–9 and Davie's 2001 team finished 5–6 on the year, the other four years on the contract meant nothing because the university chose to replace him.

Establishing and building a (family) business is an extraordinarily challenging, stressful, and daunting proposition. Yet Americans continue to do so every day, often relying on the inspirational and storied histories of companies like McDonald's and Harley-Davidson. In the sports business world there has been no better personification of a family business that has achieved the pinnacle of commercial success than NASCAR. NASCAR's history, track record, and extraordinary accomplishments have provided the requisite incentive for many to give entrepreneurship a try.

Now that many of the issues facing start-ups have been considered, it is useful to consider them along with the aforementioned stages of the business cycle. Following is a case study of sorts that chronicles how NASCAR has adeptly built its business by identifying—like other successful businesses—opportunities and threats that shape the organization and its future.

BILL FRANCE: SEIZING THE OPPORTUNITY (INFANCY)

During the prohibition era of the 1920s and early 1930s, the undercover business of whiskey running began to boom. The secret transportation quickly became more of a problem than making it. The common term for these runners was bootleggers, men who illegally ran whiskey from hidden stills to markets across the Southeast. Driving at high speeds at night, often with the police in pursuit, bootleggers were taking enormous risks.

As bootlegging boomed, the drivers began to race among themselves to see who had the fastest cars. Bootleggers raced on Sunday afternoons and then used the same car to haul whiskey on Sunday nights. Inevitably, people came to see the races, and racing cars became extremely popular in the backroads of the South.

Seizing on what he thought could become compelling sports entertainment, William H. G. "Bill" France—a driver and promoter who owned a local gas station—organized a race on the wide, firm sands of Daytona Beach, Florida, in the summer of 1938. The winner received such items as a bottle of rum, a box of cigars, and a case of motor oil (precursors to present-day sponsor involvement in the sport). France was a visionary; he realized for stock car racing to grow, an official organization had to exist to list champions, maintain statistics, and memorialize records and record holders.

FINANCIAL AND ORGANIZATIONAL GROWTH: NASCAR-A-GO-GO

By 1947, Bill France realized the time was right for a national sanctioning body to govern stock car racing, so he gathered influential promoters to gain their input. Over a three-day period, rules were drawn up and specifications were agreed on. The name of the organization would be NASCAR.

Through the 1950s, NASCAR began to flourish. Corporate sponsors, such as Pure Oil and Champion Sparkplugs took an active role in the sport. Even the major automobile manufacturers, such as Ford, Chevrolet, and Chrysler gave "factory backing" to individual drivers whereby the drivers would receive money from a manufacturer to drive its product. The car companies realized the marketing potential of racing to sell cars. In fact, a common motto for these automobile manufacturers emerged: "Win on Sunday, sell on Monday."

In 1959, because he knew the importance of properly packaging his product, France founded the International Speedway Corporation (ISC), which constructed the Daytona International Speedway in 1959 and Talladega Superspeedway 10 years later. These tracks allowed France the opportunity to control the presentation of his product as he continued to methodically grow the sport throughout the South.

This marked the beginning of NASCAR's vertical integration, a business decision that served the sport well beyond its formidable years. What were once merely loosely affiliated tracks and events grew to become an extensively organized group of assets. The importance of bundling these assets, which today include NASCAR's own cutting-edge TV channel and Internet programming, was not lost on corporate America.

France realized that for NASCAR to become a booming success it needed three elements: a cohesive governing body, television exposure, and corporate support. For most businesses, this translates into leadership, distribution channels, and financing.

NASCAR'S ADOLESCENT YEARS

The American gas crisis in 1974 not only led to increases in gasoline prices and the need for rationing, but also led many people to believe racing wasted precious gas. So NASCAR cut back the number of miles in most races by 10 percent; therefore the Daytona 500 was only 450 miles that year. Through the 1970s, and despite the gas crisis, racing continued to grow.

It did so because the France family knew the inherent value of television rested in its ability to broaden exposure for the sport beyond the South. The first race that piqued corporate interest in the sport was the 1976 Daytona 500, the final laps of which were broadcast on ABC. This was followed in 1979 when CBS became the first network to televise an entire NASCAR race—an event that attracted an estimated 15 million viewers. However, it wasn't so much the race itself that endeared the sport to so many fans.

On the back straightaway of the last lap, Cale Yarborough attempted to pass Donnie Allison on the inside, and Allison pulled down to block him. The two cars collided and careened into the third turn wall, then spun into the infield grass and stopped. Richard Petty, A. J. Foyt, and Darrell Waltrip drove past and Petty won the race by a car length. By the time Petty crossed the finish line, Yarborough and Allison had already climbed out of their cars and started fighting. Then Bobby Allison pulled up and entered the fistfight to defend his brother—all of which happened on live national television as several safety crew members attempted to break it up.

Many racing historians credit that race and its exciting finish for helping bring NASCAR to where it is today. Arguably one of the most bizarre incidents ever witnessed in sports, this nonetheless proved to be a defining moment for NASCAR.

NASCAR ENTERS "PRIME" TIME

Over the next 20 years the France family continued to capitalize on its momentum by focusing on the customer experience, whether that customer was a corporation or a racing fan.

Propelled by superstars such as Petty in the 1980s, and Dale Earnhardt and Jeff Gordon throughout the 1990s, the sport boomed in popularity and found itself with the most brand-loyal fans in all of sports. Research indicates that approximately 70 percent of NASCAR fans consciously choose NASCAR sponsors' products over other brands. The reason for the NASCAR fan brand loyalty is that fans know that the sport wouldn't exist without sponsors, and their driver couldn't compete if he or she didn't have money from a sponsor.

This fierce loyalty has enabled NASCAR to secure more than 900 sponsors that, at the beginning of 2001, were investing $400 million in the sport. Because of this sponsor and fan loyalty and the fact that NASCAR doesn't have strikes or lockouts like the rest of the major sports leagues (there is no "players union" in motorsports), it was able to negotiate a six-year, $2.8 billion television contract with Fox, NBC, and Turner, as well as a five-year Internet rights deal with AOL for a reported $100 million. On the merchandising front, NASCAR has entered into merchandising deals with more than 45 companies, which has allowed it to increase its licensing revenue from $80 million less than 10 years ago to more than $1 billion today, thanks in large part to its themed restaurants and die-cast collectible cars, among other licensing initiatives. NASCAR, once a fledgling regional business, has grown to become an international sport because it keenly focused on its customers and what they sought from their affiliation with racing.

"PRIME" CHALLENGES

Earlier in the chapter mention was made about how NASCAR survived both the 1974 gas crisis and the "crisis" at the Daytona 500 five years later, which, by the way, proved to be more of an opportunity than a crisis when examined on a historical basis. Making that key leap from an adolescent company to one in the prime often requires getting past the moments that can turn into crises. Those companies, no matter how many years they have been in business, and even if they've reached their prime years earlier, won't get back to the top if they don't implement the right measures in tough times.

For most companies moments of crisis, many of which are defining moments in the organization's history, present themselves out of nowhere. Yet for others, moments of crisis—if and when properly manufactured—can help the organization.

In 1998, Hasbro manufactured its own crisis when it restricted the supply of its newly released Furby dolls during the winter holiday season. Most companies that manufacture trendy holiday gifts want to produce enough product, fearing that if there is not enough product available the company might miss its golden opportunity. Hasbro, however, made sure that scarcity was a huge factor in the company's marketing of the Furby, a decision that served the company well. Although this is certainly a risky business strategy, it worked for Hasbro.

Hasbro knew that lack of supply could drive demand, especially in the toy business. In 1982, Coleco acquired the rights to Cabbage Patch Kids from a young man named Xavier Roberts. Even when the toy was mass-produced around Christmas 1983, supply could not keep pace with demand. Every child wanted a Cabbage Patch Kid. A great many of those searching for the toy, including adults, wanted one not because of the merits of the toy itself, but for the bragging rights and the story that went along with acquiring the doll. Some parents drove for hours to find one, and others paid up to $5,000 for an original doll. Some parents even trampled children while running full speed through the aisles at their local toy store.

The Cabbage Patch Kids became the fastest selling toys of all time, generating $1.2 billion in sales from 1983 through 1985. The company benefited by the fact that it was always behind demand. However, when the fad faded and Coleco went bankrupt, another toy company—Hasbro—acquired Cabbage Patch Kids.

All business strategies must be guided by a capable group of leaders, particularly during periods, whether unexpected or manufactured, of crisis. Beyond successfully emerging from crises, a major step in continuing to grow a business is precisely how that company handles the stepping down of the leader who founded the organization. The passing of the corporate baton down from family member to family member isn't necessarily the toughest test. That comes when the top leadership position is given to an "outsider."

THE CHANGING OF THE GUARD

Refinement in senior management is critical for companies if they are to become market leaders. Once they attain a market leadership position, reviewing and refining the ownership and management structure is instrumental in staying ahead of the competition. Certainly every organization faces change, but for family businesses, facilitating the necessary change is frequently an even more daunting task.

As is the case with so many businesses built from the ground up by the family's patriarch, there comes a point when success has been established and the baton must be passed to others who are charged with sustaining the momentum. It happens in sports, such as when Rick Pitino replaced Denny Crum at Louisville, and it frequently happens in big business.

In 1901, Charles Walgreen started his first drugstore in Dixon, Illinois. Through low prices, stellar service, and even good food—his wife Myrtle cooked everything in the early years—Walgreens grew impressively over the years. In 1919, Walgreen's had 20 stores; a decade later it boasted 525. By 1934 when Charles Walgreen turned 60, he was ready for his son to take over as president. Growth under Charles Jr. continued. Charles Jr. then groomed his son, Charles III, who oversaw the opening of the 1,000th Walgreen's store in 1984.

Walgreen III handed over the reigns to the first non-Walgreen to head the company, Daniel Jorndt, in January 1998. By the time Walgreen III left office as Walgreen's chief executive and became chairman emeritus, the company had a streak of nine years in a row in which it increased the number of store openings. By 2001, with the help of Jorndt—who would step down in January 2002—the number of stores surpassed 3,500, the annual streak of an increased number of openings was up to 13 and the company was listed 90th on *Fortune's* list of America's largest companies. Despite having fewer stores than CVS or Rite Aid, it was still number one in sales.

To its credit, NASCAR, like Walgreen's, has grown because of its willingness to hand over the reigns when other businesses might have remained reluctant to do so.

NASCAR's complete family leadership lasted for more than 50 years. When Bill France, Sr. retired in 1972, his family took over the business. Bill Jr. was named president and Sr.'s other son, Jim, became executive vice president and president of the ISC.

Bill Jr., who had a stroke in 1997 and survived cancer in 1999, ran NASCAR until November 2000, when he became chairman of a five-member board with Jim, Brian France (executive vice president of NASCAR), Lesa France Kennedy (executive vice president of ISC)—Bill Jr.'s son and daughter—and significantly, Mike Helton, whom he named COO of NASCAR in February 1999 and president in November 2000. Even though NASCAR's board remained 80 percent "France," the top position now belonged to a nonfamily member.

While a more in-depth look at NASCAR's handling of Dale Earnhardt's death on the final lap of the 2000 Daytona 500 can be found in Chapter 7, important managerial issues surfaced following the accident. Among these issues was how a rapidly growing business would deal with the largest tragedy to ever befall the industry.

Helton, the highest ranking non-France-family member in the organization, has been widely credited with opening up the Association's management style by being more accessible and forthright about NASCAR matters. He did so as the increasing popularity of the sport brought with it added scrutiny, particularly from the media.

This "opening up" even included outsourcing much of the investigation into what caused Earnhardt's death, a decision lauded by many as a defining moment for NASCAR now that it had penetrated mainstream sports.

Helton said he viewed that moment in NASCAR's history as being as much a tribute to Dale Earnhardt as it was to NASCAR's changing style.

Even drivers and car owners such as Kyle Petty acknowledged the management style of Helton during a period of intense growth and scrutiny. Petty thought NASCAR had undergone a philosophical change in their attitude and in the way they did business, and the majority of it was due to Mike Helton. Petty also noted that when Bill France, Jr. ran NASCAR some drivers had difficulty relating to him, whereas most people in the garage had seen Mike come up through the ranks and were comfortable with his presence.

Rick Hendrick, owner of cars driven by Jeff Gordon, Terry Labonte, and Jerry Nadeau, said he felt more like a partner than an adversary. In years past, Hendrick felt NASCAR made the rules and enforced them with little or no input from its constituents. He now notices that NASCAR solicits input from everybody, making for an improved working environment.

Unilateral decision making doesn't foster confidence within organizations, especially when small or family business structures begin to depend on outsiders for input and resources.

The change from the France family to Helton enabled NASCAR drivers to feel as if they were more a part of the process and the product that they helped build, even if four of five board members were still from the France family. When France announced Helton as president he said that Helton would be given the final word. This did not mean, however, that France would be completely out of the picture. After his successful battle with cancer, France continued to assist NASCAR by helping to fine-tune and clarify the organization's mission when necessary.

Decision makers all too often make unilateral decisions without helping their employees to understand the reasoning behind them. Employees don't need to be involved in every decision but they must at least feel as though they are being engaged in the company's business.

Managers might think that their control suggests to the others that they are more personally involved and hope to be given complete credit for the successful implementation of a company's agenda. However, if the employees don't feel as if they are part of the process, and they can't predict the direction in which managers want them to go, the company's growth could be slowed as employee "buy-in" could prove difficult to secure. Control is a big issue in taking businesses, which have typically been controlled by families, to the next level.

Working for a family-controlled business can be very trying, as in the case of Carly Fiorina, who took over as Hewlett-Packard CEO in 1999. Throughout 2001 and much of 2002, Fiorina tried to complete a $19 billion merger with Compaq to help Hewlett-Packard grow beyond its core competency in printing and further penetrate the personal computer and computer repair business. But Walter B. Hewlett, the eldest son of company cofounder William Hewlett, reneged on his "yes" vote, setting the stage for a highly public face-off.

Fiorina wasn't scared of Hewlett's lack of support and, after launching a national advertising campaign, as well as a Web site, and making her opinion known in the press, she eventually prevailed.

GROWING PAINS

NASCAR provides another lesson for the business world: Successfully growing a business induces growing pains. Now that NASCAR is as firmly entrenched in America's sports scene as any of the so-called "big leagues," it must redouble its efforts to manage its growth, identify emerging opportunities, and fend of new competitors like Team Racing Auto Circuit (TRAC), a longshot that hopes to chip away at NASCAR's dominant position.

NASCAR began hitting its marketing stride during the mid-1990s while the economy was strong. It capitalized on its fan loyalty and generated hundreds of millions of dollars in corporate support. However, as the economy entered a mild recession in 2001 and rumors of corporate fraud were becoming a reality, many sports sponsors began to reel in their sports marketing budgets. Two drivers, Todd Bodine and Joe Nemechek, were forced to find a new sponsor only days before the 2002 Daytona 500, the first race of the Winston Cup season, after their main sponsor, Kmart, filed for bankruptcy.

Against this backdrop, NASCAR found itself wrestling with growing pains that threatened to limit its impressive growth. As with any company that grows, it must sometimes learn how to shed its old partners to establish more profitable relationships. When NASCAR sold its broadcast rights to Fox, Turner, and NBC, it had to limit long-time partner ESPN, which was so integral to NASCAR's growth, from conducting trackside interviews for ESPN's bellwether NASCAR show, *RPM2Night*. To protect the investment of a network like Fox, which was starting up its own competitor to *RPM2Night*, NASCAR had to limit ESPN's access to races. Although it handled the situation awkwardly by allowing the story to play out in the press, NASCAR had little choice because it had to demonstrate an extraordinarily high level of commitment to those networks that were now financing the sport's ongoing growth.

New business relationships also require their share of massaging. Just as NASCAR was protecting Fox's investment in it by blocking out ESPN, NASCAR also put its foot down when it believed Fox was compromising a critically important component of NASCAR's business model.

In the first month of broadcasting under the new deal, Fox's computer-generated cars—shown for less than a minute in the Budweiser Shootout race—only featured the logos of companies that had purchased ads on their broadcast. As discussed earlier, sponsor investment in NASCAR is integral to the sport's growth, both past and present. Fox never did it again. In this case it was Fox that was forced to deal with growing pains of its own. Although Fox had televised most major sporting events and leagues, it did not fully appreciate NASCAR's sponsorship culture, an oversight that generated significant attention throughout sports business circles.

Accordingly, when businesses grow they must appreciate and acquiesce (when appropriate) to the wants and needs of strategic partners if growing pains are to be transformed into profitable, long-term business relationships that increase shareholder value.

CHAMPIONSHIP POINTS

Small but growing businesses, regardless of ownership structure, evolve in stages and work their way through the business life cycle. They survive infancy, and make it to the go-go stage prior to reaching adolescence and then, with a little luck and a tremendous amount of hard work, they reach their prime. Throughout it all, businesses and business people must do the following:

- Appreciate and pay keen attention to your business life cycle and the strategic vision required to ensure success, as did Vince McMahon and WWE, and Bill Rasmussen and ESPN.
- Create, monitor, and refine the strategic plan as necessary. Along the way, be sure to revisit and, if necessary, alter organizational goals and the approach to business as demonstrated by Jerry Colangelo and the Arizona Diamondbacks.
- Identify all the key people who are driving the business and create incentives for each of them to grow your business for you. These could be season ticket sellers or broadcast TV partners.

■ Focus on leadership. Make sure you have a Howard Schnellen-berger around—someone who has a tradition of starting from scratch and is willing to work hard to deliver the same magic for your company.

■ Once you've reached the top, continue to evolve and deter-mine what it will take to always stay there. Don't become Converse or Polaroid; think Arm & Hammer.

■ Have owners or top executives who are willing to transition themselves into the role of master strategist, especially if there are people in the organization who know more about key areas than you do.

■ Work to solve your moments of crisis by turning them into solutions for your business future. Realize when your own Daytona 500 is unfolding in front of you.

■ Refine senior management much like you refine the attributes of your organization's product or services. Recognize the need for your Mike Helton and capitalize on the timing of manage-rial transitions.

■ Be prepared to address growing pains head-on; a failure to promptly do so will result in lost opportunity.

An organization's ability to build a successful business—and work its way through the four phases of the business cycle—will be compromised if it lacks the keen ability to attract and retain custom-ers. To attract customers, many businesses rely on sports marketing, usually enlisting the aid of advertising and sponsorship of sports teams and leagues, as well as specific events.

Accordingly, the issue of reaching customers through the use of sports marketing is the focal point of Chapter 2.

2 REACHING THE CUSTOMER

The Point: Businesses and organizations that have successfully utilized sports marketing to sell their products and services have been able to do so because each clearly understands how and why sports can be an effective medium to use when communicating the marketing message. Those that have risen to world-class status as sports marketers know that they cannot maximize their marketing efforts unless or until they segment desired markets.

Successful marketers recognize that viable market segments allow companies to forecast demand and determine precisely how many resources should be allocated to not only accessing a particular market, but also to ensuring a sufficient return on its marketing investment.

Along the way, these marketers have understood that the company's brand name is attached to all those that help it get the word out and, consequently, they select their marketing platforms carefully. These organizations are also aware of the importance of protecting the integrity of their marketing message at all costs.

REACHING CUSTOMERS

Reaching customers through the broad use of marketing has never been easy. Billions of dollars are spent annually by companies on advertising and sponsorship in the hopes that their message will break through the marketing clutter that surrounds our daily routines. This includes small businesses that allocate significant portions of their budgets to getting the company name better known within local communities.

We are bombarded by thousands of commercial messages every day, some direct, others subliminal. Most of them either go unnoticed or are intentionally deflected. A distinct minority are actually remembered. Fewer still stick with us and lead us to want to learn more about the company and its products. Occasionally we are compelled to purchase the advertised goods we have seen on TV or been exposed to through sponsorship. Why? Was it the ad itself or was it the culmination of a company's well-thought-out and integrated marketing strategy?

During the TV era, a handful of memorable commercials, advertising campaigns, and characters have emerged. Great ads have always struck an emotional chord, relying on humor, fear, sex, and other emotions to make a close and long-lasting connection with the viewer.

Do you recall the public service announcement in which an Indian cried a single tear as litter, tossed out a car window, landed at his feet? What about the famous "Daisy" commercial that portrayed an innocent little girl picking daisies destroyed by an atom bomb (one presumably dropped by Barry Goldwater)? This political ad was so good at playing on people's fears that it was pulled off the air after a single showing.

On the lighter side, who can forget those old Bartles & Jaymes guys, pitching Ernest & Julio Gallo wine coolers while, "Thanking you for your support"? Or what about the Wendy's "Where's the beef" lady, Clara Peller? Or Mikey and his Life cereal?

Why do you remember these ads and marketing campaigns? Was it their compelling message or just their status as advertising legend?

Did you buy a hamburger at Wendy's because it was bigger, because you had a coupon, or because you liked Dave Thomas, the chain's owner? Or maybe it was because your local Wendy's is simply more convenient than other fast food restaurants? Regardless, advertising likely played a role somehow.

In 1926, Wheaties was the first product to ever use a jingle on the radio. However, the cereal became much more than cereal flakes thanks to its commercials, which implied that athletes like Hank

Aaron and Mary Lou Retton couldn't do what they did best without eating "The Breakfast of Champions."

General Mills, which made Wheaties, is also responsible for positioning Cheerios such that it transcends the "toasted oats" label. As the brand was on the rise in the 1940s and 1950s, General Mills boosted sales by associating the cereal with the ever-popular Lone Ranger through advertising and prizes that could be found in the cereal box. Both Cheerios and Wheaties cost significantly more than the generic toasted oats and wheat flakes found on the grocer's shelves but, for some reason, many consumers feel better picking the more established brand name—even if it does cost as much as 50 percent more.

Did any of the ads or marketing campaigns linked to these products motivate you, assuming you were the targeted customer, to want to sample the product? Were you more inclined to buy that particular product than that of the competitors? Did the ads or marketing campaigns make you more inclined to become brand loyal? Or did they just entertain you, allowing you a brief respite from everyday hassles?

If these ads in fact influenced your purchase decision, what else played a critical role? Sponsorship? Promotion? Something less overt? We "know" the ads and are familiar with the campaigns, but we are even more influenced by the strategic marketing behind them. As critical—and fun—as advertisements can be in "hooking" potential customers, they alone are seldom enough to get the entire marketing job done.

Creative and entertaining advertisements have routinely incorporated sports—or used sports as a backdrop—to make their case to consumers. In fact, sports-oriented ads and marketing campaigns have been among the most heralded. Although it is certainly debatable which have best utilized sports, at least four over the last 30 years have shaped how corporations use sports to get their message to the masses.

These masses have been properly segmented by the companies seeking to reach them and have been communicated to through advertising, and in many cases, buttressed with a comprehensive sports sponsorship strategy. Each used a breakthrough TV ad to support its broader marketing campaign. And each is in our marketing hall of fame for its ability to reach its intended audience. Their message was clear and the plot was both engaging and memorable.

Miller Lite leveraged the personalities of dozens of former athletes, whereas Coke focused on just one: "Mean" Joe Greene. Apple Computer relied on its "1984" ad, which it ran only once, during Super Bowl XVIII, to introduce the Macintosh. By the 1990s, it was Gatorade encouraging everyone to "Be Like Mike."

When considering the following examples, understand that a single great commercial seldom makes a brand, and that great brands must work diligently to see that their marketing message evolves, often relying on different messengers to woo target markets through the years. In essence, successful brands, including those that incorporate sports marketing when reaching customers, establish and extend comprehensive marketing campaigns.

MILLER LITE

"Everything You Always Wanted in a Beer and Less" and "Tastes Great, Less Filling" remain among the most brilliant taglines in advertising history. For 15 years beginning in 1973, Miller Beer's brand extension, Miller Lite, delivered an extraordinary advertising campaign that relied on retired athletes to promote its low-calorie beer.

The campaign featured numerous athletes as regular beer-drinking guys. Miller used, among others, Tommy Heinsohn, Bubba Smith, Dick Butkus, Larry Csonka, Carlos Palomino, and Billy Martin.

Another Miller Lite campaign, one featuring legendary baseball personality Bob Uecker, was equally memorable. "I must be in the front row," crowed Uecker in one TV spot, to an usher at Yankee Stadium. Instead, Uecker, who assumed he would be given a preferred seat because he thought everyone remembered him from his playing days, was taken to a seat in the farthest reaches of the ballpark, a section still referred to by fans as "Uecker seats." Coincidentally, Uecker now announces for the Milwaukee Brewers, the National League team that now plays in Miller Park.

Miller successfully linked its product to its primary consumer—the weekend warrior and avid sports fan who enjoyed a touch of irreverence. The campaign was also advantaged because it was able to leverage sports' long-standing and historical relationship with the breweries, one dating back more than a century. These ads worked not only because they simultaneously communicated multiple product attributes to the company's core consumer, but also because they did so in a tone these targeted consumers welcomed.

COCA-COLA

The 1979 commercial featuring Pittsburgh Steelers defensive lineman "Mean" Joe Greene, in which he gives his game jersey to a thrilled young boy after drinking the fan's Coke, is among sports' most memorable.

Because of its simplicity, one linking generations and ethnicities in an extraordinarily emotional context, the impact of this ad has endured. In the ad, Greene is offered a Coke by a young boy as the hall of fame player limps his way through a stadium tunnel. Greene initially declines the gesture, but eventually gives in and drinks the entire Coke in one fell swoop. As the child turns to walk away, Greene smiles and, in appreciation, tosses his game jersey to the child.

The ad was so widely acclaimed by Coke, its loyal consumers, and the advertising community that Coke initiated similar campaigns around the world, using sports heroes from Brazil and Thailand in customized international spots.

Coke's ability to link its product to the emotional side of sports while reinforcing the company's close attachment to it provided Coke an additional measure of authenticity to its targeted audience. After all, what is more universal than a child learning a life lesson from a sports hero and, to some, a role model?

APPLE COMPUTER

With a single airing during the third quarter of Super Bowl XVIII, Apple Computer's "1984" ad redefined the power of TV advertising by delivering unparalleled production value and cinematic style.

The ad opens on a gray network of futuristic tubes connecting blank, inauspicious buildings. Inside the tubes are legions of drones marching toward a large, nondescript auditorium, where they bow before a Big Brother figure that is lecturing to them on an oversized TV screen. One lone woman's spirit remains unshaken. Undeterred by the storm troopers that are chasing her, she runs up to the huge screen and, with a determined motion, throws an enormous hammer at it, destroying the TV image. As the screen explodes, the stunned audience basks in the light of its new freedom, while a voiceover announces, "On January 24th, Apple Computer will introduce the Macintosh. And you'll see why 1984 won't be like *1984.*

"1984" was supposed to air during a college bowl game, but a last-minute switch was made because Apple wanted the commercial to air closer to the product's launch date.

Excluding production costs, Apple spent $1.5 million for this one-time, 60-second spot. Today, the same ad would cost more than twice as much to run, which makes the Super Bowl the costliest sports programming during which to advertise.

Although most companies lack the financial and human resources to advertise during the Super Bowl, Apple made it clear that timing and placement is everything, particularly when an ad such as "1984" was a stand-alone event and not part of a comprehensive marketing and sponsorship program.

GATORADE

Prior to signing Michael Jordan to endorse its products in 1991, Gatorade—which celebrated its 35th anniversary in 2002—was already experiencing tremendous marketing success with the help of its great jingle, "Gatorade is thirst aid, for that deep down body thirst!" Yet its product relied solely on its relationship with sports leagues and didn't have a specific face for consumers to associate with.

When Gatorade signed Jordan and launched the "Be Like Mike" campaign, it extended its connection to sports by linking its products in an even more personal way, leveraging an even catchier jingle that begins: "Sometimes I dream ... that he is me ...," and concludes with, "Oh, if I could be like Mike..."

Whereas Nike implied that fans could fly if they bought Air Jordans, Gatorade—utilizing the same sales theme as Wheaties—said that if you, too, wanted to excel in sports, drinking Gatorade was the answer. After all, can there be a true victory celebration in sports without Gatorade being poured over the coach's head? This intimate and powerful attachment of the leading sports drink brand to the top sports personality in the world further reinforced Gatorade's impressive 84 percent market share.

Miller Lite taught us that it can be beneficial to explain the benefits as quickly as you can, whereas Coke demonstrated just how compelling a simple message can be. The simpler the message, the easier it is to absorb. Are your marketing efforts communicating a message that is too complicated for your target consumers to easily grasp?

The Apple ad caught viewers' attention better than any other to date. It immediately followed its attention-grabbing intro by telling you what to expect from its new computer. What cost-effective marketing initiatives is your business undertaking to avoid ever-increasing advertising clutter? What is it that makes your message stand out to potential consumers? Have you identified not only the proper advertising medium for your company's products, but also the most appropriate time to advertise?

Creating, implementing, and servicing marketing campaigns are extraordinarily challenging. Before any company can rise to the level of Miller, Coke, Apple, or Gatorade, it must clearly understand how and why sports can be an effective medium to use when communicating the marketing message because advertising alone seldom gets the job done.

It is also important to realize that three of the aforementioned companies—Miller, Coke, and Gatorade (now owned by Coke's competitor, Pepsi)—that incorporated a sports theme have invested significant resources throughout the sports world to further establish and legitimize their brands in the eyes of sports fans. They have done so because these companies realize that a single TV ad or campaign might very well be insufficient.

Miller had been the official sponsor of the NFL for 18 years until Coors signed a four-year, $300 million deal with the league in 2002. However, Miller still maintains individual sponsorship deals with numerous teams.

Coke, too, was the official soft drink of the NFL for 22 years until Pepsi signed a five-year, $160 million deal with the league in 2002. Like Miller, Coke still has the rights to many individual teams.

Gatorade, for its part, continues to invest in the latest generation of athletes—including Indianapolis Colts quarterback Peyton Manning, Toronto Raptors forward Vince Carter, New York Yankees shortstop Derek Jeter, and Washington Freedom forward Mia Hamm of the Women's United Soccer Association. Additionally, and to complement this presence, Gatorade's logoed cups and coolers still adorn sports sidelines, benches, and dugouts. Moreover, it has been a partner of the NFL for nearly 35 years, and has partnered with MLB and the NBA for decades.

Your organization might not have the money or inclination to utilize athletes or advertise during major sporting events. In fact, most companies are relegated to regional or local campaigns, whether it includes advertising, sponsorship, or promotion. Nonetheless, much can be learned from successful sports marketing powerhouses such as those just highlighted.

Affording the likes of Michael Jordan to help personalize your product is a pipe dream for all but a handful of companies. However, local and regional businesses of all sizes have accomplished similar results by featuring their own hometown sports leagues, teams, and athletes in their marketing campaigns, often by sponsoring a local Pop Warner football team or by purchasing signage on an outfield wall at the local Little League field.

Using Sports to Reach Your "Fans"

Much can be learned from how companies use sports to reach their end users. It is undeniable that big business in this country actively pursues consumers in virtually all demographic groups through sports marketing. This "cradle to grave" exposure—from Little League to the senior leagues—targets every consumer that has, or is likely to have, purchasing power.

Corporations use sports marketing to achieve numerous, and often times simultaneous, objectives when targeting these customers. Knowing they have a relatively captive audience tuned in during "TV timeouts," fast food companies, for example, frequently reinforce their relationships with sports fans by running commercials intended to persuade couch potatoes to buy the advertised brand of burger or pizza the next time they need their fast food fix.

Appreciating the sheer volume of people in attendance at sports venues, it is not unusual for cell phone companies to distribute surveys to sports fans or have them test market new products to assist in the product development process.

Knowing that sporting events can be used as a relaxing backdrop to conduct external business development, many companies lease luxury boxes to close important deals. These same companies often rely on the cache of a luxury box to reward employees for their achievements or dedication to the company.

Regardless of which objectives or combinations of objectives are sought, the primary goal of sports marketing is to drive sales and increase shareholder value. This is frequently accomplished by supplementing great advertising with showing (potential) customers that your brand is prevalent where targeted consumers expect to see it, namely, attached to sports via sponsorship, promotion, or other mar keting vehicles.

To validate that the use of sports makes sense in an organization's marketing pursuits, successful businesses revisit their corporate mission and goals, and identify internal and external strengths and weaknesses before giving sports marketing serious consideration.

Once this review is completed to management's satisfaction, attention can then be turned to conducting the requisite research to validate that the organization's customers can indeed be reached because of their connection to sports. Companies, regardless of their size or resources, that are successful in sports marketing then turn their attention to segmenting markets.

MARKET SEGMENTATION

To properly segment markets, marketers must divide potential customers into homogeneous groups. Doing so is more expensive and complex than simply taking a mass-market approach, but it makes it easier to reach customers while differentiating a firm from its competitors.

In addition to targeting particular customer groups for the express purpose of selling them a product or service, successfully segmenting markets will also enable a company to gather valuable feedback from, and information about, potential customers.

There are five primary techniques that marketers use to segment markets.[1] Some techniques require more time and resources than others, but these typically yield more valuable information that makes it easier for companies to reach intended customers. The five primary segmentation techniques are based on the following factors:

- Geography
- Demographics
- Usage patterns
- Lifestyles
- Benefits

1. Tellis, Gerard, *Advertising & Sales Promotion Strategy* (p. 21). Addison-Wesley, 1998.

The most basic of the segmentation techniques utilizes geography to differentiate consumers. Marketers understand that preferences can vary greatly from country to country or, for that matter, from neighborhood to neighborhood. Marketers routinely use geographic segmentation as a starting point from which they further narrow the customers they seek.

Segmentation occurs when a new business determines how many local publications it can afford to advertise in, or how many and which mailboxes it should be dropping its take-out menu into. It continues with regional stores that have effectively used hometown professional athletes that have a strong connection to the community. They utilize these athletes at store grand openings and in local cable ads blanketing the region where the team plays.

The Wiz, an electronics chain in New York, New Jersey, and Connecticut, has used former Jets and Giants quarterbacks Joe Namath and Phil Simms as spokesmen, both of whom were used on special editions of the chain's phone cards.

The next method of segmentation is more refined and considers a potential market's specific demographic qualities. This includes grouping consumers by age, ethnicity, gender, income, education, or occupation.

Ace Hardware and Tinactin antifungal foot products not only utilize former NFL coach and current ABC broadcaster John Madden as their spokesman, but they also run commercials featuring Madden during games, clearly targeting football-watching males.

Simply segmenting a market by age, such as middle-aged men, might not sufficiently narrow a market. However, combining it with the previous geographic technique, such as the New England area, might yield an adequately segmented target market.

A local Lexus car dealership can target an age group of 35- to 54-year-olds, but it also has to determine a cost-effective territory in which to advertise. Does it have a database that reveals that customers have come from 30 miles away because Lexus dealerships are few and far between? What information, if any, does it share with other dealers outside its core territory? What is the dealer's relationship with other car dealers in the same area? Is it purely adversarial or might the Lexus dealer also own the Volvo and Saab dealership in a neighboring city? Are the potential buyers of these three models a homogeneous group? How much will it cost to find out?

Another valuable way to segment markets is by lifestyle. This technique groups individuals based on their personal values and the way they live. It is more time-consuming and cost-prohibitive, but if done successfully, this technique provides marketers with target rich segments. Combining the previous two techniques with lifestyle segmentation delivers a more distinct homogeneous group that marketers strive to reach.

For instance, if a baseball team wants to sell a grandstand seat to a blue-collar worker it should focus on how inexpensive the seat is. This same team would be well advised to focus on the proximity of the seats to the action when attempting to sell a field-level seat to a small company hoping to impress a client. For a team's most affluent potential customers that are considering the purchase of a luxury suite, the amenities—such as how comfortable the seats are, the promptness of the wait service, and the variety of exotic hors d'oeuvres—might be stressed.

Usage segmentation further refines the target marketing process by grouping consumers based on how they use or consume a certain product. This segmentation technique can reveal the extent to which customers are brand loyal or even provide information about why customers choose to switch brands.

For example, credit card companies can customize and direct promotional campaigns based on where and to what extent its cardmembers use its credit cards. Billing inserts sent to American Express Platinum cardholders differ from those found in American Express' standard "green" card billing statements.

Defining markets based on the product benefits customers seek can be the most useful segmentation technique. A primary example of this is the aforementioned Miller Lite beer. Two different consumers might buy the same beer for different reasons. One might be inclined to purchase a six-pack because the beer "tastes great" whereas the other might make his purchase decision because it is "less filling."

Consumer perceptions and values are changing more rapidly than ever because the sheer number of commercial messages consumers are exposed to continues to increase. If a company can access and understand the wants and needs of its customers, it will be poised to market its product to the ideal segment(s).

Each of these techniques has its own merits and advantages. Marketers have to make sure that they utilize the appropriate number of segmentation methods and weigh the feedback accordingly. Ideally, marketers will segment based on perceived product benefits and then combine remaining techniques to create an ideal segmentation mix.

Once potential markets are segmented, marketers must turn their attention to selecting the best target market to pursue. Selecting the right segment of the market is critical if a business is to survive. Accordingly, viable market segments have three important attributes:

- Quantitatively measurable
- Reachable
- Able to generate sufficient sales volume

At their core, viable market segments allow companies to forecast demand (quantify) and determine precisely how many resources should be allocated to not only accessing a particular market (reach), but also to ensuring a sufficient return on investment (sales volume) exists.

MasterCard, which has been consistently among the top 25 highest spenders in sports marketing, uses sports to target middle to upper class adults ages 18 to 44. As evidenced in its "Priceless" advertising campaign, MasterCard has targeted parents that not only possess discretionary income, but also have families that enjoy conveniently located sports and entertainment events.

It is useful to consider a company such as MasterCard because it has not only extensively used sports marketing, but has done so effectively, forging one of the closest relationships between corporate America and the world of sports.

CASE STUDY: MASTERCARD

Based in Purchase, New York, MasterCard is a global payment services company that, thanks in large part to its brilliant use of sports marketing, is one of the most recognized and respected brands in the world. The company manages the relationships between cardholders, businesses, and organizations that accept the card, and financial institutions.

More than 1.7 billion MasterCard (and its affiliate cards) logos are present on credit, charge, and debit cards in circulation today, with more than 28 million businesses accepting it as a payment option.

MasterCard began in the late 1940s when some American banks started giving customers paper that was as good as cash and could used to make purchases with local merchants. Within a couple of years, a New York bank started issuing actual credit cards. After other major city banks followed suit, the Interbank Card Association—which eventually became MasterCard—formed in 1966 to organize payment across the country. Now, nearly 40 years later, MasterCard has more than 30 worldwide offices.

By the late 1980s, MasterCard recognized that it needed to review and refine its corporate strategy if it was to increase its market share. It had to narrow its focus and decide which geographic areas the company would target. MasterCard also had to differentiate itself from other credit card issuers in what had become a fiercely competitive segment of the financial services industry.

Once MasterCard's marketing executives identified the company's desired target markets, it had to communicate a marketing message that would allow it to successfully compete within these markets.

Company executives then determined that an appropriate way to do so was to allocate tremendous human and financial resources to sports marketing, a strategy that it believed would send the right message about its evolving image and the financial services it offered. At the same time—and to this day—MasterCard's archrival, Visa, has been omnipresent throughout the world of sports, providing an added dimension to both companies' strategic marketing efforts.

Aligning with the sports world works for companies offering financial services because doing so gives the credit card brands an opportunity to strengthen their relationships with existing customers. Using sports as a marketing vehicle—typically in the form of sponsorship and promotion—also provides these companies an opportunity to access new customers, as well as provide incentives for new businesses to accept their card.

Like their global counterparts, local companies and organizations must similarly understand that a disciplined process is called for—even if the decision at hand is whether to donate to the refurbishment of the local park or volunteering your employees' time to help register kids for the local roller hockey league.

MASTERCARD: USE OF SPORTS

MasterCard has prominently utilized sports sponsorships to increase its domestic and global reach. Company executives say they believe that their use of sports can influence large, dedicated sports fan bases in major markets around the world. Its sponsorships currently include World Cup Soccer, MLB, the NHL, the Canadian

Hockey League, the Professional Golf Association (PGA) Tour, and the Jordan Grand Prix Formula One auto-racing event.

In 2001, the company spent $52.8 million in sports sponsorships, which made MasterCard the 16th largest sports spending company according to Nielsen Media Research. But Bob Cramer, MasterCard's vice president of global sponsorships and event marketing, maintains that "it's not just about writing the big checks. You don't want to sell caviar to NASCAR fans, because they probably won't consume it."

Companies that sponsor sports routinely spend three to five times the cost of their "official" sponsorship to adequately promote and market their relationship with the sports property, whether an event, league, team, or even an individual athlete.

Consequently, when major corporations such as Coca-Cola become official Olympic sponsors at a cost of about $55 million, it is not unusual for them to spend another $200 million supporting their connection to the Games. In addition to attempting to capitalize on global sports marketing platforms such as the Olympics, companies also spend money to fend off competing brands that do their best to ambush their rival's official relationship by confusing the public with "Olympic" images associated with their product or service.

MasterCard officials say they believe that for the company to sponsor a team, event, or sports organization, the property in question must enable the company to simultaneously allow it to reinforce its brand image and awareness, deliver increased card usage, and provide value to its cardholders.

Many companies that rely on sports marketing prefer to sponsor events rather than use other, more risky forms such as retaining athletes as spokespeople. One prominent sports management executive went so far as to remind marketers that events cannot break a leg or sprain an ankle, nor do they fail drug tests or lose six-love, six-love.

For companies lacking MasterCard's resources, these events can include sponsoring a single hole at a local golf tournament, the proceeds of which benefit the local children's hospital, or even by making a modest cash contribution to help facilitate sports at the neighborhood YMCA. By doing so in a targeted and well-considered fashion that includes delicately balancing philanthropy with target marketing, small organizations can attain the same three objectives relied on by MasterCard.

MasterCard executives say they believe that its sports sponsorships provide the company with an important source of brand differentiation and help the company position itself in an industry where many consumers view the various credit card alternatives as interchangeable. Not only has MasterCard bought into the merits of sports marketing, but it has devoted the necessary time and energy to leverage the resources it allocates. This has enabled the company to reach—and often surpass—its quantifiable marketing objectives. Most notably, MasterCard has done this through soccer's World Cup and the company's "Priceless" advertising campaign.

WORLD CUP SOCCER

By the 1990s the payment service industry was reaching the saturation point in the United States. Therefore, MasterCard and its primary competitors, Visa and American Express, allocated more time and resources to extending their global reach.

For MasterCard this meant the company needed to develop, extend, and manage a worldwide image. It also had to accomplish this while repositioning itself from a domestic credit card company to a global financial payments organization.

To accomplish this, MasterCard sought to sponsor a global property that would allow it to differentiate itself from the competition by linking the consumers' affinity to the event to the MasterCard brand.

It selected World Cup soccer. The company's primary objective in sponsoring the 1990 and 1994 World Cups was to increase the brand's awareness on a worldwide basis. MasterCard's decision to market itself abroad is not unlike small companies who hope to get the word out in neighboring communities or regions by sponsoring youth soccer, Little League, or even a 10K run that benefits a local charity. Like MasterCard, small businesses must support their sponsorship of these events by glad-handing parents or working the water station at mile three.

MasterCard not only has the money and resources to use large global sporting events to reach its international consumer base, but also has the integrated strategy and corporate vision to support its high-profile sports marketing endeavors. Companies, regardless of size, that lack an understanding about how to properly segment— and then exploit—target audiences through an integrated marketing campaign are opening themselves up to failure.

The World Cup, which is played over a four-week period, includes teams from 32 countries. The 1998 World Cup was played in France and delivered a cumulative viewing audience of 37 billion across 200 countries and, in 2002, that number was believed to surpass 40 billion. To put this number in perspective, the World Cup was viewed by approximately 50 times the cumulative number of worldwide viewers (800 million) tuned in to watch that year's Super Bowl.

In addition to the event's unparalleled reach, soccer's popularity in numerous strategically important MasterCard markets also contributed to the company's sponsorship decision.

These two important pieces of information led MasterCard to pay approximately $25 million to become an official event sponsor during each World Cup. Beyond this initial investment, MasterCard spent tens of millions of dollars supporting its sponsorship in an effort to primarily build brand awareness among the billions watching on TV. In fact, in 1998, MasterCard was the only on-field sponsor with corporate signage behind the goals.

Following each World Cup, MasterCard quantifies what the sponsorship has meant to the company. The 1998 World Cup in France reportedly doubled card spending outside the U.S. while also increasing the company's brand equity. In addition to having extensive in-venue signage and running numerous TV commercials throughout the tournament, MasterCard differentiated itself by utilizing the services of Pele, soccer's greatest icon who helped Brazil win three World Cups. MasterCard, which has used this global sports icon as an endorser for more than a decade, also issued a commemorative collector's card featuring soccer's greatest legend.

MasterCard's favorable results made its decision to sponsor the 2002 World Cup, jointly played in the vital MasterCard markets of Japan and Korea, an easy one. There was much to be gained because Japan and Korea were clearly the most untapped World Cup host cities since MasterCard began its association with the event (1990 in Italy, 1994 in United States, 1998 in France). In fact, MasterCard believed that less than 1 percent of the Southeast Asian population used credit cards in 2002.

Total spending by MasterCard users leading up to the World Cup in the Asia-Pacific region reportedly grew by 20 percent in 2001, despite the fact that the company was challenged due to an unwillingness among the majority of Japanese banks to accept overseas bank cards. MasterCard understood this marketing challenge and hoped to leverage its sports marketing activities to overcome it.

Although most companies can never expect to leverage a sports marketing event like the World Cup to drive business, the same principles and processes used by MasterCard are utilized by small businesses everyday. Local nurseries, after analyzing their town and the potential customers that live there, might determine that sponsoring a local Little League team is its version of the World Cup. Or, perhaps, it's the dry cleaner inserting a coupon in the tournament program distributed at a local bowling alley. Sports marketing tenets are universal for both the MasterCard's and the "Joe's Burgers" of the world, but their application and implementation no doubt requires refinement on the local level.

MasterCard carefully analyzed the merits of becoming a World Cup sponsor. It followed this analysis by devising a strategy that had clearly defined and measurable goals and objectives. The company implemented its marketing programs using tactics that it believed would help it penetrate already segmented markets. The results of MasterCard's systematically planning its work and working its plan were impressive.

The same cannot be said for a high-profile sports marketing campaign undertaken by Progressive Auto Insurance. Utilizing 30,000 sales agents, Progressive is a company that sells its service in the U.S. and Canada. It spent a reported $3 million to become the official sponsor of the 1999 Super Bowl halftime show. As part of its sponsorship, Progressive had its name mentioned throughout the broadcast and supplemented this exposure by purchasing an ad during the telecast as well. The company also had its name at the base of the stage as Stevie Wonder and Gloria Estefan sang during the game's intermission.

Progressive's CEO, Peter Lewis, later admitted that he learned a lot from his company's haphazard foray into sports marketing. And, in a 1999 briefing to investors, Progressive executives said "inexperience" and "hubris" led the company to "incur significant losses without achieving proportionate benefits."

What did Lewis learn? He learned that his sponsorship didn't increase interest in, or sales of, his insurance products because viewers weren't thinking about buying auto insurance during the halftime show. Having learned an important lesson about target marketing from this high-profile mistake, Progressive now sponsors traffic updates on local newscasts, a much more appropriate medium through which potential consumers can make a connection to the company and its products. Some local businesses, when they see that their advertising efforts aren't working, reduce the amount they are spending. However, as Progressive has demonstrated, it's not only about the total dollars allocated; it is as much about where those advertising dollars are spent.

Although the Miller Lite, Coca-Cola, Apple, and Gatorade commercials helped build their brand names, it's a sustained integrated sales and marketing effort that made these companies what they are today.

Relying on a single great ad or one big event to increase sales, seemingly the strategy of Progressive, seldom works. The greatness of Apple's 1984 commercial certainly didn't allow the company to hold off the Microsofts and the Gateways of the world. However, it bears mention that had Apple not leveraged its 1984 commercial and continued to correctly segment its customers and promote its brand appropriately, the benefits from having run the ad would have quickly diminished.

A "PRICELESS" SPORTS MARKETING CAMPAIGN

After successfully segmenting markets, MasterCard created, relied on, and then extended a particularly compelling advertising campaign—its extraordinarily successful "Priceless" campaign: "There are some things money can't buy. For everything else, there's MasterCard." The brilliance in this tagline lies in its exceedingly basic message, a message that sports fans, a great number of whom are credit card users, can readily relate to.

McCann-Erickson developed and subsequently launched what has since been dubbed MasterCard's "Priceless" campaign in 1997. Within four years, the advertising campaign has aired in over 80 countries in 36 languages.

Although credit card companies might measure their own financial success based on the amount its customers charge to their cards, MasterCard's ad campaign suggested that the best moments are not in fact those that can be easily purchased. In addition, the company found that its ads were more likely to be absorbed if they came off as genuine, purposeful, and resourceful, and resonated with both casual and avid fans.

The first ad showed a father and son at a baseball game. The father uses his MasterCard to pay for tangible items, such as two tickets ($28), two hot dogs, two popcorns, and two sodas ($18), and one autographed baseball ($45). The conversation between the son and the father, MasterCard implies, is priceless.

These spots were followed by an ad where the "priceless" experience was taking a Little League team to its first big league game and another capitalized on the priceless experience of witnessing the 1998 home run derby between Mark McGwire and Sammy Sosa.

Yet another commercial opens with a mother using a camcorder to show her husband and two children leaving for a game. After calculating the cost of the camcorder, the videotape, and the required battery, the conversation ultimately recorded on the videotape between the children and Hall of Famers Hank Aaron and Willie Mays is deemed "priceless" by comparison.

Although these baseball-themed campaigns were very successful, companies associated with another event—sports or otherwise—have to be prepared for fallout should something detrimental occur.

In essence, the sponsoring company can be deemed an accomplice if there is a "marketing" crime. MasterCard experienced this firsthand when its sponsorship of MLB's All-Century team turned sour in 1999. Less than three years later, with the company still having a major investment in the sport, it was forced to contemplate scaling back its $100 million promotion when considering a potential work stoppage in MLB.

During the pregame show for Game 2 of the 1999 World Series, the top 25 players from the past 100 years were revealed. The players, which were selected as part of a promotion overseen by MasterCard, included Pete Rose. However, when NBC's Jim Gray grilled Rose about the documented reports of his gambling in his first sanctioned appearance at a major league ballpark since Rose's lifetime ban from baseball in 1989, the situation turned ugly.

When Rose wouldn't admit to betting on baseball, Gray continued to prod question after question, to the point where viewers felt awkward and put off by the reporter's approach. The situation and the handling of it by Gray quickly got back to MasterCard.

Five thousand fans contacted MasterCard to register their disgust and the company felt it was necessary to issue a press release urging NBC and Gray to apologize.

The point here is that even though an event cannot break a leg, sprain an ankle, fail a drug test, or lose six-love, six-love, it does not mean that a brand cannot and will not be harmed by developments seemingly beyond its control. This is why the use of sports—or any medium that is susceptible to "human error"—must be entered into with great care and managed to the satisfaction of (potential) customers and shareholders.

Approximately three years later, MasterCard found itself in another precarious situation. Throughout the 2002 season, the company allowed fans to rank their most memorable moments in baseball history from a list of 30, with the intention of unveiling the list during the World Series. In addition, one lucky voter and fan would win a trip for 10 to the 2002 World Series.

The launching of this campaign was marred by the ill-fated All-Star Game in Milwaukee. The infamous game, which ended in a 7–7 tie after the 11th inning due to both teams running out of players, overshadowed anything and everything else associated with this annual baseball showcase. The rollout of MasterCard's campaign—which included the company's retaining Barry Bonds as an endorser—was further jeopardized as a result of an anticipated player strike in September, a mere month before the most memorable list was to be unveiled.

Although a strike was averted at the last minute, thanks to the agreement on a new four-year collective bargaining agreement between the players and the owners, MasterCard had already begun to scale back its promotion by canceling some scheduled press interviews with Hall of Famers. Additionally, the company had to devise a full contingency plan in the event the World Series would not be played. Ultimately, the company's promotional campaign concluded with Cal Ripken's consecutive games played streak being voted by fans as the sport's most enduring moment.

For most companies involved in sports marketing these risks translate to affiliating themselves with community-focused and supported events that lack significant risk but yield much needed exposure.

In MasterCard's case, this much-heralded exposure led to something else: litigation.

Protecting "Priceless" Messages

Imitation is widely considered the most sincere form of flattery. However, after several years of running its "Priceless" campaign, MasterCard finally became fed up with both the magnitude of, and tone used in, a variety of spoofs.

In an effort to protect the campaign's brand name, as well as its own, MasterCard began to take legal action against those using the "Priceless" format without the company's permission and using the campaign's trademark tagline for commercial gain without the company's consent or license.

The company did so by initiating litigation to halt the spoofs by emphatically stating that the success of the "Priceless" campaign required the company to insulate its campaign and tagline from those who sought to use it for their own promotional purposes.

MasterCard officials recognized that being hypersensitive to protecting the images and messages contained in the "Priceless" campaign was essential to protecting the integrity of the entire marketing program. MasterCard does this on a global basis; small businesses must similarly do so on a relative scale.

For example, that local coffee shop that builds traffic by marketing its frequent diner program must be equally sensitive to the management of its marketing message. In fact, it might be even more important for small, family-run businesses to protect their marketing message—especially when the family name is on the door. Similarly, small businesses must be careful not to intentionally copy, as a major lawsuit by a corporate behemoth could easily put them out of business.

Knock-off "Priceless" campaigns appeared everywhere and were used by adult and humor-oriented Web sites, as well as prominent politicians. MasterCard claimed that the spoofs, many of which were in poor taste, hurt its brand name, causing it significant harm in the hearts and minds of consumers.

For instance, one knock-off spoof made light of the high school massacre in Columbine, Colorado, and another slightly less grave—but just as politically incorrect—high school spoof addressed the trials and tribulations of the high school sports scene. In this knock-off, prominent mention was made about how a football team's cheerleader, impregnated by the star quarterback, could use the card to pay for an abortion.

MasterCard even sued the Green Party's presidential candidate Ralph Nader for $5 million, alleging "unfair competition" and "deceptive trade practices" resulting from Nader's parody of the "Priceless" campaign, one aimed at his political adversaries George W. Bush and Al Gore.

MasterCard's legal counsel sent a letter to the Nader campaign explaining that the company had no involvement in the presidential aspirations of Nader. MasterCard was also concerned that its cardmembers could be left with the mistaken impression that MasterCard was involved with or endorsing the Nader candidacy. In September 2000, Nader prevailed after a federal judge ruled that MasterCard failed to show how it harmed them.

Many felt that the company was being hypersensitive about the spoofs and that the company should "lighten up" or "get a sense of humor." For MasterCard, however, that was hardly the point.

Seldom has a company struck such a strong marketing chord with a message aimed at such highly segmented markets. Master-Card's ability to effectively target market customers with a creative campaign mimicked worldwide speaks to the company's extraordinary marketing efforts.

The company's intense policing of its "Priceless" campaign vividly demonstrates that companies that have developed unique and invaluable marketing themes must devote resources to ensuring their integrity. Companies, including Cyveillance Technology and Delahaye Medialink, now provide corporations with the tools necessary to track their brand names and logos should they appear on unauthorized Web sites.

These developments reinforce the fact that once a stellar brand is established, in this case an ad campaign, it must occasionally be micromanaged to ensure its continued success and build shareholder value.

THE COMPLETE MARKETING PACKAGE

MasterCard has matched its uncanny ability to create a great emotion-based ad campaign with its ability to devise a fully integrated marketing program to ensure its continued success.

From a sports marketing perspective, this included the company's $81 million, five-year renewal of its MLB sponsorship. Rather than simply airing its "Priceless" ads on Fox and ESPN during games, MasterCard is supporting the campaign by attaching itself to MLB's international and online marketing initiatives, as well as the All-Star Game and World Series, none of which comes without measured risk.

Organizations can put themselves in a position to successfully use sports marketing to help build shareholder value provided they confirm that the use of sports is consistent with their mission and goals and that they have the resources necessary to implement and service the sports marketing programs.

Regardless of a company's size, stature, or resources, great effort must be taken to segment markets prior to attempting to reach them with a well-constructed marketing message. This segmentation can be done based on geography, demographics, usage patterns, life-styles, product benefits, or any other constructive criteria.

MasterCard has used the World Cup and World Series as success-ful marketing platforms; small mom-and-pop businesses might be well advised to use youth soccer and 10K fun runs.

Companies must also determine that targeted audiences repre-sent viable market segments that allow them to forecast product demand, determine precisely how many resources need to be allo-cated to accessing a particular market, and ensure a sufficient return on their marketing investment.

Reaching customers through the broad use of marketing has never been easy but, thanks to the sports marketing lessons provided by MasterCard, it has become a little easier to understand.

CHAMPIONSHIP POINTS

The companies highlighted throughout this chapter have used sports as a backdrop to market their products and services; some have succeeded beyond anyone's wildest expectations, and others have failed. Those in the sports marketing Hall of Fame, including Miller, Coke, Apple, Gatorade, and certainly MasterCard, understand the following:

- Great ads can make you laugh, cry, or even make you angry. However, absent a coherent marketing strategy, a single ad—regardless of its brilliance—will seldom lead to sustainable sales.
- Successfully investing marketing dollars in the sports world often includes initial spending on advertising to associate with the team or league, and is followed by allocating even more resources to reinforce this presence to important market seg-ments.
- A keen working knowledge and understanding about precisely what should be communicated in the marketing message is essential.
- Determining the best medium to communicate the marketing message is critical; it might be sporting events for MasterCard and Gatorade, but what is it for your company?
- Market research is invaluable. How can you successfully sell a product if you don't know what consumers seek?

- Market segmentation is required. How can you successfully sell a product if you don't know who or where the (potential) customers are?
- Marketing and financial limitations exist and must be considered when contemplating the totality of a comprehensive marketing strategy.
- The company's brand name will be attached to all those that help it get the word out and, consequently, must select their marketing platforms carefully.
- The importance of protecting the integrity of their marketing message at all costs.
- "Auditing" marketing campaigns to determine the return on investment of the marketing dollar is essential.
- There are inherent risks associated with any and all marketing alliances, including those that include the sports world.

Once businesses and organizations successfully identify and market to their customers, attention must be turned to providing stellar customer service. All the fancy advertising, market research, and integrated marketing efforts will be severely compromised if newly gained customers are not provided with adequate customer service.

3 CUSTOMER SERVICE

The Point: Businesses and organizations of all sizes often overlook the importance of delivering great customer service. In today's business world, being able to truly serve those on the other side of the counter is often the major differentiator. However, poor customer service remains as prevalent an issue in big-time sports as it does in any other industry and has been exacerbated by the recent trend of the white-collarization of sports.

Certain sports leagues, especially Minor League Baseball, serve to remind us of the positive impact great customer service can have on an organization's bottom line. The minor leagues remind us that businesses are built one customer at a time and that catering to your customer's wants and needs—however large or small—is more important than ever. Minor League Baseball officials also realize that loyal customers are worth every penny it takes to keep them and that providing customer service is everyone's responsibility, regardless of where they are on the corporate ladder.

CUSTOMER SERVICE

Beyond paying lip service, far too many businesses pay scant attention to their customers, causing severe and unnecessary long-term damage to these delicate relationships that finance their enterprises.

In sports, customer service begins from the time you pile your family into the minivan or cram your face-painting, beer-guzzling cronies into the ramshackle Jeep and head off to the stadium. Either way, from the time you leave for the game (and listen to the pregame show on the radio) until the time you finally make it out of the stadium parking lot (listening to the postgame show), the issue of customer service should prevail.

It seldom does, however. Gridlock, the $8 beer, and unappreciative team management seem to lurk around every corner. Parking lot attendants, ticket takers, ushers, concessionaires, and even an athlete or two make fans feel as though they are inconveniencing them. It is not unusual for customers—the fans—to feel marginalized by the big business that sports has become.

However, Minor League Baseball, due in large part to its folksy feel and community orientation, has juxtaposed itself favorably against the major sports leagues by providing affordable, customer-service-focused, family entertainment in the process.

Unlike most Minor League Baseball fans, many fans of big-time sports have become disenfranchised due to the way they are treated once they arrive at the game. Still fewer can afford the freight to even check out their favorite teams in person. For more than a decade Team Marketing Report has published its Fan Cost Index (FCI).[1] This index tracks the cost of attending a game for a family of four and includes four average-price tickets, four small soft drinks, two small beers, four hot dogs, two game programs, parking, and two adult-size caps. The FCI suggests that a trip to the ballpark requires quite a financial commitment, as indicated in Table 3-1.

TABLE 3-1   Fan Cost Index for Four Professional Sports Leagues

SEASON	LEAGUE	FCI ($)
2002	NFL	290
2002–03	NBA	255
2002–03	NHL	240
2002	MLB	145

---

1. Team Marketing Report's Fan Cost Index. For more visit www.teammarketing.com.

Another way to look at these FCI totals would be to compare them to the other demands for a family's time and resources. A family can attend a NFL game or buy a couple of weeks' worth of groceries. It can take in a NBA game, or make that minivan payment. The same family can cheer on its favorite NHL team in person or take their son's entire Boy Scout troop to the latest Harry Potter movie. Although MLB remains relatively affordable, its FCI has increased 36 percent over the last five seasons.

The mythical family of four that Team Marketing Report likes to reference has become a rarity at many professional sporting events. The corporatization, or white-collarization, of sports as it has been called, began in earnest in the 1990s as teams and leagues realized they could make more money by catering to corporate America, which gobbled up luxury boxes and club seats in an effort to use sports as a backdrop for business development. Along the way, convenient parking, affordable concessions, and decent seats became scarce for Joe Average and his family.

As if this wasn't bad enough, professional sports has had more than its fair share of labor problems. Whether it's the players going on strike or owners locking their employees out, professional sports manages to constantly damage its relationship with fans. Billionaire owners suggesting that their multimillionaire employees are bleeding them dry sit on one side of the table. Spoiled athletes who seem to forget their privileged lifestyle—but not the trappings that come with it—sit on the other side of the table bemoaning their slave wages. Yet working families, who cannot relate to either side's position, are expected to finance each.

It's important to note that not all of pro sports, has succeeded in bundling an expensive product with abysmal customer service. Bill Veeck, owner of the St. Louis Browns, Cleveland Indians, and Chicago White Sox from the 1950s through the 1970s, broke attendance records, in part, because he was the best at customer service. The father of the modern-day promotion understood that he was constantly competing for the entertainment dollar and, to win that battle, he had to give his customers the feeling that there was no better place to spend their money.

Veeck wrote in his autobiography, *Veeck as in Wreck,* that a baseball team is a commercial venture operating for profit, and therefore, the idea that they didn't have to package their product as attractively as General Motors packaged its product, and hustle baseball the way General Motors hustled its product, was baseball's most pernicious enemy.

Veeck is best known for hiring little man Eddie Gaedel, who measured 3-foot-7, to step up to the plate as a stunt for a game in 1951. Gaedel naturally walked on four straight pitches, then sat on the bench and never played in another baseball game.

Veeck was known for doing anything that made his product stand out, always positioning his team to garner great newspaper coverage. That meant giving away dozens of live lobsters, a 200-pound cake of ice, and having zany promotions such as allowing everyone with the last name of either Smith or Jones free admission.

What Veeck should be remembered for are the little things he did that proved that he went out of his way for his customers and valued their time and hard-earned money. For example, Veeck figured out that baseball had neglected women as customers, saying that baseball treated women as men in dresses.

Veeck went out of his way to make the ballpark a better experience for women. As they entered the stadium they had a pretty good chance of receiving nylons or orchids, and sometimes even a Hawaiian lei. Every time he took over a team, he made sure the ladies rooms in his stadiums were perfect—something other male managers never considered. In Cleveland, he spent $40,000 to convert a stadium tower into a nursery school and had a dozen registered nurses on staff to watch children during games. Then he worked on making the kids in the nursery happy, making sure they received their milk and cookies.

Veeck did this because it was good for business. He quantified the returns and determined that when the customers were satisfied they spent more, as indicated by their spending on concessions.[2]

As shown in Table 3-2, Veeck calculated that x was the minimum amount of money that he would make on a given night, and, after reviewing his books, he figured out that a winning game would yield twice as much in postgame sales than a losing game. However, Veeck could increase sales regardless of the game's outcome provided he kept his focus on the customers by providing them with a postgame fireworks display.

2.   Veeck, Bill, with Linn, Ed, *Veeck as in Wreck* (p. 120), G.P. Putnam and Sons, New York, 1962. Reprinted by permission of Sterling Lord Literishi, Inc. Copyright 1962 by Bill Veeck, Estate O.

TABLE 3-2   Postgame Revenue

Outcome	Promotion	Impact
Lose game	None	x
Lose game	Fireworks	$1.4x$
Win game	None	$2x$
Win game	Fireworks	$3x$

Within the last couple of decades, Minor League Baseball teams have featured their version of Veeck's fireworks as much as they can to make fans happy and to keep in touch with their fan base. Teams have gone out of their way to ensure that customers enjoy a safe, affordable, family-friendly trip to the ballpark. The Minors offer a sporting experience reminiscent of the old days, when ushers greeted you by name and ballplayers signed autographs for free.

Accordingly, Minor League Baseball has seen its total attendance increase by 50 percent over the last decade and has a total annual attendance approaching 40 million fans, enabling many teams to become quite profitable, simultaneously increasing franchise values in the process.

It was 100 years ago that a group of baseball men got together in a hotel room in Chicago. They were the presidents of seven minor leagues who met to discuss the damage being done to the sport as a result of team owners fighting over players and territories. Following a series of meetings in which solutions to the sport's early problems were recommended, the seven emerged having created the National Association of Professional Baseball Leagues, Inc. (NAPBL), or its more widely known name, Minor League Baseball.

The presidents clearly had more than just organization on their minds, although they understood the importance of devising a workable structure for the sport. They showed amazing foresight by helping devise systems to honor each other's contracts (as well as penalties for violators), establish territorial rights in their cities, and put in place a salary structure, a player draft, a classification system for the different levels of leagues, and a reserve list of a specified number of players for each team.

These remain integral parts of Minor League Baseball. They are prime reasons the organization has been able to carry on for 100 years, going through boom times and depression, wars and natural disasters, while steadily moving forward to the thriving industry of today.

In the beginning, Minor League Baseball was an isolated organization, fighting for the preservation of its own rights. A hundred years later, it has grown into a formidable partner of MLB, serving not only as a feeder system to the Major Leagues, but ironically, as an exemplar of how to treat the customer to both its professional counterpart and other businesses alike.

CUSTOMER SERVICE 101

Hundreds of responses exist to the question, "What is customer service?" Depending on whom you ask—or which side of the counter you are on—you will hear a wide range of answers. Through all these responses, three prevailing principles have emerged.

First, every company must determine for itself the role and importance of customer service. Next, every employee must add value to the buying process. Finally, customers ultimately determine the value attached to service.

Once these principles are communicated and reinforced throughout a company it will be positioned to deliver the high levels of customer satisfaction that will enable it to not only retain its current customer base, but also to extend it. Customer retention experts JoAnna Brandi, Howard Hyden, and Chuck Reaves believe companies that excel at customer service have addressed and considered the following eight service principles, tenets, and issues:[3]

- Building customer loyalty
- "Moments of truth"
- The value of service
- Employees: The internal customer
- Customer service makes the difference
- What do your customers think?
- Turning complaints into devotion
- The customers who got away

3. Adapted from TEC Worldwide, Inc.'s, "Best Practices: Customer Retention."

BUILDING CUSTOMER LOYALTY

Establishing customer loyalty is one of the most overlooked yet critically important elements in building a successful business. Companies traditionally allocate resources to gaining customers, not keeping them. Once a customer is gained, his or her loyalty must be nurtured and never taken for granted because the costs of replenishing, or churning, customers is simply too high.

If you want to know how to treat a customer, look no further than the Kane County Cougars, a Midwest League single-A minor league affiliate of the Florida Marlins that plays in Geneva, Illinois. Located within an hour's drive of both Wrigley Field and Comiskey Park in Chicago, the team claims to have sold out almost every game since it began play in 1991.

The Cougars drew about 3,500 fans per game during the team's first year, leading the team to expand its stadium's seating capacity to 4,800 seats. Even that expansion was insufficient. The per-game average hovered around 5,000 fans when standing room and other special tickets were included in the count. During the Cougars' first five seasons in the league, total attendance increased 97 percent. Year after year the team has continued to post impressive attendance levels even as a single-A team. It now routinely finds itself among the top 15 in attendance throughout the entire minor league system, averaging close to 8,000 fans per game.

Fans weren't showing up in droves because the Cougars had great players; Marlins first-round draft pick catcher Charles Johnson is one of only a handful of recognizable players to have been on the Cougars' roster. Minor league teams can't market their players easily because their function by nature is to develop them enough so that they'll be promoted to the "big leagues."

This creates an interesting dichotomy, because a winning team with great players obviously helps, but those teams that learn how to cater to their customers, like the Cougars, have no problem with player movement. The team didn't win its first league championship until 2001. However, three seasons before, the *Sports Business Journal* named the Cougars the top fan-supported team in the Minors. Each minor league team's 1998 box office performance was analyzed in four categories: average attendance, on-field record, area population, and stadium capacity.

So, what's the secret? It starts with affordability. Inexpensive ticket prices, ranging from $5 to $10, are combined with fun, fun, and more fun as the team constantly provides a great game-day experience. In addition to the game itself, the between-innings breaks are loaded with great family entertainment. Water balloons are fired into the stands by giant slingshots. Perhaps Jake the Diamond Dog is retrieving foul balls for the umpire. There might even be a peanut butter sandwich-making contest or pigs dressed in costumes running bases.

The Cougars set out to fill a family niche, and do so while appreciating that baseball is a slow game. The team is aware that it has to do something for the kids, and for moms in particular. The Cougars know that although they might play baseball, the team is, in fact, part of the entertainment business.

If there's any star that's constantly being promoted for the Cougars, it's the team mascot Ozzie T. Cougar, who—in what is perhaps the embodiment of a winning proprietor–customer relationship—races kids around the bases and always finds a way to let them finish ahead of him.

The Cougars have realized how to build their customer base. It's often the child that brings the parents in but the team has to give mom something to do while dad watches the game and the kids play.

To draw first-time customers, Ozzie sponsors a reading program that started in the mid-1990s with 40 Chicago-area schools and has expanded it tenfold, with about 125,000 potential customers who can each beg parents to go see Ozzie at the ballpark.

Once in the ballpark, the emphasis on bringing something Ozzie-like home, to remind that child of the experience, is very strong. During the 2001 season, the Cougars provided free Ozzie tattoos, Ozzie growth charts, Ozzie baseball cards, Ozzie posters, Ozzie bobbleheads—you get the idea.

Building loyalty extends beyond the initial or on-site sales experience. Providing customers with a positive and lasting experience puts companies in a positive light and keeps them top of mind to consumers.

For minor league teams, it's the promotional item that fans can take home to remind them about the fun time they enjoyed at the game and about their affiliation with the team. Other companies might hand out calendars or sticky notes with their address and phone number. For a department store like Nordstrom's, that extra something is a business card with your particular salesperson's name on it. The card not only formally establishes a relationship with the customer after the sale, but it also subtly reminds them to return when they see the card in their wallet.

Whatever it takes to build customer loyalty, even if it's something small or potentially perceived as inconsequential, should be undertaken. Failure to do so jeopardizes a business's chance for success.

"MOMENTS OF TRUTH"

Building on this first principle, "moments of truth" can make or break a company's chance to gain loyalty. Every time a customer comes in contact with a firm, there is a chance to gain—or lose—that customer for life. It is necessary to make sure that customer feels special every time. Conventional wisdom says that one usually remembers the beginning and end of an event, not the middle. Appropriately, sports teams have taken advantage of these moments of truth to improve customer service.

How teams help fans when they lose or misplace their tickets can provide a positive "moment of truth" experience. Season ticket holders for the Saskatchewan Roughriders of the Canadian Football League, for example, can show up without their tickets once and still get into the game. The second time, they have to pay the game-day price, but if they find their ticket a couple of weeks later, they can get a refund. Many teams reissue stolen tickets to a customer as long as he or she comes with a copy of the police report.

Moments of truth also arise during events and can have a profound effect on how organizations are viewed by (potential) customers.

The University of Southern California (USC) had a basketball season ticket holder who had been attending games since 1950. After submitting his credit card order to pay for season tickets to the Trojans 2001 season, he received a letter from USC informing him that unless he joined a booster club costing an additional $2,000, his seats would be moved from the section he had occupied since the Sports Arena opened in 1959.

The ticket holder was terminally ill from cancer and apparently too sick to call USC himself, so his son contacted the athletic department and informed them of his father's condition, but was told that other options did not exist. Apparently the school had a policy, and that was that. An athletic department representative was even reported to have told the son that he'd have to pay $2,000 or be reassigned to nondonor seats.

An executive of the Better Business Bureau even volunteered the bureau's services to investigate USC after hearing the story. He believed that it was possible that USC was breaching a contract with the fan because he already had paid for tickets.

When school officials became aware that the *Los Angeles Times* was looking into the incident, it reacted swiftly to quell any further damage by moving the ticket holder only 20 seats away—without requiring the $2,000 payment. However, by that point the damage had been done. Although USC believed that extenuating circumstances went unreported, the dollar amount of the ill will and bad publicity generated by the paper's coverage of this customer service debacle greatly surpassed the additional revenue sought by the athletic department.

"Moments of truth" can also be sought out.

Just weeks after USC created ill will through its handling of this basketball season ticket holder, it was presented with a golden opportunity to demonstrate its commitment to, and appreciation for, its fans.

A USC student who thought he had won a $10,000 scholarship during halftime of the Trojans' game against UC Santa Barbara later learned that he would not get the money because he was over the line on two of the four shots (a three-pointer and a half-court shot) he had to make.

The student, a sophomore broadcast communications major, later acknowledged that he was over the designated line after reviewing the videotape. USC's director of event marketing said the decision was out of the school's hands because USC hired a promotions company, SCA Promotions, to handle the contest.

The USC executive indicated that he'd like to pay the student, but the money wasn't the school's to give. USC said it understood the student's disappointment, but stated that he was so far over the line on his half-court shot that it couldn't feel sorry for him.

Although USC was under no legal obligation to make good on the promotion, it could have stepped up and honored the spirit of the promotion, generating a customer for life. USC had several options at its disposal. First, it could have honored the promotion. Next, and in tongue-in-cheek fashion, it could have honored part of the promotion. Because the half-court shot was from 50 feet and apparently the student was 2 feet over the line, USC could have paid the student $9,600, or 96 percent, and generated tremendous goodwill in the process. Alternatively, the school could have worked the phones, calling on its list of athletic department sponsors to see if any of them would be willing to pony up by funding a scholarship for this student.

Although the issue of customer service in this case rested squarely with SCA Promotions, ultimately it was USC that was vulnerable, leaving many fans to think, "There they go again." Just because a particular customer service experience falls outside of a company's legal obligation doesn't mean they won't face a backlash from customers who perceive them as responsible.

SCA Promotions later demonstrated that it understood this concept when it decided to give the student the full prize. The company considered the circumstances and felt it was the right thing to do. SCA Promotions thought that because the contestant made the shots, and handled himself pretty well when he was told he wouldn't get the money, it would honor the commitment even if the company technically didn't need to.

During the 2000 season, San Jose State football player Neil Parry had to have his right leg amputated below the knee after a teammate rolled over on it during a kick return. Two seasons later, Parry—having endured some 20 surgeries—was determined to return to play again even though he would be forced to do so with a prosthetic leg. A month before his scheduled return to the field, the NCAA's insurance carrier, Mutual of Omaha, informed Parry that if he were to play his medical bills (which had already risen to $400,000) would no longer be covered under its catastrophic injury policy.

Outrage filled the air on sports talk shows across the country once Parry's situation was made public. Because they realized they had an opportunity to create a "moment of truth," Mutual of Omaha, received approval from the NCAA the next day and reworked Parry's insurance to include lifetime coverage of his medical bills, averting what would have rapidly been perceived as a monumental breach in customer service.

In some cases, organizations actually go out of their way to ensure that customers have that "winning" feeling about their business.

Buck Rogers, one of the most innovative GMs in Minor League Baseball, provides a compelling example of this. While serving as GM of the Lake Fear Crocs, Rogers ran a promotion in which if a player hit for the cycle (a single, a double, a triple, and a home run all in the same game) any time during the season, a lucky fan would win an $8,000 gift certificate toward a new Harley-Davidson motorcycle. One night, a Crocs player named Noah Hall came up in the ninth inning having already hit a double, triple, and home run. Hall, in a close game, was given the assignment of bunting to advance a runner. However, when the third baseman bobbled the ball and Hall was called safe at first, Rogers made sure the official scorer knew to give Hall a hit, so that a fan could win the prize. "We'd like all our fans to win," said Rogers, noting that the insurance company didn't have a case because the bunt was officially scored a hit.

How businesses create or respond to moments of truth has a long-lasting impact on the way they are perceived by customers and noncustomers. Accordingly, it is critical for these high-profile events to be handled professionally and with the utmost concern for the customer.

The Value of Service

The third principle of customer service is the value of the service itself. Customer service must be valued by the firm and considered as important as any of its products. It must consistently meet the demand for service or risk long-term damage to the customer relationship. The sale itself is not the only part of customer service that is important, but a company must offer great after-purchase service to earn that loyalty.

Before the salesperson closes the sale at your local electronics store, odds are that he or she is going to ask you if you want to buy an extended warranty after the product's initial guarantee expires. Retailers that offer this service might be missing an opportunity to establish a long-term relationship with the customer. Because the odds of the retailer having to go out-of-pocket are minimal, the store can afford to pay these marginal costs in exchange for differentiating itself from the hundreds of electronic stores selling the same exact product.

Want another reason? What do you think happens when customers have to bring a product back for repair? They have to walk into the store again and they might see something else they like. Because not enough people choose to take the extra guarantee, once the initial warranty lapses—and assuming the customer has bought nothing else—the store has jeopardized the link with that particular customer.

If the customer doesn't have a problem with the item, the electronics store that offers a free extended guarantee has, nonetheless, favorably positioned itself. At the point of purchase, they established a relationship that many other electronics stores hadn't because they saw the immediate revenue possibilities of selling product insurance instead of the long-term revenue generated by loyal customers.

Kansas City-based electronics retailer BrandsMart took this concept one step further. For the week of October 31, 1999, BrandsMart took out a conditional rebate policy with a sports insurance company. The promotion they ran in area newspapers stated that if the Kansas City Chiefs shut out the San Diego Chargers (who hadn't been shut out in seven years) on Sunday, everything bought in the store from Wednesday through game time for more than $399 would be given a full rebate. That's right—it would all be free.

Business flowed that week and, thanks to the promotion, Brands-Mart Director of Advertising Rick Burt said that the day before the game was the most profitable sales day in history. However, the company got its best value when the Chiefs blanked the Chargers, 34–0 and 325 customers walked away with a total of $425,000 worth of electronics. Plus, there was the uncalculable publicity. After the game, word circulated throughout the Chiefs locker room about the promotion and BrandsMart made its way onto ESPN's *SportsCenter* that night.

Putting a price tag on the value of stellar customer service might not always be as easy as it was for BrandsMart, but quantifying the return on investment associated with service is becoming as important as tracking any other measurable part of a business.

EMPLOYEES: THE INTERNAL CUSTOMER

Companies can attempt to incorporate each of these initiatives into their business, but if they don't have the right people implementing them, customer service won't be handled properly. Companies must invest in their hiring and training. The first step is to hire people who will thrive in the firm's culture. Firms must continue investing in their employees by continually training them and giving them the opportunity to be experts. This training must focus on the customer while challenging employees to think of ways to simultaneously create value for the customer.

When companies hire interns they often allow them to dabble in many capacities throughout the organization. After a couple of months, an intern spending a little bit of time in each department and communicating with a variety of people can learn more about the current state of business than a middle manager, who sits in his or her office and "manages" without surveying the work environment.

Solid training programs, regardless of various entry levels, should enable the worker to understand all aspects of related company business. After all, the more an employee knows about the company and the business environment in which it operates, the better able the company is to adequately service its customers.

Minor League Baseball teams train their employees well by all but mandating that they participate in every aspect of the organization. A radio broadcaster for single-A team is often the same person charged with designing and writing features for the game program, as well as selling advertising in it. Ticket takers also sell merchandise and concessions.

One of the most important details, providing stellar customer service, is everyone's responsibility, including the team owners and GMs. Buck Rogers, who planned and executed invasions as a member of the 82nd Airborne Division, compares his employees to private agents, in that they know so much about everything. "Even the interns know a little bit about their boss' job ... and their boss' job ... and on and on and on," Rogers said.

In addition to overseeing all aspects of the game's operations, Minor League Baseball owners—unlike some of their counterparts in MLB—seek out fans to solicit their input on everything from the quality of the hot dogs to the cleanliness of the restrooms.

Because Minor League Baseball appreciates the importance of showing new employees how the whole system works, it puts itself in the enviable position of better understanding the wants and needs of its fans.

Business owners and managers must decide for themselves how important it is to the company that its employees are well rounded and can pitch in to accomplish just about any task. It's certainly important to companies that sell services, such as Kinko's. Most people don't walk into their local Kinko's because the company necessarily has the best equipment in the world. They come because they need help doing something they can't do—or don't have the time to do—on their own. Should one or two of the five employees not know how to complete a specific task, it can significantly slow down business and frustrate harried customers in the process.

Companies like Kinko's demonstrate that competence is the most important attribute the company has to offer. These companies appreciate the importance of listening to customers, understanding their problems, and applying the company's knowledge to come up with creative solutions critical to success.

CUSTOMER SERVICE MAKES THE DIFFERENCE

The fifth principle suggests that customer service makes the difference. These days, product quality does not always translate into a competitive advantage. With technologies improving, the differentiation between the qualities of certain products has decreased. Firms are realizing that service can be the competitive advantage that keeps customers coming back. With the amount of entertainment available to the average consumer, it is necessary for professional sports teams to get a leg up on customer service. With customer-friendly new stadiums, a seemingly endless number of ushers, and other value-added offerings, many teams are taking this step and trying to provide value to their customers.

Rogers never forgets the competition he's up against in Daytona, where trips to the beach represent an inexpensive entertainment alternative. Once, while walking through the stands, an elderly man spilled all four of the beers he was carrying on Rogers. As the man was cleaning himself up, Rogers asked him what type of beer he spilled. "Bud Light," he said, confused why Rogers cared. Within a couple of minutes, Rogers had introduced himself and offered four new beers to the man. For $3.12 (actual cost of the 72-ounce beer refill), Rogers made a customer (a fan) for life. In this case, it meant much more because the man was the CEO of a nearby company and told the story at a board meeting the following week.

Increased customer service in stadiums and arenas can be seen in the growth of gourmet food over the past decade. Since the gourmet trend at sporting events took off with new stadiums and luxury boxes in the early 1990s, upscale caterers Levy Restaurants and Sportservice have each expanded their accounts to more than 20 sports facilities each.

At Veterans Stadium in Philadelphia, fans in luxury boxes can order roasted vegetable napoleon. At St. Louis Cardinals games, if fried raviolis aren't good enough (they make 12,000 per game), a food service company can provide affluent patrons almost anything if given a couple days' notice. Rolf Baumann, executive chef at Busch Stadium, said that venison and fois gras aren't out of the ordinary. How far will he go to get the right item? "We had people coming from different countries and whatever a person wanted, we had to have ready," Baumann said.

To the Outback Steakhouse chain, delivering something of value includes its curbside/drive-by service. To make picking up an order easier, Outback restaurants across the country simply opened a 60-square-foot separate entrance on the side of the building with its own designated parking area. When placing orders, customers are asked for the make, model, and color of their car and, on arrival, courteous employees hand customers their order. Outback executives were clearly thinking outside the box. Why can't non-fast-food restaurants have drive-up windows? By offering this service to customers, Outback has seen takeout orders increase. Not only do customers not have to get out their cars, but Outback now has less congestion in the restaurant and can save valuable parking spots for those that are dining in.

It doesn't matter what products or services a company offers when it comes to customer service making the difference. Providing customers what they want—particularly if it cannot easily be found elsewhere—adds value to the purchase experience and enables companies to differentiate themselves from the competition.

Unless management makes it clear, and then constantly reinforces to employees that customer service is important, line employees—those in direct contact with customers—won't attach the requisite value to it. It's hard for an employee of the Seattle Supersonics, for example, not to realize how important customer service is after watching the actions of their owner and Starbucks chairman Howard Schultz. Schultz spends time on the phone talking to former season ticket holders about why they didn't renew and has allowed young fans to congregate courtside before the game for the pregame warm-ups. He even allows them to spend time on the court after the game.

WHAT DO YOUR CUSTOMERS THINK?

A company might think it is doing right by its customers but it seldom knows for sure. Accordingly, the managers and decision makers must get feedback from their customers to confirm their beliefs. Customers, employees on the front lines, and even prior customers, can be great resources for this feedback. It doesn't matter how you get the feedback, just as long as you get it.

Most firms measure success by profit, but in a customer-intensive firm, customer satisfaction must be a primary contributor to overall success. Besides the obvious feedback, referrals, and repeat business, firms must take other steps to measure satisfaction.

Washington Capitals owner Ted Leonsis and Dallas Mavericks owner Mark Cuban are leaders in the sports business world because they listen to their customers and regularly communicate directly with them via e-mail.

Leonsis and Cuban also benefit because each demonstrates that he is in touch with his customers. One fan e-mail a day directed to Cuban goes straight up on the team Web site, DallasMavericks.com.

Leonsis frequently recounts the story of a fan who asked him if he could tell a vendor to change his route so that he could get some cotton candy during the second period. "I forward it to the facility department and copy the sender of the e-mail with a note such as "make it so," Leonsis wrote via e-mail. "And then I get a response (from the facility department) that says 'it will happen next game.'" Two days later, that fan e-mails Leonsis, copying 15 friends saying, "Wow, I can't believe you took care of my request so fast and so efficiently."[4]

Leonsis says he learns more directly through fan feedback than from studies or even his own employees. Feedback includes comments about the arena's sound system, wait time in concession lines, and player wish lists.

For Leonsis, knowing if he is doing a good job doesn't just include e-mail interaction. "I also have my box and me put on big screen from time to time," he said. "If they boo, we need to improve. This is the best indicator of how we are doing."

Mark Cuban is among those owners sensitive to the white-collarization of sports and its impact on fans and their in-arena service. Cuban's Mavericks play in the American Airlines Center, a corporatized arena (of which Cuban owns 50 percent) that opened in 2001 at a cost of $420 million, making it the most expensive indoor sports venue ever built in the United States. With its 142 suites, some priced as high as $300,000 annually, and 1,936 club seats ranging in cost from $7,000 to $18,000 each, the arena has a decidedly corporate feel to it.

Despite the arena's corporate look and feel, Cuban remains intimately involved with his team and its fans. He believes that there's a difference between running a business and owning a business. In the case of the Mavericks, Cuban is doing both and paying keen attention to customer service in the process.

Cuban knows that the fans are the whole reason he's in the coveted position he is in. He recognizes the symbiotic relationship

---

4. Rovell, Darren, "With Jordan and Jagr, Leonsis Is All Offense." ESPN.com, March 12, 2002.

whereby the more fun the fans have, the more fun the players have. Cuban realizes he can't make any game-winning shots, but as far as the fans are concerned, he certainly can respond to any issues they have. Because Cuban believes his fans are the best quality-control mechanism available, he freely hands out his e-mail address to gain feedback. Fans will tell Cuban if there's bubble gum on the seats. They'll tell him if there aren't enough signs in the parking lots and if they can't find their car. He'll listen and fix any concerns immediately. Cuban remains hopeful that his immediate recognition and response approach will spread to the entire NBA.

Cuban understands that, at its core, owning a sports franchise cannot be a long-term, profitable venture without listening to customers. Although corporations are paying most of the bills, Cuban realizes that sponsors are only doing so because they believe the Mavericks provide them a great marketing platform. Should Cuban alienate Mavericks' fans, it would have a serious financial impact on his business because corporations would be less interested in linking their brands to his.

Letting customers know that you are personally engaged in their experience is more critical than you think. Customers often fail to provide important feedback because they don't believe organizations are paying attention to them.

Survey postcards that are sent out in the mail to patients following a hospital stay or to guests after they stay at a hotel don't have a very high response rate. Once someone sees the generic corporate address as the return address, rather than a particular customer service representative's handwritten name, the sentiment is, "Why bother if it doesn't look like they are going to read it?"

Like the Kane County Cougars, the Dayton Dragons is another single-A Minor League Baseball team that routinely sells out, but they never take customer feedback for granted. Fans who have a complaint or a suggestion simply fill out a "One-to-One" contact form, which goes directly to team president Rob Murphy. Team policy dictates that every letter and e-mail is answered and every phone message is returned within one business day. Employees who follow through on great service are recognized with a certificate of excellence, and managers who service customers exceptionally well are rewarded by team management with a Dale Carnegie class of his or her choice.

Establishing an environment in which employees benefit from redoubling their customer service efforts can literally and figuratively pay dividends.

One of the best companies that shows it bothers to read feedback is Whole Foods Market, now the largest retailer of organic and natural food products in the world. Whole Foods started as a small store in Austin, Texas in 1980, but now has more than 120 stores across the United States.

When you walk into a Whole Foods store you will likely see a big bulletin board that features customer comments, as well as timely staff responses to shoppers' questions. This service not only gives customers a sense of worth with Whole Foods management, it also empowers other customers that see that Whole Foods is committed to addressing any and all concerns of its shoppers. The bulletin board also serves as a high-profile reminder that customer service matters.

The more contemporary version of the traditional bulletin board is, of course, the Internet. Popular online auction site eBay, which has more than 1 million sales postings a day, is merely a "marketplace" where people bid for others' goods. Although none of the money for the actual items changes hands through the company, one of the reasons eBay has survived the dot-com collapse and become the leader in online auctions is because its customer service is unrivaled by competitors.

Over time, thanks to feedback in its early days from the site's message boards, eBay developed an effective system of response. If a customer is unhappy with the service he or she is getting from the seller, they can leave negative feedback, which will often affect the seller's ability to make future sales. eBay even provides sellers with the ability to send a reminder of payment due to buyers, who can also be influenced by negative feedback. Without the site's support of mechanisms like these, a lack of trust and inability to make the sale in person could limit eBay's success.

In the sports world, the Internet has even been used in an attempt to get rid of a hometown's goods. A disgruntled group of Chicago Bears fans created www.tradecade.com, which asked their beloved Bears to unload the team's 1999 first-round draft pick, quarterback Cade McNown, after he went 3–12 in his first two years in Chicago.

During an eight-month period in 2001 more than 15,000 signatures were collected on the site. In August 2001, McNown was finally traded to the Miami Dolphins. The following season, without the much-maligned McNown, the Bears made the playoffs for the first time since 1994. Did the Bears management make the trade just because of the online petition? Of course not, but it allowed customers the opportunity to express their frustration about the product, and to do so in a way that got management's attention.

Paying for feedback also works well, provided you spend wisely. At the end of the 2001 season, Buck Rogers, while with the Daytona Cubs, spent less than $100 on sodas, hot dogs, and a keg of beer, and invited all fans to attend "a feedback session." About 50 or 60 fans turned out and Rogers learned quite a bit about issues and concerns that had never crossed his mind (e.g., one season ticket holder said that four games were rained out, so Rogers refunded him four games on the following season's ticket). When Rogers told his friend, who worked at a large Internet server company, the friend responded, "I work for a Fortune 500 company. By tapping a couple kegs and cooking some hot dogs who would have known that you could get feedback so cheap?"

Understanding what your customers think about the company and the products it offers is so important that any means necessary should be explored to ensure that accurate feedback is being generated.

Turning Complaints Into Devotion

Turning complaints into devotion can be a great opportunity for a firm to learn from its customers. Learning from these complaints, appeasing the situation, and doing so quickly should help protect the customer relationship.

One Thursday night (the day of the week when the Daytona Cubs have 99-cent beer night) a mother approached Rogers and told him that the man in front of her and her young child wouldn't stop swearing. When Rogers offered to change her seat, she told him that the rowdy fan was so loud that she thought she would hear him swearing from anywhere in the park. Because of this experience, she said, she would never come back. Rogers, unable to kick the man out, gave the woman his number and said that the belligerent fan was not a "regular" and that she and her son could come back on his dime. Not only that, Rogers said that when they did, her son could throw out the first pitch. Not surprisingly, the woman and her son returned—and more than once.

Customer concerns also arise prior to making the purchase decision and can have grave consequences on an organization's viability.

Tim Eernisse, an executive with the Continental Basketball Association's Grand Rapids Hoops, wasn't expecting to see 15- to 20-minute lines at the ticket window for the Hoops opening game of the 2001–2002 season. He carefully watched for fans that decided to balk at the long lines. When he saw one man and his family give up before getting to the box office, he ran after them, sat them down free of charge and gave them hot dogs and sodas. "They came to at least six of the first seven games and I honestly don't think they would have ever come back if I didn't go after them."

It is also prudent to have a strong internal system for handling complaints so that upset customers don't voice their dismay in a much broader forum. After not receiving an adequate response to two letters complaining about service during a trip to Hawaii and Japan on United Airlines (UAL) Jeremy Cooperstock started a Web site called Untied.com.

"Have you suffered a bad experience with United Airlines?" the Untied.com complaint forum asks. "It might come as a small consolation to know that you're not alone. Since Untied.com has been collecting them, we've received thousands of letters from people like you, who have been treated with disdain by a company getting rich from your travel dollars. These pages probably won't solve your problems, but they do provide a forum where you can share your experiences with others, and hopefully, embarrass UAL into making amends."

At Untied.com approximately five complaints are received per day ranging from refund problems and airplane food to employee rudeness. United spokespeople have said the best way to get a quick response is to contact United directly, but apparently that hasn't worked satisfactorily because the need for the site still exists.

If United had an appropriate forum for customers to voice their complaints, Cooperstock's site would not be receiving 20,000 hits a month—20 of which he says come from United's headquarters on a daily basis.

When UAL CEO James Goodwin stepped down in October 2001, Cooperstock, who says his site isn't meant to be an anti-United site, offered to help new CEO John Creighton create a more adequate system to field complaints. However, the site is still actively taking complaints and forwarding them to the customer relations managers at United.

Remember that it costs less to keep a customer than it does to replace one. Although only 10 to 15 percent of all customer complaints are voiced directly to the company, if these complaints are not resolved to the satisfaction of the customer, significant damage is inflicted on the company's brand name and balance sheet.

Identifying, acting, and following up on complaints will help a company turn disgruntled customers into devoted ones.

THE CUSTOMERS WHO GOT AWAY

The last principle a firm should observe is which customers are "getting away." It might be acceptable to allow certain customers to walk away provided they are being replaced with more desirable ones. A company's strategy helps dictate which customers it can afford to lose and does so by providing a framework for valuing each customer. Minor League Baseball values the "everyday" fan, whereas much of big-time sports seems to cater more to the corporate fan, allowing these everyday fans to get away.

By most accounts, Los Angeles' Staples Center has been a tremendous success. Since its opening in 1999, it has hosted an extraordinary number of diverse nonsporting events ranging from concerts featuring Bruce Springsteen and the Eagles, to major international gatherings, such as the 2000 Democratic National Convention and the Latin Grammys. In addition to hosting hundreds of Los Angeles Kings and Clippers games, the Staples Center claims the three-time defending NBA champion Los Angeles Lakers as its premier tenant.

This compelling and unparalleled combination of sports and entertainment events—more than 200 annually—has enabled the venue to market itself as "The Entertainment Capitol of the Entertainment Capitol."

Prior to establishing itself as the premier venue for sports and entertainment's top events, the Staples Center had to create and market its vision to corporations and Los Angelenos alike. Given the region's unwillingness to allocate tax dollars to the pursuit of sport, those desiring to provide Los Angeles with a world-class entertainment venue had to turn to corporate America to finance their vision.

Once this decision was made, everyday sports fans were allowed to get away as they possessed neither the influence nor cash to materially affect the process. In the overall scheme of things, they became less important than corporate America.

Revenue streams pledged to financing the construction of Staples Center came from the following categories, with a distinct and disproportional corporate feel:

- Luxury suites: 33 percent
- Corporate sponsorships: 29 percent
- Premier seats: 17 percent
- Naming rights: 11 percent
- Concessions: 9 percent
- Ticketing agreement: 1 percent

It should come as no surprise that the Staples Center was built by and for corporate clientele, resulting in the need for the venue's management team, which also maintains an ownership stake in both the Kings and the Lakers, to consistently cater to that corporate clientele to ensure its long-term cash flow. The apparent marginalization of the everyday fan at many of America's sports venues makes industry observers squeamish because they believe it could lead to a long-term erosion in traditional fan bases.

Many franchise owners have become overwhelmingly reliant on corporate customers while pricing everyday fans out of the in-venue experience. This has taken place because many modern-day owners are more preoccupied with maximizing short-term revenue than they are with protecting the long-term viability of the leagues in which their teams compete.

Understanding precisely who the core customers are is essential when crafting customer service relationships. Once core customers are earned and kept, attention can then be devoted to accessing additional customer bases. In the case of Minor League Baseball, this begins with families and then extends to corporations. Throughout much of big-time sports, the reverse is the case. Customers, whether everyday fans or corporations, must be identified and properly serviced if a business is to prosper.

CHAMPIONSHIP POINTS

Customer service is an all-too-often overlooked aspect in business. Shoddy customer service remains a prevalent issue in big-time sports and has been exasperated by the recent trend in the white-collarization of sports.

Minor league and amateur sports have provided, and will continue to provide, a great backdrop from which to gauge the growing importance of customer service. It enables businesses of all sizes to appreciate the following:

- Businesses are built one customer at a time. Just as significantly, businesses are dismantled one customer at a time. Make the customer feel that there is one-to-one service and create the illusion that there is one employee for every customer at all times.

- Knowing your customer's wants and needs is more important than ever before. Are you neglecting your version of the ladies bathrooms?

- The little (customer service) things still matter.

- When realizing "moments of truth," it is more important to take the appropriate action than simply worry about the immediate impact on the bottom line.

- Giving customers something more than a receipt after a purchase is a great way to make them want to come back.

- Loyal customers are worth every penny it takes to keep them. Not only is customer feedback essential, it should be sought out.

- The more your employees know about the business and its various operations, the easier customer service becomes. Remember that employees at all levels of an organization are de facto customer service representatives.

- The more your employees feel like they have a stake in your brand, the more interested they are in doing whatever they can to satisfy an unhappy customer.

- Acting on customer service issues is invaluable. Surprise customers by paying more than lip service—give them a "cotton candy vendor"-like response.

Great service can go a long way to building customer loyalty and, by extension, improving the bottom line. Establishing and maintaining customer service as a priority pays extraordinary dividends for companies that have succeeded in convincing all of those people who represent the business that doing so helps extend the brand name. Variations of these same tenets also apply to individuals, particularly star athletes.

4 THE PERSONAL BRANDING PROCESS

*The Point: Everyone, whether a superstar athlete or business execu-
tive, has a personal brand. In today's business environment where
character and reputation have become invaluable currencies, the
development of a great personal brand must be a priority for those
who wish to succeed in business. Over the years, athletes—often
unwittingly—have helped us understand the role that personal
branding plays within the business community.*

The personal and professional lives of athlete endorsers provide great insight into the personal branding process. Great personal
brands, whether associated with star athletes or revered executives,
evolve regardless of whether they are actively managed. The most
revered professionals obsessively protect their personal brands (reputations) at all costs, recognizing that any indiscretion—no matter
how inconsequential it appears—can wreak long-term havoc.

Regardless of how harmless an under-the-breath comment might
appear, or how insignificant a lack of other social skills might be, it is
important for business people to manage their careers as if they are
public figures—such as star athletes. Just like an athlete's attitude or
indiscretion can reflect negatively on the league, so too can your
behavior reflect on your company's reputation. This is especially
true with higher-level executives because they are routinely charged
with officially, as well as unofficially, representing the organization in
highly public settings such as press conferences, shareholder meetings, and during times of crisis.

When business people don't manage the little things that define their personal brands, such as how they dress or how they handle themselves after a few cocktails at a company party, they run the very real risk of having no personal brand worth managing.

PERSONAL BRANDING

Emulating our favorite athletes is as American as apple pie. Pretending to be Ted Williams, Roger Staubach, Chris Evert, Wayne Gretzky, or Mia Hamm has provided an escape for generations of sports fans while providing valuable lessons about the personal branding process.

Growing up as kids it was not unusual to place that Johnny Bench rookie baseball card in the spokes of your bike (such a reckless activity would be viewed as heresy in today's sports trading card market). We not only wanted to be our stars, we wanted to let everyone know that we had a special, unconditional relationship with them.

We knew these athletes on the field and whether we—or even they—realized it or not, we learned about what qualities they most exemplified off the field through sports marketing and endorsements.

Sports marketing is defined as using any level or type of sport or sport-related activity to promote, advertise, or otherwise communicate the attributes of a corporation's products or services. There is little doubt that, given the intimate relationship fans believe they have with star athletes, their endorsements not only fit neatly into this definition, but they routinely go one step further: Endorsements add a personal touch to the communications process.

It takes a mere moment or two for consumers to form opinions and beliefs about the products and services pitched by athletes. Their observations impact consumers' feelings about the particular athlete and the company he or she is representing. Consequently, a compelling match between the athlete's personal brand and the corporation's brand became increasingly important. This holds true throughout business and industry today, as organizations tend to hire people that reflect their values and project the company's carefully crafted image.

By using the sports endorsement model to show how athletes have used their affiliation with companies to shape their own personal brands, it becomes easier to see how a person can shape his or her own personal brand, or, even more specifically, how a business decision maker can effectively choose the right spokesperson for a company's brand, whether that spokesperson is a star salesman or athlete.

It is constructive to look at the role of athlete endorsements because, unlike most private executives, star athletes enable us to study very public, and often debated, personal brands. When reading this chapter on athlete endorsements, consider the evolution, positioning, and ongoing management of personal brands as they relate to business managers.

When athlete images are presented in ads only one or two of their qualities shine through. The same is true in professional settings where people quickly form an opinion about a manager's core qualities. Consequently, it is important for managers to take the necessary step to communicate their most important attributes. After all, it is widely believed that "you never get a second chance to make that first impression." Managers must reflect on what they are doing day to day to earn—and then extend—that initial endorsement from colleagues, superiors, and the company.

You might wonder why athlete endorsements are reflective of the personal branding process. Even though athletes who companies choose are pitching a carefully crafted message about a product and not themselves, the most effective athletes, with the help of their agents and sports marketers, choose which companies they align themselves with and such endorsements become an equal reflection on the athlete and the company. It is easy to forget that the most effective endorsement is one that is consistent with an already established personal brand.

The businessman's endorsement world is subtler because he is not pitching someone else's products, not being paid extra for doing so, and not broadcasting it to the world. Yet managers still make equally important choices about the company and the people they keep.

Managers who are aware of personal brand building have the opportunity to present a consistent message about themselves and gradually shape that message over time. They realize that—like star athletes—some of the personal branding process is developed while on the field (at work) and an equally important amount is developed off the field (at company functions, dinner meetings, etc.).

The first athlete to endorse a bevy of products was "The Galloping Ghost," Red Grange, a three-time All-American halfback at the

University of Illinois, who, after leaving Illinois, brought prominence to the NFL. In 1925, Grange reportedly earned an outrageous $100,000 for a nine-game tour. Thanks to Grange's agent, C. C. "Cash and Carry" Pyle, an Illinois theater owner and promoter, Grange secured product endorsements that included meatloaf, ginger ale, and candy bars. He also made radio and personal appearances and earned roles in three movies, all of which reportedly earned this early marketing duo more than $1 million.

Among the reasons he was a successful endorser was that his reputation and standing was left largely to the imagination of national audiences. His appeal was built in an era when people read day-old accounts of ballgames or heard his voiceovers on the radio—a far cry from today's around-the-clock sports and advertising cycles.

Grange was followed a few years later, in 1930, when Babe Ruth made $73,000 in endorsements for Spaulding, Quaker Oats, Pinch Hit Tobacco, and All-American Athletic Underwear. Ruth, widely considered the ultimate indulger, took advantage of the rapidly evolving media and was positioned as an All-American hero—one capable of selling almost anything.

The biggest corporate spenders in the early years of the endorsement market were cigarette companies. Ruth and the Chicago Cubs were Old Gold; Joe DiMaggio, Early Wynn, and Bob Lemon pitched Camel; Willie Mays had Chesterfields; and Frank Gifford and the Brooklyn Dodgers were Lucky Strike men. The combination of high-profile, successful athletes and the classy images associated with smoking made for an ideal marketing relationship.

DiMaggio, in addition to his cigarette deal, was among the first to have an incentive-based endorsement contract. Heinz—as in 57 different varieties—was scheduled to pay DiMaggio $100,000 if he hit safely in 57 consecutive games. Close, but no (your company's name here) cigar.

JACK, JOE, MICHAEL, AND TIGER

Over the last 40 years, four athletes have significantly contributed to shaping the endorsement landscape. Jack Nicklaus, Joe Namath, Michael Jordan, and Tiger Woods each refined—and redefined—the attachment of athletes to products and services. Like today's executives, each crafted a personal brand that enabled him to excel.

These athletes recognized that the right marketing relationships would further their careers. They also knew that the products and services they endorsed said as much about their own brand names as they did about the companies they promoted, much the same way people project, accurately or not, personal qualities onto you based on the company you work for or the decisions you make.

With the guidance of Mark McCormack, the founder and chairman of International Management Group (IMG) and patriarch of the sports business industry, Jack Nicklaus became one of the sporting world's greatest brands. While Nicklaus battled with Arnold Palmer, another equally prominent McCormack client, on the golf course throughout the 1960s, 1970s, and 1980s, the man dubbed "The Golden Bear" captivated audiences in the galleries and on TV.

Along the way, and because of his credibility and believability, he established numerous business relationships with companies who shared the golfing world's target market, namely men 40 years of age and older who earned in excess of $100,000 annually.

Forty years after his professional debut, Nicklaus' name has been associated with about 30 companies and products, including Lincoln-Mercury, Rolex, Visa, Pepsi, Drexel Heritage (furniture), and Gulfstream Aerospace. Notice how all of these endorsements are for middle-class or upscale products. By virtue of being a golfer, Nicklaus has somewhat excluded his personal brand from being associated with fast food companies or cleaning products. Nicklaus still earns twice as much from endorsements on an annual basis as he made in his entire career on the PGA Tour ($5.7 million).

Joe Willie Namath, the following generation's superstar spokesman, was no Nicklaus, nor did he want to be. Namath was a showman; he positioned himself as a "personality" as much as an athlete. He literally and figuratively played to a different crowd. The New York Jets quarterback and cocky bachelor is most remembered for one game and one moment—his guarantee that his Jets of the American Football League would defeat the 18-point favorite Baltimore Colts of the NFL in Super Bowl III.

The man who wore a full mink coat on the sidelines starred in three movies. He was among the first athletes to recognize that being outrageous would put money in his pocket. Namath also knew his sex appeal commanded attention. His most famous spot was in 1974 for Hanes Beautymist pantyhose, where he admitted that although he didn't wear them, if Beautymist could make his legs look good, imagine what they could do for women.

Although one could say that Namath's endorsement of pantyhose was inconsistent with his job as a football player, Namath's guarantee of winning—something truly ridiculous at the time—allowed him to be seen as a wild and wacky character.

Namath understood the importance of winning in the nation's largest media market and seized on the marketing platform provided by the combination of his brashness and a still evolving media, TV. Companies also appreciated the powerful combination of winning and market size, and realized products could be elevated to a winning status by association with a sports winner. In short, Namath's familiarity, whatever its origin, was worth a lot of money.

TV gave you the feeling that you knew Joe Namath as an outrageous, yet endearing personality. The commercial star of the late 1980s through the 1990s, Michael Jordan, went one step further—he made you feel as if you were his friend.

The ultimate in personal branding is when you are simply known by a single name, and such was the case with "Michael." He was one of the most competitive athletes the world has ever seen, a quality revered by all who believed they knew him.

But it was Michael's soft side, shown in playful spots like Nike's Mars Blackmon "Do You Know? Do You Know?" commercial with Spike Lee (1989) and his McDonald's "Nothing But Net" spots with Larry Bird (1993) that made the marketing difference. These commercials made Jordan appear more human, allowing legions of fans and consumers to relate to this "regular guy."

Jordan, like Namath, turned to film to extend his personal brand. In 1996, Jordan teamed up with Looney Tunes characters in *Space Jam*, which grossed more than $220 million at the box office and sold more than 8.5 million home videos.

For an entire generation of TV viewers, Jordan morphed between superstar athlete and media personality, relying equally on both to extend his brand name beyond compare. In fact, Jordan needed the symbiotic relationship with the entertainment industry as much as it needed him.

Through this cobranding, which legitimized both Jordan and the properties he attached his name to, the endorsement business reached new heights.

Although Tiger Woods was afforded a brief introduction in his first professional season with Nike's "Hello, World" advertisements in 1996, he fully emerged during Michael Jordan's second retirement nearly three years later. Despite his talent and global appeal, it took a while for Tiger to be on the same level as Michael because of Woods' constant intensity. Sure, it was that intensity that enabled him to win major tournament after major tournament on his way to becoming the best golfer of all time, but his seriousness was hindering consumers' ability to forge a close relationship with him.

Jordan's personality was reinforced by his style of play and infectious smile. Tiger, on the other hand, only occasionally exuded the personality that everyone assumed he had.

The issue facing Tiger, much like the employee who misses company gatherings because he or she is always the first one to the office in the morning and the last one to leave at night, was that his intensity contributed to his success on the golf course but limited his ability as a marketer. He could concentrate more than anyone else; he could block out the crowd, focus on the shot, and forget about the surroundings. Golfers might respect that, but to transcend the sport Tiger had to communicate something else off the course: fun.

Like Jordan, it started with Nike. A tape of Woods bouncing the ball on his club and then smacking it for a long drive, "proved" that Woods could have fun and introduced millions to a newer, more approachable Woods. Tiger not only started having fun in Nike commercials but he also had lighter scripts written for him for his Buick and American Express commercials as well.

Don't think it wasn't a conscious decision to show Tiger's smile. His agent, Mark Steinberg of IMG, the same sports management firm that built the Nicklaus and Palmer brands, told Tiger that it was okay for people to see the real side of him—that it was alright for people to view Woods as human—smiling, laughing, and joking—away from swinging in a robotic fashion and hitting every drive perfectly.

Made-for-TV events orchestrated by IMG, such as "The Battle at Bighorn," enabled Woods to show a more relaxed and light-hearted side. Competing against David Duval, Sergio Garcia, and teaming with Jack Nicklaus in these exhibitions that aired in prime time on ABC allowed Woods' personality to shine.

Managers seeking to make a name for themselves should heed Steinberg's advice. They need to know how and when to show their clients' lighter side in otherwise serious business settings.

Collectively Nicklaus, Namath, Jordan, and Woods shaped the endorsement industry and, in the process, shed enormous light on the process of personal branding.

By studying which products certain athletes endorse and understanding why companies enlist their support when representing a corporation's products or services to consumers, you can observe how athletes, with the guidance of their handlers, create, develop, and reinforce their personal brands.

We mostly know Lance Armstrong because of his amazing comeback story and we seem to know Barry Bonds as a selfish jerk. We all want to relate to Cal Ripken's consistency, both on and off the field. At times, we wish we could exude Andre Agassi's flashy style and infectious personality. Although none of us would admit it, we're somewhat envious of Anna Kournikova's success—even if it has little to do with her athletic prowess.

All of these athletes have successfully shaped their own brand image and those who have done so most successfully understand that defining moments on—and away from—the playing field go a long way in establishing and reinforcing personal brands.

Executives can and must appreciate this. Managers must ask themselves what they are doing day-to-day to establish, build, and protect their own brand name.

Athlete endorsers are concerned about how they are perceived by fans, teammates, and corporations. So too should business people be aware of how they are perceived by customers, colleagues, and (potential) employers.

CORPORATE AMERICA AND THE ART OF ATHLETE BRANDING

When corporations set out to hire an employee, whether an athlete for an endorsement campaign or a seasoned executive to lead the sales effort, the hiring decision routinely comes down to personal brand name enjoyed by the job candidate. Company decision makers don't just look at a list and say, "Who's the cheapest available?" or "Who is my favorite?"

Corporations seek to increase profits or enhance shareholder value when integrating athlete endorsements into their marketing mix. Using athletes as spokespeople—marketing channels, really—can be an integral part of any or all of a company's sports marketing activities.

These same companies hire executives, another variation of spokesperson, to reinforce their corporate brand names. Management, like athlete-spokespeople, is hired to play diverse roles with the primary purpose of increasing profits and shareholder value.

Corporations are essentially a collection of personal brands and, as such, employers must evaluate how a particular candidate will impact the organization's chemistry and, by extension, its brand. In sports, coaches routinely weigh the pros and cons of signing great athletes that might lack a "team" orientation or otherwise exude selfishness.

In much the same manner in which corporations rely on great salespeople to market their products, they also utilize star athletes as vehicles to promote, advertise, or otherwise communicate the attributes of each organization's products or services. Retaining the right athlete—just like hiring the right salesman—can be an excellent means to increase an organization's visibility, sales, and, ultimately, profitability.

Although there might be as many reasons why corporations use athletes to market their products and services as there are athletes themselves, athletes—or even traditional salespeople for that matter—with strong personal brand names are primarily retained to help do the following:

- Establish the organization's brand
- Increase awareness about the organization's products or services
- Authenticate a particular product or service line with consumers
- Enhance credibility with retailers
- Assist in product development
- Create a positive association between customers of all types (i.e., retail, wholesale, etc.) and the corporation

It is generally accepted that consumers are more likely to purchase goods and services endorsed by famous individuals, including star athletes, than those without accompanying endorsements.

Essentially, establishing the product as a winner by associating it with a winner—an admired athlete in this case—creates a compelling connection between consumers and the products they purchase.

If this were not the case, multimillion-dollar endorsement contracts would not exist. Additionally, it is believed that the use of high-profile endorsers helps maintain viewers' attention, increasing the impact of marketing campaigns.

Athlete spokespeople are uniquely qualified to provide insight about products or services, especially when promoting those that contributed to their achievements. Essentially, the more familiar an endorser, the more likely consumers are to buy the endorsed product.

Consider the owner of a single hardware store in suburban Houston that sells basically the same items as the large home improvement chains. Having a more conveniently located store, when combined with competitive prices and better customer service, might help the single store differentiate itself. However, having a Houston Astros player say, in a free-standing insert in the local paper, that he always shops there is yet another way to differentiate the small business while allowing customers to associate that ballplayer with the company.

Most small businesses cannot afford star players, such as the Astros' Jeff Bagwell, but they might be able to afford other local, second-tier players such as Lance Berkman or Billy Wagner, both of whom are readily identifiable in the community.

Not only can retaining an athlete to endorse a product be cost prohibitive; it can also bring with it the significant risk of bad publicity—especially for smaller or regional businesses. The same can be said about a company that makes an inappropriate or dreadful hiring decision that backfires and forces the company to retrench.

For instance, former Dallas Cowboys All-Pro wide receiver Michael Irvin was arrested with drugs and prostitutes. For Nike, with whom Irvin had a modest marketing relationship, the damage was minimal. However, for the 13 small Toyota dealerships that had retained Irvin's services for $500,000 and integrated him into a series of commercials, the damage was considerable. Not only did the dealerships suffer the direct losses associated with retaining Irvin, but they also incurred additional costs when replacing the campaign.

Numerous criteria are taken into account when a corporation is contemplating retaining an athlete to serve as its spokesperson—or when an organization is hiring its next vice president of sales. Regardless of which (and in what order) criteria are evaluated, the preferred outcome of using an athlete as an endorser remains the same: Integrate his or her personality into the corporation's image, accentuate the association, and build a competitive advantage over the competition.

Four criteria are typically considered when analyzing the marketing merits of an athlete—or any executive for that matter. Once issues relating to cost and appropriateness of fit are satisfactorily addressed, attention is turned to an athlete or executive's:[1]

- Familiarity
- Relevance
- Esteem
- Differentiation

Each of these attributes also plays a role when an organization seeks to hire the right candidate for a specific job. The professional attributes, or personal brand characteristics, of job candidates are similarly measured, with the individual proving the best overall "fit" usually getting the job.

At the core, targeted customers must recognize the athlete and find him or her friendly, likable, and trustworthy. Further, a compelling connection between the athlete and the product and the athlete and the audience must be established. For the endorsement to be effective, the athlete must be held in high regard, respected, and deemed credible by potential customers. Finally, successful sports marketing campaigns that incorporate athletes must do so by retaining athletes that stand out among the public, whether this is attributable to charisma, athletic achievement, or an ability to convey a message.

These same premises also hold true in "regular" business settings. That is, employers prefer job seekers who provide the right mix of personality, integrity, and product knowledge. More important, potential customers must recognize these traits if a company's salesperson is to prosper.

However, two additional points warrant mention. First, familiarity can breed contempt. An inverse relationship usually exists between the number of products or services endorsed and the credibility of the pitchman. As the number of products promoted increases, positive consumer perceptions about the athlete's trustworthiness may decline. This explains why most well-managed superstars prefer quality over quantity in their corporate relationships.

---

1. Dyson, Amy, and Turco, Douglas, "The State of Celebrity Endorsement in Sport." *The Cyber Journal of Sports Marketing*, Volume 2, Number 1, January 1998.

The second point that needs to be made about the endorsement market is that there are exceptions and awkward applications to the aforementioned rules. In short, a "personality" like Dennis Rodman is the exception that proves the rule. Or is he? Maybe he was intentionally positioned to maximize his marketing opportunities by locating himself at the Jerry Springer end of the spectrum.

Lance Armstrong, Cal Ripken, Andre Agassi, and Michael Jordan all possess the coveted marketing traits just highlighted. Each has made a unique connection to sports fans and consumers alike. Each knows personal branding as well as anyone and each provides great perspective on how to build a personal brand that transcends their respective roles in professional athletics.

THE FAMILIAR LANCE ARMSTRONG

It's remarkable that a guy who rides a bicycle commands any attention at all, especially because the only live coverage in North America of the sport's biggest event is on niche cable channel, the Outdoor Life Network. Then again, Lance Armstrong's life, not just his athletic career, is about as incredible as they come. His extraordinary achievements have not only been well documented, but they have been positioned in a way that enhanced his reputation as a friendly, likable, and trustworthy professional. Along the way, and because of these traits, he has become a familiar face, a symbol of what can be achieved if someone really sets his or her mind to it.

Armstrong rose quickly up the ranks among the most known sports figures thanks to his four consecutive Tour de France titles between 1999 and 2002. His total domination, among so many riders, amazed Americans, and his comeback story was even better.

In 1996, Armstrong had brain, testicular, and chest cancer and was given very little chance to live. Not only did he live, but he came back to become one the world's greatest athletes. So good in fact, that fans along the tour's route, other cyclists, and sports writers claimed he must have been cheating, although he never failed a drug test.

His story remains so compelling that the media continues to cover it, and cancer patients and survivors look to his example to provide hope in their lives. Armstrong also continues to discuss his life and career, most notably in his best-selling book *It's Not About My Bike: My Journey Back to Life.*

For the most part, mainstream Americans don't think of cycling as a sport—let alone a major sport. Moreover, Armstrong's story is only resurrected for three weeks a year as the country sees brief recaps of the Tour de France.

How many miles is the Tour de France? Where does it take place? When? Can you even name somebody else who's known for bike riding other than that 8-year-old brat down the street who throws your morning paper in the bushes?

It is because of cycling's anemic following in this country that Armstrong's accomplishments are so amazing. The nature of his story, when coupled with the way he has let us in on it, has led millions to feel that they know Lance Armstrong better than Ken Griffey Jr. or Peyton Manning. Ironically, these are the very same people who couldn't tell you how many stages make up the Tour de France or even what drafting is.

According to a list published in 2002 by sports consultancy firm Burns Sports, Armstrong trailed only Tiger Woods, Michael Jordan, Kobe Bryant, and Anna Kournikova among the sports world's most desired endorsers.

That's right, a cyclist was ranked ahead of NBA star Shaquille O'Neal, and tennis players Andre Agassi and Serena and Venus Williams.

Armstrong's endorsements, which include Nike and Wheaties, are worth about $10 million annually. Speed and reliability are connected to the U.S. Postal Service, which sponsors the U.S. team and pays him about $2 million a year, and Armstrong continues to tell his life story by the companies he chooses to endorse.

His second biggest endorsement deal is with Bristol-Myers Squibb, which manufactures cancer drugs. He is also tied to medical companies like Brainlab and medical content provider Web MD.

The Tour de France is three weeks out of the year, and Armstrong then seemingly disappears. So why is America so familiar with him? His story is simply too good. It would be un-American to bash Armstrong. To his credit, he has not allowed his name or reputation to be overly commercialized, or voiced over by John Tesh. He has provided the media, corporations, and people of all walks of life with one of the most compelling sports and human-interest stories of this—or any—generation. He hopes this incredible story is not entirely overshadowed by his sheer athletic prowess. Armstrong has capitalized on this groundswell of support without alienating a single audience. No athlete has garnered so much familiarity while generating so little contempt.

Business managers must strive to accurately and succinctly refine their "story." It must be communicated in interviews, meetings, and even offline. For CEOs that are comfortable talking about themselves—and have the ability to connect their story to their customers' needs—emotional and personal branding can become a sizable competitive advantage.

In short, business people of all backgrounds and pursuits must invest adequate time and resources to ensuring their own level of familiarity.

BARRY BONDS: THE ANTI-ARMSTRONG?

Armstrong has established and managed his personal brand with great effort. The same cannot be said for perpetually scowling San Francisco Giants outfielder Barry Bonds. Without a doubt, Bonds is among the very best athletes of any generation. Between his incredible on-field performance that culminated in his breaking Mark McGwire's single season record by hitting 73 home runs during the 2001 season and the size of the Bay Area media market, one would expect this future first ballot hall-of-famer to be a familiar, sought-after spokesman.

A five-time MVP and 11-time All-Star, Bonds alienated Madison Avenue for many years and has limited his value as an endorser.

This, of course, assumes that he wanted to build a personal brand. Bonds seldom signs autographs for fans. He has consistently failed to even be courteous to those who shape his personality for the masses, namely the press. His lack of team focus has angered many who have played with him.

Building, maintaining, and extending a personal brand is not important to everyone, and perhaps Bonds is a great example of this. Until the final months of the 2001 season, as the media surrounded him during his pursuit of the single-season home run record, he seemed unconcerned about his personal brand. However, that didn't mean he hadn't been branded. Accordingly, as he sought to reposition himself to sports fans and advertising executives during the home run chase, he might have recognized that what he failed to say and do for himself, society said and did for him in its own way and on its own terms. Basically, you either define yourself or allow others to do it for you.

Bonds contends that it was not his personal brand that had alienated people, but rather it was the media's—and the white media in particular—portrayal of him that was causing the real harm to his personal brand.

Why would companies attempt to be hands-on with him, retaining Bonds to build their corporate brand, when he had been so aloof and disinterested in building his own? He has a black leather massage recliner in the "Barry Section" of the Giants clubhouse, which includes four lockers, a VCR, and TV. Bonds, when asked about relationships with teammates at the 2001 All-Star Game, responded by asking reports whether they in fact liked everyone they worked with. Bonds quickly noted that neither did he.

Because of this alienation, Bonds, as he was ready to break Mark McGwire's home run record, had only modest endorsement deals with Conagra Refrigerated Foods for Armour Hot Dogs, Fila, and Pacific Bell.

Brands that have been developed over 15 years can seldom be reinvented in a matter of months. However, with guidance from his agent Scott Boras and a new sports marketing agency, Bonds had success persuading corporate America that he could pitch their products in 2002. Bonds was portrayed as happy-go-lucky in advertisements for Kentucky Fried Chicken and Charles Schwab and his baseball achievements were highlighted during MasterCard commercials. But Bonds was still a liability. For every good moment, there was a clubhouse fight with Jeff Kent or an idiotic comment like when he said he believed a strike in 2002 wouldn't significantly hurt the game.

Managers must go out of their way to make sure they aren't perceived as the company's Barry Bonds during those Monday morning staff meetings. Conversely, senior management teams are routinely forced to deal with their own Barry Bonds—that awesome but rogue salesperson who puts up huge numbers but alienates everyone in the process. When businesses consider forging an association with an athlete (or employee), they must make sure to research his or her personality and determine what people think of him or her, and not merely rely on his or her athletic prowess (ability to sell).

THE RELEVANT CAL RIPKEN

Long before race car drivers were thanking sponsors in victory lane, baseball's original ironman, Lou Gehrig, was busy plugging one of his endorsements. In April 1935, with his consecutive games played streak nearly 10 years old, Lou Gehrig told magazine readers how to be successful. Gehrig made it known that for any boy or girl, or mom or dad for that matter, a big bowl full of Wheaties every morning was a good way to start the day out right.

Gehrig might have been the first athlete to appear on a Wheaties box (he did so three times between 1934 and 1936), but the man who surpassed Gehrig's consecutive game streak of 2,130 games, Cal Ripken—himself a Wheaties box alum—is among the sports industry's most credible spokesman today.

In 2001, Ripken's final season, he earned about $6 million from endorsements. Ripken's agent noted that as his Hall-of-Fame career with the Baltimore Orioles was coming to an end, he had received more than 250 proposals from companies that wanted to associate with him, leading him to believe in Ripken's long-range marketability.

He has attained this lofty position thanks to his savvy decision making and stellar presentation, perhaps best summed up by the perspective of many sports fans. These fans think that although many Americans pay to see flashy guys living the rock 'n' roll and millionaire lifestyle, just as many revere blue-collar types with whom they can more readily identify. It is these fans that watched Ripken out there every night giving everything he had without being an over-paid prima donna. They viewed him as a guy who did everything he could to let the fans know that he appreciated the fact that they paid his salary. It was for those reasons that scores of sports fans look for-ward to telling their grandchildren about Cal Ripken, Jr.—and hop-ing that they emulate him.

Ripken's consistency on the field has been matched by his con-sistency away from it. Generally believed to have character beyond reproach, Ripken has emerged over the last decade as the consum-mate athlete–dad and credible pitchman.

Part of the reason for this is that his product choices have been predictable, delivering an unparalleled level of believability.

He also overdelivers in the area of relevance. Ripken constantly forges a connection between himself and the products he endorses. This connection spills over to audiences that respect his work ethic and embrace his aura as a parent. The type of products he endorses reinforce this favorable positioning.

To risk-averse corporate America, a guy like Ripken appears right out of central casting: a great athlete that possesses class, dig-nity, and a commitment to work and family.

He has pitched everything Ward Cleaver would pitch: McDonald's, Coca-Cola, John Deere, Century 21, Chevrolet, and of course, milk. Ripken has even included his family in the message. In Coke's "Life Tastes Good" campaign, Ripken is seen walking off the diamond arm-in-arm with his daughter. Very Norman Rockwellian.

His agents coordinated the marketing of the Cal Bar, a Ripken candy bar sold as a fund-raising vehicle for schools and Little Leagues throughout Maryland, which generated more than $500,000.

Thanks in part to his great brand, the new minor league team that he purchased, the single-A Aberdeen Ironbirds of the short-season New York Penn League, was almost completely sold out prior to the opening of the 2002 season.

Because Ripken recognized early in his career that building and maintaining a great personal brand would enable him to succeed both on and off the field, he served as a great ambassador for the sport of baseball, particularly to those kids shagging fly balls on fields he helped finance.

Ripken's "show up everyday" mentality and work ethic spoke directly to the value he placed on commitment to his team. His entire career was predicated on the fact that there are no easy solutions—no shortcuts to success or self-esteem. Even though his productivity waned toward the end of his career (his batting average only surpassed .300 during one of his final 10 seasons), his daily presence inspired all those that worked around him. Corporate America, understanding this, tabbed him the Iron Man of Relevance.

Because many small companies have their own "personalities" and are readily known throughout the community, they must retain athletes that actually have a believable connection to the company. For businesses that seek to be respected corporate citizens within their communities, sending the right (i.e., relevant) executive to give that Rotary or Kiwanis Club speech is just as critical.

STEVE GARVEY: THE ANTI-RIPKEN?

Unlike Ripken, most athletes struggle in their attempts to be relevant. However, this doesn't always limit their ability to successfully pitch products, provided they *seem* credible.

Case in point: 1974 National League MVP, 10-time All-Star and 19-year baseball veteran Steve Garvey, who in 1998 and 1999, helped sell Enforma system products Exercise in a Bottle and Fat Trapper, earning a reported $1 million in the process.

According to the Federal Trade Commission, the infomercials ran 30,000 times in 10 months, or 100 times a day. Garvey, who enjoyed a stellar reputation for many years with the Los Angeles Dodgers, along with purported nutritionist Lark Kendall claimed that the products helped block fat and burn calories without exercise.

Garvey stated in the pitch that he'd always been an athlete and that he was aware of what exercise can do for the body. He later said that using the product could keep everyone skinny—without even needing to exercise.

That's right, whole pizza pies, buckets of fried chicken, and all the hamburgers we wanted, provided of course we used the products religiously. Finally, the magic pill couch potatoes and a nonathlete like Garvey was needed. This truly revolutionary product was available for the amazingly low price of $69.90, plus shipping and handling for a two-month supply.

It was after the company had amassed a customer base of more than 1 million that it was uncovered that the supplements the product contained were in amounts too small to deliver the extraordinary benefits promised despite the fact that Garvey claimed he conducted his own due diligence and that the products worked for him and his wife. In short, the company had made false claims and laundered them through Garvey and Kendall.

In April 2000, the company was forced to repay $10 million to its purchasers and although Garvey was eventually cleared of charges by a federal judge, his flagrant statements about the product were not forgotten. Perhaps a great athlete like Garvey can help legitimize a product that initially lacks credibility, but ultimately it was his personal brand that suffered because he allowed himself to be attached to a brand that lacked believability.

Garvey's very public marketing relationship with Exercise in a Bottle and Fat Trapper provides a vivid example of just how devastating a single lapse in professional judgment can be to one's otherwise strong personal brand.

Business people must assess their careers and determine if there are aspects of their daily job responsibilities where they lack credibility. Does the business card say one thing while daily activities demonstrate something quite different?

THE ESTEEMED ANDRE AGASSI

For an endorsement to be effective, the athlete must be held in high regard, respected, and deemed credible by potential customers. Add to these traits a bit of flair and a touch of personality, and the makings of a great spokesperson are in place.

In the late 1980s and early 1990s, American men dominated the tennis scene, but there was one distinct problem. Most of its star power was as about as vanilla as you could get, especially when compared to the sport's earlier characters, Jimmy Connors and John McEnroe.

Many tennis players, including Michael Chang, Jim Courier, and Pete Sampras could win, but only Andre Agassi did so with style. In business, plenty of executives can put up big numbers, but few do so with the Agassi-like optimal blend of flair and personality.

Agassi quickly climbed up the ranks. After turning pro in 1986, he improved from being ranked 91st in the world to 25th. In 1988, he won 63 of his 74 matches, six titles in seven finals, and found himself ranked third in the world with an increase in earnings from prize money and endorsements of $2 million.

He was the only one among the new young group that actively played to the crowd, and did so while taking full advantage of his status as a sex symbol. After a win, he'd brush back his bleached long hair, blow kisses to the crowd, and throw them his pink and yellow Nike shirts and leftover denim shorts.

Competitor and fellow American Jim Courier believed that because Agassi was from Las Vegas he understood show business and that Agassi knew what the people wanted and knew how to give it to them. Agassi came from the school of giving the people what they wanted and understood that innately. Courier, for one, thought that Agassi just knew something most didn't about pleasing crowds.

In 1988, Michael Jordan was already 25. Many teens could relate better to Andre Agassi, who was just 18. Norm Salik of Bausch and Lomb understood this sentiment and set up a booth at the U.S. Open where it was swarmed by kids asking for "the kind of Ray-Bans Andre Agassi wears."

In a Canon commercial, Agassi told his fans that "Image is Everything," and it seemingly was. Because of his age and pizzazz, Agassi joined Jordan and Bo Jackson as Nike's most marketable stars in the late 1980s.

Tennis great Pete Sampras maintained the sport's top ranking from 1993 to 1998, but fans had a closer relationship with Andre. They felt as if they knew his girlfriends, including his future wife, Brooke Shields.

Sampras didn't fall out of the top 10 at any time in the 1990s, yet it was Agassi who provided the story line. In 1997, due to a wrist injury, he plummeted to 141st in the world. At 27, he could have quit, but he didn't. Returning with a shaved head, we rooted for him to come back and he did, jumping to No. 8 in 1998 and winning both the French and U.S. Opens in 1999.

He was familiar to us—he'd been a star on the American sporting scene for 15 years. Agassi was fresh in our minds because he won, but more so because we viewed him as "real." On the other hand, he struggled on occasion with this perception.

Much of Andre's early marketing exposure was linked to a tagline that he didn't think accurately portrayed him. Agassi indicated that the "Image Is Everything" phrase used in the Canon commercials wasn't reflective of who he was, even then. It was sad to say, according to Agassi, that even in saying the line and filming the campaign, that it never quite occurred to him what was being said or expressed. In essence, he sought to be esteemed and believed that he could grow to earn this designation, but believed his portrayal as a pop culture icon with a trendy catch phrase limited his ability to transcend pop culture and truly be esteemed by mass markets.

Agassi's assessment highlights an important point in the personal branding process. Regardless of how harmless a passing remark or politically incorrect e-mail might appear to be, it is important for business people to try to manage their careers as if they are being covered on the front page of *The New York Times* on a daily basis. If they don't manage the little things that define their personal brands, they might find that, over time, there will be no personal brand—or personal or professional endorsements—to manage at all.

Throughout business, those executives who garner respect, and do so while showing just the right amount flair and personality, find themselves esteemed by colleagues and customers alike.

ANNA KOURNIKOVA: THE ANTI-AGASSI?

We know Andre Agassi for the politically correct reasons: He plays tennis, he wins, and many of his fans aspire to be like him.

We know Anna Kournikova because boys and men fawn over her—but hardly for her ability on the court. Since the fall of 1999, when Lycos' search engine started tracking athletes on a weekly basis, she's consistently been among the most searched athletes.

Sports Illustrated dubbed Kournikova "Pornikova." Others were a little more diplomatic, noting that Anna proves that you don't have to excel as much as you have to be well-rounded—both literally and figuratively. Some sports marketers even went so far as to say that talent is no longer the driving force and that, like Jennifer Lopez and Britney Spears, it's all about how Kournikova's packaged.

She has appeared in numerous television ads, including promoting Lycos fantasy sports. One of the spots, which plays on the word "fantasy," has her agent and a crowd of men believing Kournikova will be playing "lingerie tennis." Fueled by the ad, which ran for the first time during ABC's *Monday Night Football*, Lycos fantasy football registration tripled from the previous year.

There's no denying that she's positioned to capitalize on her sex appeal and her agents have done a good job of selecting the products she endorses. In addition to having a computer virus named after her, she appeared on the cover of June 5, 2000 edition of *Sports Illustrated* seductively grasping a pillow on a bed. Would Billie Jean King have done that? Would it have sold additional copies of the magazine if she had?

Kournikova's name was also featured on the cover of the June 2002 *Penthouse* magazine when the publication said it believed it had 12 topless photographs of the tennis player. In fact, the photos were not of her, and she subsequently sued, seeking $10 million for defamation of character. The irony of this development was not lost on many who believed she had been subtlely promoting her sex appeal on the tennis court.

She makes more money in endorsements (roughly $10–$15 million a year) than her long-time doubles partner, Martina Hingis, who was consistently ranked number one in the world. Underlying all her product pitches is what we already know—that she's merely an above-average professional tennis player.

Kournikova was supposed to be great. From 1998 to 2000, the Russian bombshell went from being ranked 13th in the world to eighth, but she never won a Women's Tennis Association singles title and injuries caused her to miss Wimbledon and the U.S. Open, resulting in her falling out of the top 20 by the end of 2001 and eventually spiraling down to number 73.

Even though she didn't play in Wimbledon, *The London Daily Star* featured "Kourny Korner," a daily pictorial that featured her in her scheduled Wimbledon attire.

Adidas officials have said they believe Kournikova transcends tennis and brings in not only the tennis consumer, but also those whose interest doesn't necessarily lie with the sport—both male and female.

Kournikova has been dubbed one of Adidas' eight "brand symbols," along with such superstars as Kobe Bryant, Martina Hingis, and Sergio Garcia. Brand symbols are endorsers whose products sell beyond the sport category in which they play. However, she's the only athlete in the group who hasn't won an individual title or championship and although Adidas officials won't admit it, there has to be concern over her record.

How should managers feel about that colleague who dresses well or otherwise makes a great entrance yet lacks substance? What does it say about a company when it allows such an individual to represent the firm to customers, suppliers, or shareholders? Businesses that allow themselves to become reliant on such individuals must prepare themselves for the consequences should the strategy backfire.

AND THEN THERE'S MICHAEL

The last of the four criteria considered when evaluating athletes as spokesman is differentiation. Differentiation addresses an athlete's ability to stand out among the public, and considers the extent to which an athlete has packaged his or her charisma and ability to convey a message with his or her athletic achievements. Michael Jordan is the personification of differentiation. He also leads all other athletes in the other three categories: familiarity, relevance, and esteem. He's the complete package.

Not only is Michael Jordan the best basketball player of all time, he might very well be one of the best communicators of all time.

With an assist from the NBA's global appeal, Jordan was afforded the opportunity to reach large, diverse audiences worldwide. He took full advantage of it and, in the process, built the most lucrative personal brand to date.

Placing an Arnold Palmer poster in the window of a fast food restaurant would never sell hamburgers, but Michael Jordan's presence in the window at McDonald's has certainly helped sell more than a few Big Macs.

When McDonald's aired Jordan's famous 1993 Showdown ("Nothin' But Net") commercial with Larry Bird, during which the two play a far-fetched game of H-O-R-S-E, people from New York to California found it funny. Both rich and poor laughed, as did parents and their children.

The other products he endorsed similarly transcended categories. His Air Jordans weren't just sneakers, they were fashion statements for older men and teenagers alike. When customers paid well over $100 and even $200 for Jordan XVIIs in 2002, they were not only buying the shoe, but they were also buying into Jordan's brand equity.

Through endorsements, the public believed they knew Jordan as a person and could somehow relate to his incredible accomplishments. Because he was authentic and extraordinarily talented, he made almost $50 million per year by leveraging his differentiation.

In 1997, Nike determined that Jordan's brand name was so strong, the company started its own Jordan division with that all too familiar Jumpman logo on all of the brand's shoes and apparel.

When you bought a particular product it might very well have been because you believed in Michael Jordan's brand—not necessarily the company's. For example, Bijan Cologne signed Jordan to produce his own signature cologne in 1996 and, in the process, featured his attributes more than the product's. When advertising the Jordan cologne, sales of which reached $130 million in the first two years, Bijan rarely mentioned anything related to the cologne's fragrance.

Even five years later the company's Web site made absolutely no mention of specific product attributes. Rather it stressed how the fragrance had captured the essence of Jordan's personality, character, and lifestyle off the court. The cologne, believed Bijan executives, was ideal for those men who could not only dream big, but also achieve.

From the very beginning it was Jordan's goal to develop a strong personal brand, one that would take time to perfectly shape. Jordan sought to establish a family image that would be enticing to companies like McDonald's. The personality he blended with his good looks and athletic achievements on global stages, such as the Olympics, appealed to companies like Chevrolet and Coca-Cola, which hoped to position their products as "all-American."

Is there any other person, let alone athlete, who could have been called "a family man" more than two years *before* he was married? Ironically, one has to wonder to what extent he will be perceived after his wife filed for divorce, and then subsequently rescinded the request in 2002. Or if details of an extramarital affair revealed in an extortion lawsuit later in the year damaged his personal brand.

How would your personal brand be affected if everyone was aware of such a personal matter in your life? Would they avoid you or welcome you at the water cooler?

The concept of differentiation applies to extraordinary executives just as much as it does to great athletes. After all, truly great executives garner tremendous positive public attention, partially due to the way they have packaged themselves and partially due to their performance in the boardroom.

SHAWN KEMP: THE ANTI-JORDAN?

If managers compromise their personal brands and, in doing so, damage the company or its reputation, they must be prepared to pay the price because great brands will aggressively protect themselves.

For athletes, this means that they must stay on their toes when endorsing a particular shoe or company; any failure to do so could bring with it immediate and grave consequences, as well as harm to the athlete's personal brand.

Corporations (employers) pay handsomely to have high-profile athletes (employees) endorse their products and services. So when athletes compromise the product or service they promote by either singing the praises of a competing brand or demeaning the one they endorse, companies are quick to step in because confusion in the marketplace cannot be tolerated. It hurts the brand and costs the company precious time and resources. This is precisely why most corporations require athletes to avoid such conflicts of interest by agreeing to exclusively endorse a specific product or service.

In the event the athlete or his or her representatives do not employ appropriate discretion in their endorsement relationships, corporations have demonstrated the value they place on these relationships by taking legal action.

In September 2000, the Cleveland Cavaliers' Shawn Kemp filed suit against Reebok, claiming the company had no grounds to terminate his five-year, $11.2 million contract two years early.

From the time he was drafted by the Seattle Supersonics in 1992, Kemp had endorsed the company and had two signature shoes, Reignman I and Reignman II, named after him.

However, Reebok terminated his deal when they saw his comments in the April 16, 2000 edition of the *Akron Beacon Journal*. When asked what his favorite pair of shoes was, Kemp, who in the article was called the "Imelda Marcos of the NBA" because he had 400 pairs, replied that his all-time favorite pair was probably the Air Force II by Nike, also worn by Darrell Griffith and Moses Malone.

Kemp continued to sing the praises of the competing shoe by saying that when he got a pair of Air Force IIs, he was the coolest kid in school. He'd wear them around just to let everybody know he was a ballplayer. Kemp then proceeded to rip the quality of today's shoes compared to those of yesteryear.

Two months later, Reebok claimed that his comments were in violation of his contract. Kemp claimed that he was just telling the truth and that the company used these comments to void his contract because he wasn't playing as well as when Reebok signed the deal.

Soon after the jury began deliberating, Kemp withdrew his suit and quickly settled with Reebok. Reebok spokesperson, Denise Kaigler, made the company's perspective well known when telling the Associated Press that the message being sent was clear: Reebok would never tolerate the disparaging comments that Kemp made.

Analyzing the world of sports endorsements helps illustrate how athletes have created their personal brands. Although certain elite corporate leaders have speechwriters and spin doctors to assist in the personal branding process, few business people have their own personal handlers. Accordingly, they must redouble their efforts to position themselves in the eyes of others.

CHAMPIONSHIP POINTS

The trials and tribulations of athlete endorsers provide great insight into the personal branding process. Great athlete spokespeople, like great executives and line employees, appreciate the following points:

- Personal brands evolve whether they are managed or not. Managers can either choose to play an active role in shaping it or they can allow others to do it for them. Regardless, personal brands bring with them lasting impressions.

- Understand the environment and circumstances in which the personal brand name is established and reinforced. Just like athletes often seek to make themselves more marketable with the increased persuasiveness of the media, business people too must understand the settings in which they will be viewed most favorably.

- Stay on point by consistently communicating and reinforcing the same positive attributes. Lance Armstrong has stayed on his message so brilliantly that he continues to have people talk about him and his story. His reputation precedes him. If managers do it properly, when (potential) colleagues and employers introduce them, they'll say, "This is the guy who. . . "

- Be relevant. This does necessarily mean showing up for work 2,631 games in a row like Cal Ripken; it merely means that people should be true to themselves and others will admire it. There's nothing wrong with being a "milk" guy, provided you are indeed one.

- Make it easy for people to respect you. Do the little things that people don't necessarily see. Help out when you're not expected to. Do the little things like Andre Agassi always has.

- Contrary to the tagline Agassi has voiced, image *is not* everything—substance matters. Managers are ultimately judged on merit, not intangibles that fail to build shareholder value.

- Stay in the information flow. Being the Tiger Woods of your office can bring with it limitations. Managers compromise their brand by not going out on occasion to have a glass of wine with a few colleagues or by not playing on the company's softball team. Employees who don't participate in activities like these routinely find themselves a step behind in the corporate communications process.

- Encourage and establish lines of communication at all levels of the corporate totem pole. Michael Jordan communicates and speaks the languages of most consumers, and built his personal brand in the process.

- Help others establish, maintain, and extend their personal brands when appropriate. Think of this as personal branding's golden rule.

- Protect your reputation at all costs. It is the most important part of your business image, and once it has been damaged it is very difficult—if not impossible—to repair.
- If a company intends on using a corporate spokesperson, it should make sure he or she is familiar with the business' customers and relevant to the brand—attributes that apply to everyone in an organization.

Personal branding is critical in today's business environment because it contributes to success in virtually all areas of enterprise. A failure to live up to personal branding's golden rule of establishing, maintaining, and extending the personal brands of not only yourself, but also your colleagues, often limits success.

When strong personal brands are lacking it becomes increasingly difficult for executives to effectively communicate their positions on critical business issues, including employee relations.

5 EMPLOYEE RELATIONS

*The Point: The dynamic created in the workplace between employ-
ees and upper management and between business owners and labor
unions frequently causes friction and, on occasion, negatively
impacts organizations' bottom lines. This dynamic is even more
intriguing in sports, where a segment of the employees, the athletes,
are also the product. Because of this, the sports industry's handling
of employee relations provides a fascinating backdrop against
which businesses can learn how to handle delicate issues involving
employees.*

The sports industry's relationship with some of its employees,
most notably its athletes, might not always closely resemble the
structure of employee–employer relations, especially the role of
unions, witnessed throughout other industries. Nonetheless, examining employee relations in big-time sports provides many compelling
examples and constructive lessons about managing people in the
more traditional workplace.

Where would business be without the co-dependent relationship
between labor and management? Most employees would be unable
to function without commiserating with peers about their abysmal
treatment (unassigned parking), unacceptable working conditions
(just how long has that broccoli beef been sitting in the department's
refrigerator anyway?), and overall lack of motivation.

According to nuclear power plant technician and animated worker bee Homer Simpson, if you don't like your job, there's no need to strike. You just show up everyday and do a half-assed job. Simpson is under the impression that's the American way.

Let's not forget about management, though. Management would be equally hamstrung without underachieving and self-absorbed employees to boss around, intimidate, and generally annoy.

The curmudgeon C. Montgomery Burns, who owns the Springfield Nuclear Power Plant and is Simpson's boss, has a slightly different perspective on business. Burns' philosophy is short and sweet; he believes that family, religion, and friendship are the three demons that must be slain if one wishes to succeed in business.

The often adversarial relationship between workers and their superiors is fundamental in business and has been memorialized in sports and business through the ages.

The back-and-forth relationship between New York Yankees owner George Steinbrenner and two of his employees, slugger Reggie Jackson and feisty manager Billy Martin—who would be hired to become the skipper of the Yankees an amazing five different times over 13 years—is one of the best examples of management versus employee quarrels in the history of sport.

The former Yankees second baseman made his debut as manager when he led the team through its last 56 games of the 1975 season. In 1976 and 1977, Martin managed the team to two World Series, losing to the Reds, but beating the Dodgers. However, in the 1976 off-season, Steinbrenner, in a move Martin did not approve of, acquired Oakland A's outfielder Reggie Jackson and signed him to a five-year, $2.9 million contract.

Throughout the 1977 championship season, Martin and Jackson were clearly at odds, with tension coming to a head in a game against the Boston Red Sox at Fenway Park. After Martin took Jackson out of the game for not hustling on a fly ball, the two almost knocked each other out in the dugout, all while the TV cameras rolled. They were two employees who simply couldn't get along, but they were too talented for Steinbrenner to jettison. Martin was one of the best in the game and Jackson became the only player to hit five home runs in a single World Series and eventually became the first living Yankees legend to receive a plaque in Monument Park at Yankee Stadium in 2002.

Martin's first managerial stint ended in July 1978 when Martin exploded, telling reporters that the two—Jackson and Steinbrenner—deserved each other because one was a born liar (Jackson), and the other had been convicted (Steinbrenner). Martin's reference to Steinbrenner related to his 1974 fine of $15,000 for funding illegal contributions to President Richard Nixon's reelection efforts.

Steinbrenner knew that Martin had talent, which is why he continually brought him back to manage the team after the relationship appeared to have soured. Martin went on to manage the Yankees in 1979, 1983, 1985, and 1988, and later became a consultant with the team before he was killed in a car accident in 1989.

While Martin was enjoying a good second season managing the Oakland A's in 1981, more than 13,000 of the nation's 17,500 air traffic controllers went on strike to argue for higher wages, shorter hours, and better pension benefits, in what would become one of the most massive employee strikes of all time. Within hours of the strike's first day, President Ronald Reagan announced that if the strikers, who were not contractually allowed to strike per their agreement with the federal government, didn't return to work within two days they would lose their jobs.

Nonstriking and replacement air traffic controllers came in while the Federal Aviation Administration (FAA) and the air traffic controller's union (PATCO) attempted to negotiate a settlement. These controllers remained on the job once it became clear a resolution would not be reached. At the beginning of the strike, during the busiest flying days of the year, many airlines reported losses of up to $30 million a day due to the large number of delayed and cancelled flights. Business eventually returned to normal, although the FAA enjoyed the freedom of not having a union to oppose for six years following PATCO's decertification.

Bitterly fought and highly contentious labor negotiations between management and employees have not been limited to the public sector or big business. For decades, professional sports has provided numerous textbook examples of how *not* to handle employee relations.

Although every major sports league has incurred highly publicized labor strife, MLB is in a class by itself. In fact, in baseball, there had a been a work stoppage at every renegotiation of a collective bargaining agreement (1972, 1973, 1976, 1980, 1981, 1985, 1990, and 1994–95) until 2002.

In September 1994 an already strained relationship between then acting MLB Commissioner Bud Selig and the Major League Players Association (MLBPA) reached an all-time low as Selig announced the cancellation of the remainder of the season, including the World Series. Selig's decision came a month after the players decided to strike following months of unproductive negotiations.

Analysts were quick to note that the sport's labor discord had managed to do what the World Wars and the Great Depression could not—namely bring the national pastime to a disgraceful and grinding halt.

The impact of the cancellation resonated throughout the sports, business, and political worlds. In addition to the projected $442 million loss of revenue to MLB, the strike wreaked havoc on broadcasters, local businesses, merchandisers, and even charities.

Disillusioned fans, believing that both sides in the dispute were consumed by greed and unconcerned about them, switched allegiances to other sports during—and perhaps well after—the work stoppage. This caused sponsors and advertisers to rethink their allocation of marketing dollars, further comprising the economic viability of MLB.

In April 1995, the players returned to work without a new collective bargaining agreement, but with an injunction that barred MLB from imposing many of the demands it had placed on the MLBPA. As discussed later in this chapter, the decision to return to play without resolving the sport's most pressing business and labor issues came back to haunt MLB during the 2001–2002 season.

The high-profile nature of sports, the structure and organizations of sports leagues, and the passion with which sports is followed are the factors that separate it from other industries embroiled in acrimonious employee relations.

A STRUCTURE FOR EMPLOYEE RELATIONS

An organization and its labor force are dependent on each other and must work together to optimize their relationship to succeed. Whether employees are represented by a union, as is the case throughout the four major sports leagues, or not, there are many other variables and issues that must be contemplated for this relationship to prosper. Employers and employees alike must correctly analyze and adequately address these issues to maximize shareholder value, whether these shareholders literally own the company or figuratively do so in the case of sports fans.

The six prevailing issues that require consideration on the labor front are:[1]

- Building of long-term relationships
- Dealing with change
- Navigating "hot-button" issues
- Acting in the best interests of the game
- Leading by example
- Managing the relationship

BUILDING LONG-TERM RELATIONSHIPS

Building long-term relationships with workforces has enabled companies and organizations of all sizes to prosper. In professional sports, success can only be attained once a league has achieved long-term labor peace. Without such peace, leagues are unable to convince TV networks to pay billions of dollars for the rights to broadcast games unless the contracts have clauses stipulating "make goods" in the case of a work stoppage. This fallout arises due to the network concerns about a sport's long-term stability and their fears that advertisers might not be able to reach as many viewers should ratings decline as fans become disenfranchised. Essentially, any sports league—or company for that matter—that is perpetually embroiled in labor strife cannot maximize profits.

This macro perspective on the impact of securing positive long-term employee relations is complemented by the need to do so on a micro level, one highlighted by individual employee or player relations.

With the exceptions of Bo Jackson, Deion Sanders, and a handful of other two-sport superstars, sports leagues seldom have to worry about their players jumping ship from league to league because the major professional sports leagues are both monopolies and monopsonies (where there is but one "buyer" for the athlete's services—the pro league) that lack significant competitors. This doesn't mean, however, that individual teams don't face extraordinary employee relations issues, particularly when dealing with high-priced free agents, players who are able to change employers when their current contracts expire.

---

1. Adapted from Blackard, Kirk, *Managing Change in a Unionized Workplace: Countervailing Collaboration.* Quorum, 2000.

In much the same way treating an employee professionally and with respect pays dividends, treating a player or coach "right" can make the difference in retaining that employee even when the money being offered is significantly less than what the competition is offering. It also leads to establishing long-term, mutually satisfying employee relations.

Dallas Mavericks owner Mark Cuban pays his players well, leading some to believe he is one of the best owners in the NBA. But it might be the creature comforts he provides his employees that really make the difference. Cuban purchased a new Boeing 757 team plane, partly because the NBA charter didn't have the amenities that would enable his players to properly recover from fatigue during extended road trips.

The Mavericks play in a new arena and Cuban has gone out of his way to do all the little things—from putting more plush in the players' courtside towels to commissioning the building of comfortably padded leather chairs to accommodate his players. What Cuban does for his players is akin to what many dot-coms did in 1999 and 2000 for employees who were asked to work long hours before (if ever) cashing in. Internet companies "compensated" employees with pool tables, video games, and customized office furniture in an effort to maintain motivation and reduce employee attrition.

An athlete might also accept less money if he or she has the option to play for a successful organization, a team that not only has the chance to win a championship, but also the commitment to seeing that it happens. Successful organizations that are doing well and are committed to doing even better find it easier to retain and acquire employees, and they are provided a measurable competitive advantage in the process.

Having a supporting cast of well-qualified people also contributes to building long-term relationships. Although Joe Sakic, Patrick Roy, and Rob Blake were unrestricted free agents immediately after they helped the Colorado Avalanche win the 2000–2001 Stanley Cup, each decided to resign with the team prior to exploring the market in search of other lucrative contracts. Of course, offering Sakic the largest contract in NHL history at the time didn't hurt, but the personnel commitment around him was certainly a factor in his decision.

Long-term, mutually beneficial, and bargained-for relationships minimize the strife between organizations and their employees. Once these ideal working relationships are formed the ability to avoid and overcome conflict is greatly increased.

Counterproductive conflicts not only contribute to the animosity between management and unions, but can also foster disdain from customers. NHL and Ottawa Senators star Alexei Yashin, after consulting his agent Mark Gandler, held out the entire 1999–2000 season. Yashin, who was scheduled to make $3.6 million in the final year of his five-year contract, was awaiting a raise from the team before playing his final season. Yashin thought he deserved more money because he was a finalist for the league MVP award.

Essentially, out of nowhere, the player who was featured on all the team's promotional materials would not be playing. In a surprising and unusual move, a group of 11,000 season ticket holders attempted to recover $27.5 million worth of damages for Yashin sitting out, claiming that they had purchased one product (a team including Yashin) but were given another (a team without him). However, as with many labor matters where the customer is affected by internal company affairs, the judge eventually ruled that the contract was between the Ottawa Senators and Yashin, and the fans had no legal standing.

Although the Senators made the playoffs (the team was eliminated in the first round) without Yashin, the fallout to the Senators thanks to his failure to honor the contract was tremendous. Yashin, legally forced to grant the Senators a final year, played as a lame duck of sorts, knowing the team would trade him when the season ended because he had so severely alienated the fans and embarrassed the team. As expected, Yashin was traded to the Islanders for the second pick in the 2001 NHL draft and signed a 10-year, $87.5 million contract.

Many Ottawans will never forget the bitter taste that Yashin's holdout left in their mouths and Yashin, despite his prospects of future success in the league, will always be associated with the holdout.

Some companies are so embroiled in their internal employee relations wars that they forget how it is all affecting the customer relationship. No matter how talented or valuable an employee appears to be to an organization, this value has limitations. No single employee exists who is more important than the organization itself and the brand name it has achieved.

DEALING WITH CHANGE

Organizations and their labor forces must work diligently to make sure that any changes that do occur, regardless of their origin or controversy, are handled as favorably and seamlessly as possible. Creating an environment where change is dealt with in a positive fashion will help both sides to accept the outcome and begin to make the best of the consequences surrounding it.

The best executives are those who strive to monitor the pulse of the changes necessary to improve their company on a daily basis. Revered managers are those who explain changes to their workforce and do their best to smoothly navigate major transitions in management philosophy.

In the sports world, major transitions involve the hiring and firing of managers and head coaches. Although it is often said that firing managers and coaches does little to improve team performance, because it's the players that play, sports economist Gerald Scully found that changes at the top, in general, actually do improve team performances, especially in baseball and basketball.

However, it's not only about the change itself, or even who the new manager is. How the change is made is actually just as important. The following illustrates one of the most botched managerial changes in modern sports history.

It was clear to many fans that Arkansas State athletic director and head football coach Joe Hollis had to go. Hollis had compiled a 13–42 record over five years and his team had lost 18 out of its last 21 games heading into the final game of the 2001 season. School President Les Wyatt reportedly told Hollis that he would be fired at the end of the season. To Hollis, that probably meant the day after the last game; but to Wyatt, that somehow meant before the last game concluded.

Late in the fourth quarter of the final game between Arkansas State and Nicholls State, Wyatt—wanting to make sure that the press knew about the firing before the media left for the postgame press conference—distributed the following memo to those in the press box:

> Arkansas State University is conducting its search for an Athletic Director. Joe Hollis has served in that position on an interim basis since March 2000. Once selected, the new Athletic Director will be asked to hire a new Head Football Coach. Joe Hollis will no longer have head coaching duties. ASU and Coach Hollis will be working together to ensure a smooth transition within the administration of the Athletic Department.

If that wasn't enough, with less than a minute to go in the game, the Lynyrd Skynard song "Gimme Three Steps" blared on the stadium's public address system. Although Chris Wyche, ASU's assistant athletic director, later told reporter Keith Merritt of Tribalgrounds.com that he wasn't aware of the words to the song, it seemed too much of a coincidence that one of the lines in the song suggests that "you won't see me no more."

If any hope of a "smooth transition" remained, it was dashed when Hollis was handed the press release as he walked off the field. He refused to talk about his firing at the press conference and when the players were asked about the firing, they, of course, told reporters that they hadn't heard the news. In July 2002, Arkansas State announced Dean Lee as its new athletic director, bringing to a close an awkward chapter in the school's sports history.

If you think that once a worker is laid off, he or she has severed ties with the company, think again. If an organization fires employees the way Arkansas State fired Joe Hollis, the damage will go far beyond a single former employee. Although in this case a new athletic director and a new coach were hired shortly thereafter, it remains the case that prospective job candidates might indeed remove themselves from consideration if they are concerned about how employees—current and former—are treated.

Earlier in the chapter it was noted that success in sports is predicated on labor stability and media distribution (i.e., lucrative TV contracts). Because the NFL has consistently anticipated change, and done so hand-in-hand with the NFL Players Association (NFLPA), the two have secured long-term labor peace. In turn, this peace has enabled the NFL to negotiate the most lucrative TV contracts in sports. Under terms of the current $18.3 billion agreements with Viacom Inc.'s CBS, News Corp.'s Fox, and Walt Disney Co.'s ABC and ESPN, payments to the league will increase to $2.8 billion in the eighth and final year from $1.75 billion in 1998.

As impressive as these totals are (they dwarf the TV revenue generated by the NBA and MLB), what is truly astonishing is the ongoing spirit of cooperation between the NFL and the NFLPA. Rather than bicker over every minute detail relating to league revenue and expenses, the two sides have recognized that working together will afford them tremendous economies that enable the sport to outpace all others in terms of financial success.

For example, the two sides agreed to set aside $342 million from 2002–2005 to make up for a possible temporary decrease in television revenue when the current TV contracts expire after the 2005 season. This was done in an effort to ensure that the players have something set aside for a "rainy day." The "rainy day" feared by the NFL and NFLPA is what each side believes to be a decline in the sport's most important source of revenue—that generated from broadcast television.

Historically, the revenue generated from the sale of its broadcast rights has provided individual teams with enough money to pay their players. Generally speaking, because the NFL and NFLPA have achieved such an extraordinary working relationship, teams basically break even before considering any other revenue streams. This has contributed to rapid escalations in franchise values and made the NFL the most profitable sports league of all time.

Despite the earlier discussion about the air traffic controllers strike of 1980, the airline industry has also demonstrated great examples of employee relations, including one involving Southwest Airlines, which has one of the highest employee retention rates in the industry.

Although Southwest—the official airline of the NFL—has routinely paid its employees below the industry average, those employees continue to perform their jobs well due to their quality of training and depth of performance incentives, as well as an extensive profit-sharing pension program. This development led some to believe that the old-fashioned bond of loyalty between employees and company might have vanished throughout much of corporate America, but remained strong at Southwest.

In December 1997, Southwest flight attendants agreed to a six-year contract that was described as one of the best (union contracts) in the industry. In September 1998, Southwest Airlines' 2,800 pilots voted to keep the second half of an unusual long-term labor contract that integrated stock options, profit sharing, and wage increases. In exchange for no wage increases during the first five years of the contract, the company's pilots received options to purchase 3.15 million shares of Southwest Airlines common stock in each year of the contract, were to receive 3 percent wage increases during the second half of the accord (raised to 5 percent during the 1998 renegotiation), and receive compensation based on the company's profitability. As part of the negotiations, the company's CEO, Herb Kelleher, asked to have his salary frozen for at least four years.

Not surprisingly, in January 2000, Southwest Airlines was included on *Fortune* magazine's list of the 100 Best Companies to Work for in America.

However, much like professional sports, and MLB in particular, sustaining long-term labor peace in the traditional business world can be very difficult, particularly because it usually requires a confluence of favorable events and developments to ensure stellar employee relations.

Southwest's stock remained, by many accounts, a good buy (due in part to relatively low employee costs that contributed to profitability), even in the wake of the terrorist attacks of September 11, 2001. Ironically, because of this, employees with whom Southwest was negotiating, including mechanics (with whom they reached agreement in August 2002 following the involvement of federal mediators), flight attendants, and pilots, were inclined to seek what they believed to be their fair share during the first half of 2002. Unfortunately, for all parties involved, this occurred during the same period in which the stock market fell dramatically, compromising Southwest's long-standing and revered track record of strong employee relations.

Keeping employees happy while holding down their base pay is a challenge, but Southwest has accomplished it. After New York and Washington, D.C. were struck by terrorist attacks, many airlines were forced to lay off thousands to avoid bankruptcy in the ensuing months. The industry, which lost more than $10 billion from January 2001 through August 2002, required serious federal aid. Nonetheless, Southwest was able to avoid layoffs and major losses partly because of the favorable relationship it enjoyed with its employees.

So, although dealing with change in labor and management matters is critical to function, working in tandem to anticipate and deal with change—whether anticipated or not—is essential to prospering.

NAVIGATING "HOT-BUTTON" ISSUES

The third prevalent part of labor and management codependency deals with the legal side of the relationship. Certain issues between parties, typically dealing with wages, benefits, and working conditions, require serious negotiation and, in many cases, collective bargaining.

With such hot-button issues, there is seldom a courteous air of give-and-take. Neither side, when thought to be battling for their very livelihoods, allows the other side much leeway, especially when lawyers are involved.

Rather than rely on litigation, some unions prefer to utilize activist groups to impact business and influence the decision-making process.

Two hundred employees of the New Era Cap Company, which is the official cap maker of MLB, were willing to sit out almost a year (from July 2001 to July 2002) in pursuit of better wages and an easing of production quotas. As a result of making the effort to keep most of its production in America, New Era attempted to leverage its American employees.

Although New Era was able to compensate for its striking workforce, those on strike—and represented by the Communication Workers of America—had gained the ultimate leverage. The union received the support of the United Students Against Sweatshops and the Worker Rights Consortium and, thanks to student activists at many major universities, more than a dozen schools said they would stop doing business with New Era until the company treated its employees better.

In July, the employees signed a new four-year deal that gave them relaxed quotas, improved health benefits, and allowed shifts to be determined based on seniority.

Hot-button issues, particularly those supported by external stakeholders such as special-interest groups, which are not adeptly dealt with early, can manifest themselves into larger, farther-reaching dilemmas.

However, with less pressing issues, both sides should bend over backwards to accommodate as doing so demonstrates a resolution-based approach to negotiations. This, in turn, can foster a dialogue that enables both sides to work together to move the relationship forward.

In 1995, NHL Commissioner Gary Bettman faced just such a situation in his dealings over a "hot-button" issue with the NHL Players Association Executive Director Bob Goodenow. Unfortunately, the outcome served to do nothing more than extend the sport's economic problems into the foreseeable future and force it to revisit its management–labor relationship years later at a time when the stakes had become even larger.

The owners began the negotiations insisting they needed a salary cap. However, the Players Association, as expected, dismissed this request. The owners countered by proposing a luxury tax. But because the luxury tax would essentially limit teams' spending on players, the union interpreted it as essentially a salary cap and declined to accept it. After missing slightly less than half the season, the owners, many of whom needed the revenue generated by playing games on a regular basis, finally tabled the request.

Bettman thought the board understood this fully—that if a cap or a tax was indeed necessary, it would have required losing at least one season. As a result, Bettman believed the board and the owners were comfortable that the agreement wasn't worth the rest of the season.

The 103-day lockout came to an end and reduced the season's schedule to 48 games. In the process of tabling the hot-button issue of player costs, the NHL and the NHLPA missed a golden opportunity to demonstrate to fans and, more important, to TV networks and sponsors, that each side was willing to bargain absent acrimony, to achieve the same level of stability enjoyed by the NFL.

Acting in the Best Interests of the Game

The fourth element of employee relations requiring attention is the premise that both sides must realize that the other has specific interests it is trying to protect or extend. Even though these issues might not be in direct conflict, it does not necessarily mean that they are mutually respected rights or positions.

Management's overriding interest usually lies in the success of a firm as viewed by its shareholders. In sports, leagues often cite the need to act "in the best interests of the game," a time period that lasts in perpetuity. Team owners, on the other hand, are concerned with increasing the value of their teams over a certain period time, one lasting only as long as their ownership tenure. Athletes, as well as their agents and unions, have an even more narrow time period covered by the "best interests" doctrine: the length of their careers, which typically average three to five years.

Once all parties involved in a labor relations matter recognize the interests of the others, they will be in a position to work to achieve a deal that benefits all involved. Typically, resolving labor disputes, such as salary and bonus levels, requires three steps. First, the parties must create and build a relationship. Next, they must plan and prepare jointly for change and the future. Finally, the parties must conduct the actual negotiation.

Although it is often recommended that neither side speak to the media in specifics during labor negotiations so as not to "open up" the closed-door meetings to the world, controlled leaks to the media can be advantageous.

Sports leagues and their unions can gain leverage by spinning their positions with prominent sports writers in *The New York Times* and *Los Angeles Times* through "on-" and "off-the-record" comments. So, too, can small companies or unions that gain the favor and sympathy of a local columnist or on-air personality. Having public sentiment in your favor can give you that much-needed home field advantage that can ultimately pressure your collective bargaining opponent to yield to demands. Because the sports world does not attempt to form picket lines to get attention, league work stoppages serve as the next best way to use the media in labor negotiations.

For both sides to effectively control their message in the media, a single point person should be responsible for the overall message disseminated in media circles. This doesn't mean that each side must be limited to only one person publicly stating the company's line. It just means that one person has to be the filter—knowing exactly where information is being placed and how it is phrased or presented.

From a sports league perspective, the filter is controlled through threats, or more simply put, large fines. During the 1998–1999 NBA lockout, Commissioner David Stern imposed a $1 million fine on owners who commented on the labor negotiations. During the 2001 and 2002 seasons, MLB commissioner Bud Selig also threatened a similar fine on any owner who talked about MLB's volatile labor situation. In 2002, MLB decided to have its executive vice president of labor relations Rob Manfred and its executive vice president of baseball operations Sandy Alderson travel around the country talking to baseball reporters about the labor situation, so as to further discourage individual owners from talking. As talks heated up in August, Manfred conducted frequent conference calls with reporters to describe the day's events. The Players Association declined to hold such conferences.

In a well-managed labor campaign, neither side grants hundreds of media interviews. There are only a select few, often to columnists that either management or the union trusts implicitly. In sports labor negotiations, a side might be as proactive as to update the situation for a *USA Today, Washington Post,* or ESPN.com reporter. This same side might only contact a local writer if he or she says that the other side has commented and the scoop could be picked up (and spun) nationally. Regardless of the media platform utilized, trust in a particular writer is also essential, as being misquoted or taken out of context can be disastrous to a negotiation.

NBA players certainly didn't gain much sympathy with the public when Boston Celtics guard Kenny Anderson decided to make himself a spokesman. For the average working man, an overrated player like Anderson who had four children with three different women couldn't have been the ideal person on the player's side to personalize what the lockout's impact meant on daily life.

While the negotiations were stalled, Anderson, who had recently signed—but was not receiving—a seven-year, $49 million contract, implied that he was going to have to start belt tightening. Anderson then explained that after his "hanging out money" ($120,000), rent for his Beverly Hills home ($12,500), alimony payments ($7,200), and taxes ($2 million), he'd only have about $2 million remaining to invest. Anderson thought his first budget cut might have to be his Mercedes—one member of his eight-car fleet that included Range Rovers and Porsches that costs $75,000 annually to insure. Anderson's comment was a disaster for the Players Association. Of course, when the lockout ended and it was time to return to work a couple months later, Anderson said he was only joking.

Having your side's leader quoted is important, but also having a different representative's voice, such as an appointed league attorney, can also be effective. David Stern and his deputy commissioner, Russ Granik, provided the press with the league's perspective in the 202-day lockout (a lockout is essentially a strike by management).

The NBA owners clearly won their public relations battle, whereas MLB management had a tougher time with its Players Association. What was the difference? First, Stern was trained as a lawyer. He knew how to choose words carefully, was adept at persuasion, and understood the art of negotiation. He knew how to portray to the fan that he and management had a genuine interest in returning to work. Selig, on the other hand, was a wealthy car dealer who lacked Stern's communication skills. With 28 years of ownership of the Milwaukee Brewers under his belt, Selig took a hard stance from the beginning and made it appear to all that heard him that negotiation was not a top priority. As a result, baseball's owners struggled in the game of public relations.

Stern and Granik held constant teleconferences to discuss how negotiations were proceeding and posted the transcripts online.

Meanwhile, Selig and MLB spent more time in the winter of 2001 being reactive to the press, calling many reporters to express how dissatisfied they were with a report or feature column instead of being a proactive part of it.

Stern also went out of his way to let fans know that he was trying, along with the players, to come up with a formula that allows the negotiating process to be a long-term success story. MLB, on the other hand, rarely let fans know that it was concerned about them.

Stern consistently gives the impression he cares about the overall state of the game, at least in the eyes of the customers—the fans. Selig, however, who began the negotiations for a new collective bargaining agreement just days after an exhilarating seven-game World Series between the New York Yankees and the Arizona Diamondbacks, didn't come off quite as well. That's because for him the first step in the new collective bargaining agreement negotiations was to announce that the owners had unilaterally agreed to fold two teams. This was despite the fact that the Players Association apparently had the right to know about anything affecting all terms of their employment. Selig then called an emergency meeting in Chicago, where owners extended his contract.

The Players Association quickly responded by filing a grievance that resulted in the Twins no longer being a candidate for contraction, at least through the 2003 season. These developments were followed by the House Judiciary Committee calling a hearing to try to strip MLB's antitrust exemption, which, if successful, would remove baseball's power to make unilateral decisions regarding franchise movement. Selig was constantly lambasted in the press, economists took the side of the union, and all the while the union's executive director, Donald Fehr, didn't have to lift a finger to achieve a public relations victory.

The point of all this isn't necessarily to be positive in the press about negotiations like Stern was. It's to realize where public sentiment lies and get your position across in a manner so you can gain the support of the national or local masses. Losing the battle of the media burdens your side when you step up to the bargaining table.

Regardless of the platform chosen—picketing, calling talk radio shows, or leveraging long-standing and strategic media contacts— successful labor relations requires that both sides acknowledge, beyond the use of rhetoric, that the other party has interests it seeks to protect or extend. Ultimately, this acknowledgment must be extended to the point where both sides act "in the best interests of the game."

LEADING BY EXAMPLE

Establishing an appropriate framework for change is also a critical part of labor relations. If there is going to be a (positive) change in the relationship between management and employees, management must work diligently to set the tone and dynamic under which any change will occur. This includes amount of effort given toward the negotiations, overtures about what sacrifices will need to be made, and leading by example by minimizing unnecessary chaos.

When establishing the tone and dynamic, it is important to bear in mind the need to improve the current working relationship, as well as envision what an improved business relationship will yield for the parties involved. Once management demonstrates it wants to (or needs to) initiate changes, it must embrace employees if it expects the new relationship to be productive and long-lasting.

This must be accomplished even in circumstances where the employer–employee relationship is only slightly jeopardized.

To make rapid changes in the company, important decision makers routinely feel the need to demonstrate that they are sacrificing something as well. During times of downsizing and lack of annual bonuses and holiday parties, many CEOs make it a point to show that they are in effect "one of the guys" by making it clear that their pay will be frozen as well. The extreme side of this was seen in 2001 when key decision makers reduced their multimillion-dollar salaries to a single dollar to save some employees from being released. John Chambers and John Morgridge, Cisco's CEO and chairman, lowered their salaries to $1. So, too, did former CMGI CEO David Weatherall. Ironically, and despite companywide belt tightening, Weatherall insisted that CMGI would hold on to the naming rights deal it negotiated with the new New England Patriots stadium despite a stock plunge of 99 percent.

Many were quick to point out that these "sacrifices" were somewhat hollow, because only a modest connection exists between executive compensation and the number of employees retained. Nonetheless, the symbolic gesture of leading by example was generally well received, a lesson begrudgingly learned by the University of Washington (UW).

As a result of a state ethics investigation, UW adopted a policy that specifies which employees and guests can be invited to postseason football bowl games at the university's expense. The investigation centered around whether the school violated state laws by using proceeds from bowl appearances to spend on airfare, game tickets, and other activities for themselves, their friends, and certain UW employees.

The investigation arose following an anonymous tip that indicated athletics director Barbara Hedges allowed colleagues in the athletic department to take their families to the game using revenue earned from appearing in the Rose Bowl. The trip included air and ground travel, four nights at the Beverly Hills Hilton, Rose Bowl tickets valued at $125 each, souvenir packages, and Disneyland passes.

UW President Richard McCormick's Rose Bowl guest list included 89 people, most of whom were university employees, UW regents, and their spouses. The list included four legislative leaders, Washington Governor Gary Locke and his family, and McCormick's in-laws.

Although the actions of the athletic department's administrators were consistent with those of previous administrations, UW revised the president's contract to allow him to bring his spouse and dependent children to postseason athletic events at the university's expense. UW also will stipulate in other employee contracts whether the university will reimburse the employees for family travel to bowl games.

In a settlement approved by the Ethics Board, UW reimbursed the board $8,500 for the cost of the nine-month investigation and agreed to adopt invitation guidelines to bowl games. Both sides, though, said they were ready to go forward and believed the new policy would prevent future misinterpretation.

The value of "black-and-white" guidelines, especially in matters dealing with perks and who qualifies for them, is enormous. The relatively minor indiscretion just described was chosen to highlight the fact that even the little, often overlooked, or otherwise deemed insignificant things matter. They matter not only to ethics boards, they matter to employees. When companies change policies, whether relating to dress code or vacation benefits, they must effectively communicate the reason for doing so with clarity and reason if the current working relationship is to be maintained, let alone improved. Not doing so breeds employee cynicism and hurts companywide morale.

Ideally management will recognize that the system it has in place is imperfect or in need of refinement. Even great organizations have their flaws—and great managers know it.

In 1998, the Bowl Championship Series (BCS) became the official framework for determining college football's national champion. The BCS, which runs through the 2005 regular season, consists of four bowls that each host the national championship game twice in rotation—the Rose Bowl presented at the time by AT&T, Nokia Sugar Bowl, FedEx Orange Bowl, and the Tostitos Fiesta Bowl.

Each year if the system isn't perfect, it is refined. Consequently, through the 2001 bowl season, there has always been a consensus national champion.

In 1999, an undefeated Kansas State lost in shocking fashion in overtime to Texas A&M in the Big 12 conference championship. The team slipped out of all of the BCS bowls, despite ending the season being ranked fourth.

That led to a change where any team ranked either third or fourth and did not receive an automatic bid because it had lost its conference championship had to be selected as an at-large BCS team.

In 2000, Florida State went to the national championship game to play Oklahoma because it had a higher BCS ranking than Miami. This was despite the fact that the two Florida schools had the same record (11–1) and Miami beat Florida State during the regular season. Fans and journalists once again called the system flawed, as they had done the year before when Kansas State slipped all the way to the Alamo Bowl.

Because of Miami, the BCS was tweaked again for the 2001 season. The formula now gave bonus points for wins over top 15 teams while replacing the two computer polls that stressed margin of victory over the quality of the opponent with two other polls that didn't place as much emphasis on margin of victory. To some degree, John Swofford, the BCS Commissioner, thought this was a necessary evolution of the formula.

However, in 2001, Nebraska, because of a late-season loss to Colorado, didn't even play in the Big 12 Conference championship game. Yet because of a series of losses by Texas and Tennessee, Nebraska played in the National Championship game. Fans and media members then said that schools from conferences with championship games shouldn't be able to play in for the National Championship if they weren't even considered the conference champion.

In June 2002, new BCS coordinator Mike Tranghese notified the computer pollsters that the BCS was undergoing another change—it would only accept formulas that did not take margin of victory into account.

Although the BCS certainly has its shortcomings, its willingness to change to provide a better relationship with its athletes and other stakeholders, especially fans, is noteworthy. What part of your company's formula, perhaps refining the criteria used for promoting employees, needs to be refined? If the media openly criticized your company's way of conducting business on its way to its "National Championship," would your organization be more willing to refine its system like the BCS has?

Improving the relationship between management and labor requires an inclusive approach to managing employee relations. This must include a willingness to work together, as well as a commitment to refine employee relations whenever possible. Leading by example and bending over backwards to do "right" by employees and the products they sell measurably contributes to productive and long-lasting labor relations.

MANAGING THE RELATIONSHIP

The final employee relations issue to consider is the constant, proactive management of this relationship. Neither side should harbor any hidden agendas at any point in the process. Even though a trusting relationship between labor and management seems an improbable feat, it always makes financial and public relations sense for both parties to try to foster long-lasting and well-managed relations from the outset.

Doing so enables each party to act in the best interests of its respective constituents while creating positive change for those involved and affected by the management changes. The parties must realize that without the other, neither could survive, let alone prosper. Appreciating this understanding begins as early as the interview phase, whether you are a company looking for a new president of marketing or a legendary sports team looking for a new head football coach.

Prior to managing the relationship, both parties must enter into it with clean hands. As the University of Notre Dame found out, entering into an employer–employee relationship that is not predicated on trust leads not only to public embarrassment, but severely damages its relationship with its constituents.

Just five days after Notre Dame announced it had selected Georgia Tech head coach George O'Leary to replace Bob Davie, O'Leary was forced to resign after it was discovered his bio in the Georgia Tech media guide, which was passed on to Notre Dame, contained false information about his athletic (it said he was a three-year letterman at University of New Hampshire, but he never played a game) and academic credentials (it said he earned a master's degree from New York University, but he only took a couple of classes there).

O'Leary stated that due to a selfish and thoughtless act many years ago, he had personally embarrassed Notre Dame, its alumni, and fans. Bearing in mind that the integrity and credibility of Notre Dame was impeccable, he decided to resign his position as head football coach effective December 13, 2001.

Notre Dame's athletic director Kevin White accepted O'Leary's resignation after making it known that he thought the inaccuracies represented a very human failing. Nonetheless, to White they constituted a breach of trust that made it impossible for Notre Dame to go forward with the relationship.

O'Leary's resume flap proved not to be an isolated case. Over the next eight months, at least seven sports executives or coaches—including United States Olympic Committee president Sandra Baldwin, incoming Dartmouth athletic director Charles Harris, incoming Georgia Tech defensive coordinator Rick Smith, and UCLA men's soccer coach Todd Saldana—were relieved of their duties because of similar résumé flaps.

The entire process by which Notre Dame handled Davie's firing and O'Leary's hiring was called into question by those impacted by the relationships' mismanagement. Among those dismayed by Notre Dame's poor employee relations included alumni, former coaches, and the media.

Because it is not possible to successfully navigate ill-formed employee relationships, they should be avoided from the outset. Few employer–employee relationships are as high-profile as coaching or managing a storied program like Notre Dame, but it is precisely its high-profile nature that mandates the school take any and all precautions when addressing personnel matters. Simply relying on word-of-mouth references can be disastrous, as such recommendations routinely focus on the rose, forgetting it might have thorns.

In business, such oversight leads to litigation arising from employee actions (and inaction) and can also damage the company's reputation with other employees or shareholders in much the same way the O'Leary situation damaged Notre Dame's reputation among coaches and alumni.

Therefore, companies should strive to be pragmatic instead of symbolic when agreeing to long-term contracts with top executives. Organizations should be candid with themselves and ask, "Are we signing so-and-so to a long-term deal to show analysts or outsiders that we are more stable than we actually are? Or are we signing this person because we truly believe shareholder value will be enhanced?"

In many cases it is not only preferred, but also less expensive to hire the right person for the right reasons rather than extending or entering into an awkward relationship.

Properly establishing and then proactively managing relationships spares organizations the time and resources associated with replacing those employees that should never have been hired in the first place.

CHAMPIONSHIP POINTS

Relative to community or public relations, the term *employee relations* does not carry with it the same upbeat tone. Rather, the adversarial message that employee relations connotes has a built-in negativity to it. However, it need not be viewed any less favorably than the other business relations such as shareholder relations or government relations.

In fact, there are numerous ways through which those charged with delivering and maintaining a great working environment can prosper. For instance:

- Avoid hiring a Homer Simpson or being hired by C. Montgomery Burns. Not only is life too short to work with or for people with these professional characteristics; such colleagues routinely suppress motivation and long-term success.

- Recognize the professional and personal value in quality, long-term relationships. What is in the "best interests" of a business in the long run must not be in conflict with what is required to succeed in the short run.

- Do what you can to maintain employee happiness. Even in tough economic times, when your employees are less likely to jump ship, employee happiness is still linked to increased productivity.

■ Just like it is cheaper to keep an existing customer than to woo a new one, the same is true with employees—it's less expensive and time consuming to retain an existing employee than to hire and train a new one.

■ Don't play hardball with an employee or his or her representatives just because you can. Conversely, realize that if and when employee representatives play hardball it can damage the long-term relationship with important constituents including shareholders and sports fans.

■ Be prepared to negotiate and bargain in good faith, as any failure to do so will alienate important constituents, including customers or fans.

■ Take a page from the NFL's playbook when dealing with change. Incorporating vested parties in the process, whether formally or merely by providing a "heads-up," will help changes be more favorably received.

■ Recognize the inherent value in the assistance of others. In sports, it's often the media that plays a critical role, but far less visible allies can also help manufacture mutually satisfying results.

■ Be willing and amenable to consider change even if it is not in your immediate best interest to do so. Imagine the pounding the BCS would have taken had it not been willing to tinker with its formula.

■ Surround yourself with people you trust, and if they are new to a company make sure you've done your homework. Getting "O'Learyed" as Notre Dame did not only embarrassed the school, it tarnished the Golden Dome's brand.

■ Proactively manage the employee relations front at all times.

Sports has provided a great backdrop to learn about dealing with employees and their labor issues. An acute matter in sports, employee relations has become equally critical throughout all business and industry, affecting not only the organizations themselves, but those with whom they seek to conduct business.

It is far easier to structure mutually beneficial strategic alliances when potential business partners believe your workforce is both stable and properly engaged in matters that materially impact business operations.

6 BUILDING ALLIANCES

The Point: Structuring strategic alliances can be a powerful way to grow a business exponentially. The economies of scale provided by carefully orchestrated alliances often allow the organizations involved to extend their product offerings beyond their core customer base. In sports, these alliances—some of which have worked, whereas others have delivered far less than the anticipated results— have included players, TV networks, leagues, and myriad other industry participants.

S trategic alliances, relationships that are formed with the intention of being mutually beneficial partnerships, have been around since Adam and Eve. Through the ages, alliances have been struck between and among individuals and organizations with all types of backgrounds and business interests.

Just as Bonnie Park had Clyde Barrow as a partner in crime, so too did Batman have Robin to help stop it. In comedy, Bud Abbott would have been nowhere without Lou Costello; some might say the same would have been true for Laverne DeFazio had she not found Shirley Feeney—but that is debatable.

How many years later would we have heard about George Harrison and Ringo Starr had they not partnered with John Lennon and Paul McCartney? Could there have even been a Rat Pack without Frank Sinatra?

At the beginning of the 20th century businessman David Abercrombie went into business with Ezra Fitch, and Bill Hewlett and David Packard partnered nearly 40 years later.

In sports, it was unspoken but understood alliances between Jerry West and Elgin Baylor that allowed the Los Angeles Lakers to build a dynasty in the 1960s and early 1970s. In recent years, West helped form the alliance among Shaquille O'Neal, Kobe Bryant, and Phil Jackson—one that allowed the team's reputation as a champion to continue. In 2002, the Memphis Grizzlies, intent on building a legacy of its own, hired West as its general manager and chief alliance builder, reportedly paying him $5 million a year.

In sports business, important strategic alliances have been formed between NBC and the WWF, AOL Time Warner and the NBA, and, to a certain and much lesser extent, this book's authors, David Carter and Darren Rovell!

Each and every alliance just noted, regardless of its outcome, was entered into with the understanding that the whole would be greater than its individual parts. In the process, the partners would prosper and, in the case of a publicly traded company, shareholders would profit.

Two online giants, America Online and Amazon.com, offer a prime partnership example. Within this alliance AOL hopes to gain more hits, visitors, and ultimately paying subscribers to its sites, whereas Amazon seeks to tap into AOL's subscriber base, one it believes to be a strong demographic match to its own, in an effort to sell more books, toys, and CDs.

Sports companies have begun to utilize this practice of alliance building as well. Nike has entered into strategic alliances with universities, including Duke and Michigan. In this relationship Nike gains large amounts of notoriety from these top schools through their extensive TV exposure and fiercely loyal fan bases. University benefits include financial gains, cost containment, and merchandising opportunities—all of which directly and indirectly assist in the recruitment of student-athletes.

In fact, after the No. 4 Chris Webber Michigan jerseys that were bought by fans of all ages and societal classes during the emergence of the "Fab Five" in 1989 contained both the Michigan name and the Nike swoosh, both organizations enjoyed increased notoriety and exposure. This notoriety and exposure took on a different and far less desirable feel throughout much of 2002, when it was disclosed that a prominent booster had given $280,000 to Webber during his playing days at Michigan. In a federal case investigating the booster, Webber said he didn't receive that much money. He was subsequently accused of lying to a grand jury and obstructing justice. As a result of the money lending, Michigan also agreed to forfeit all the games that Webber and three other players played while ineligible.

Alliances can provide opportunities to enter into large-scale marketing efforts that normally would carry too high of a price tag on a stand-alone basis. Movie studios, such as Disney, and fast food restaurants, like McDonald's, often utilize this form of marketing partnership to help promote the newest summer blockbuster. These deals provide McDonald's the opportunity to run in-store promotions in exchange for contributing marketing assets to help publicize the film.

In the sports world, sports leagues are now working intimately with movie studios to try to use films to reach their demographic. In the summer of 2002, the NBA and 20th Century Fox teamed together in producing *Like Mike,* a story about a young orphan, named Calvin Cambridge, who makes it to the NBA thanks to putting on a pair of Michael Jordan's old shoes. The league gave the filmmakers access to NBA players, arenas, and trademarks, hoping that the young demographic interested in the movie will in turn think about the NBA. In the end, these integrated deals provide both organizations ideal marketing platforms for reaching shared target markets.

Certain alliances are created to strengthen negotiating positions with suppliers, customers, or regulatory agencies. Global corporations might utilize alliances for this purpose when attempting to penetrate a new market in a foreign country. For instance, because businesses are angling for a better way to penetrate the large Chinese market, many are turning to China-based partners to help procure local supplies, deal with the Chinese government, and reach Chinese customers. This development has become particularly pronounced leading up to the 2008 Olympics in Beijing.

Gaining access to critical or scarce resources is yet another primary reason businesses seek strategic partners. Many industries, such as the diamond industry, remain monopolistic. Currently, DeBeers owns a majority of the world's diamond mines, and has the ability to influence product scarcity. Not surprisingly, jewelers and watchmakers, in an attempt to address the issue of scarcity, hope to establish preferred relationships with DeBeers. Gaining hard-to-replicate access to this coveted product provides jewelers and watchmakers a competitive advantage.

Cost containment is often the most dominant reason to enter into a strategic alliance. By outsourcing certain aspects of their operations, companies—especially those in the home computer industry—can reduce costs. Because it would be far more expensive for IBM to create its own processors, it outsources this function to Intel, the established market leader, resulting in a powerful and lucrative business alliance. Occasionally alliances are constructed such that one entity finances the operation of another. In the dot-com world, both Microsoft and Cisco partnered and invested millions of dollars in cutting edge technology to align their products online.

If entering into a strategic alliance is to be beneficial it is imperative that organizations analyze their industry, competitive environment, and customer wants and needs carefully before entering into one. It is also critical that the partnership is crafted to the mutual benefit of both companies. If utilized correctly, strategic alliances provide companies valuable competitive advantages that would not exist independent of these arrangements.

In the ultracompetitive sports business and media marketplace, industry leaders such as ABC have capitalized on the importance of strategic alliances, crafting some that have worked famously like the network's historic relationship with *Monday Night Football*. Other networks, although enjoying their own measure of success when forming alliances, have on occasion fallen short, including NBC, whose relationship with the XFL failed miserably.

STRATEGIC ALLIANCES

Three ways typically exist to grow a business: internally by ramping up, through a merger or acquisition, or via the creation of a strategic alliance. Strategic alliances are simply business-to-business relationships designed to enhance, among other things, joint marketing, sales or distribution, production, design collaboration, technology licensing, or research and development activities. Strategic alliances are prevalent throughout today's business landscape because companies seek out and enter into partnerships in an effort to diversify risks and increase benefits.

Analysts estimate that in the year 2000, 20 percent of all business conducted was done so through alliances—a fivefold increase from 1990. Significantly, this percentage is expected to double, reaching 40 percent by 2010.

The move toward strategic alliances is pervasive because three powerful forces today are simultaneously assaulting so many industries. First, competition is becoming more intense than ever. Next, many companies seek to conduct business globally. Finally, many operate in industries that are rapidly converging.

Whether an alliance is structured vertically between a vendor and a customer or horizontally between (local, regional, or global) vendors, many are formed to achieve economies of scale, increase competitiveness, or improve product development. Still other alliances are established with an eye toward business development, penetrating new markets, or reducing costs, among other factors.

In addition to these potential advantages, disadvantages also exist. Key among them is the reduction in control and the damage this causes. In baseball, this might be best characterized by the fly ball hit into the shallow portion of the outfield. When converging on the ball, the last thing a second baseman wants to hear from the outfielder is, "I got it—you take it!"

Further, issues relating to the hasty formation of alliances, as well as differing corporate cultures (and personal chemistry), and increased government oversight also provide challenges. To avoid these problems associated with strategic alliances, it is important to develop search criteria that dovetail with the business objectives sought through an alliance. When conducting the search for an ally it is constructive to bear in mind the essential building blocks to any well-structured alliance:[1]

- Complementary interests
- 1+1 had better equal 3 (or more)
- Great chemistry
- Both sides earn a "W"
- Compatibility
- Quantifiable opportunity
- A clear game plan
- Commitment and support

---

1. http://www.strategic-alliances.org/pubs/BPWBpreview.pdf.   Reprinted with permission from the Association of Strategic Alliance Professionals, Inc.

COMPLEMENTARY INTERESTS

Companies are measured, and by extension, their share prices determined, by how strong their relationships are with employees, customers, and competitors. They are also valued by the strength of their alliances. For an alliance to be successful, each company must complement the other, both strategically and operationally, if they are to take advantage of industry developments that impact employees, customers, and competitors.

Jim McCann bought the telephone number 1-800-Flowers in 1986. After opening 14 flower shops in a relatively contained New York area, McCann began to envision a nationwide network of florists that would fall under the 1-800-Flowers umbrella.

Today, 1-800-Flowers only owns about 150 stores, but the company has become an extraordinary brand thanks in large part to a brilliant strategic alliance with more than 2,000 independent local florists that, when an order is placed in their assigned region, quickly accommodate it. This enables 1-800-Flowers to markedly reduce both rent and delivery costs.

When searching for a florist, many consumers immediately think of the 1-800-Flowers brand, yet have little or no idea about the local florist involved in the process. However, both 1-800-Flowers and the local florist share in the revenue generated, which helps foster an atmosphere of cooperation.

Still, for the partnership to work, the local florist has to be as willing to commit itself to the same level of customer service for the 1-800-Flowers orders as it would give its own in-house orders. Because 1-800-Flowers is the company the customer has placed the order through, 1-800-Flowers has to make sure that the local florist is conducting its job professionally because it's not the neighborhood florist that loses the business if an order is misplaced or delivered late. Rather, when something is wrong with an order it is the 1-800-Flowers name that wilts.

McCann's interests are closely aligned with those of mom-and-pop florists nationwide. Each delivers critical strategic and operational benefits to the other, leveraging the alliance's merits to increase their combined clout through increased market penetration and cost containment. Sports apparel and equipment makers recognize the same opportunities within their industry.

Nike dabbled in the golf industry for years, lurking on the fringe waiting for the ideal opportunity to emerge. Since the mid-1980s it had make golf shoes and, with the signing of Tiger Woods in 1996, Nike developed a clothing line and debuted a slew of company-branded golf novelty items that appealed to the casual golfer. However, in 1999, Nike determined that it should provide products aimed at the serious golfer. It selected golf balls as the product it would use to penetrate the "serious golfer" market.

Initially uncertain about its prospects to achieve success in the $800 million golf ball market, Nike chose not to allocate significant internal resources, either financial or human, to the cause. Rather, Nike golf formed an alliance with Bridgestone, a Japanese company that was third in market share behind Titleist and Callaway, to make its balls. Bridgestone complemented Nike in that Nike didn't have to start from scratch and that it had partnered with a premium golf ball company. At the same time, Nike complemented Bridgestone by allowing it to align with Nike's potential success, positioning Bridgestone to produce more balls as the venture grows.

Although the average golfer didn't know of the alliance, it was heavily debated in the golf trades. Some questioned why Bridgestone, which owned 13 percent of the premium ball market, would make a ball that might be better than its own—and possibly cannibalize its own brand in the process. Others questioned whether Nike's ball was merely an imprint, like a generic supermarket brand made by a company with a sizable share in the market, and whether Nike's own research and development made the ball any better than the Precept, the name of the Bridgestone model.

Nike knew that the company could not merely slap a swoosh on an inferior product, for doing so could ultimately harm its reputation and diminish its brand name. However, the company also believed that when someone sticks a golf tee in the ground they don't care who owns the factory.

In the early going, Nike executives were sworn to secrecy so as not to expose that Bridgestone was producing the balls. However, when Tiger Woods switched from Titleist to Nike in the summer of 2000 and won the 100th U.S. Open by 15 strokes, the company—which only had a 1 percent share of the market—was clearly on the rise, as pro shops and retailers called from around the world to place orders for the Nike balls. Bridgestone reportedly wanted to take credit but Nike executives wanted consumers to think that the product was entirely Nike's.

Bridgestone's response was a typical one in a strategic alliance where suppliers do well due in part to the name behind the visible brand. It causes some tension, but the bottom line is that this relationship allowed Nike to develop new business opportunities and increase exports, and Bridgestone improved its competitiveness and positioned itself favorably to extend its position in the golf industry.

1+1 HAD BETTER EQUAL 3 (OR MORE)

If a strategic alliance is to be mutually advantageous, the organizations must have complementary strengths that allow the whole to be greater than the parts. Such strategic synergy puts allies in a favorable competitive position.

Few alliances since peanut butter met jelly have rivaled the symbiotic relationship enjoyed by sports and television. Baseball, in particular, has become a strong ally of media companies hoping to use the sport's history and tradition to increase the value of their collective programming assets. Today, media conglomerates including News Corporation (Los Angeles Dodgers), the Tribune Company (Chicago Cubs), and AOL/Time Warner (Atlanta Braves) own MLB teams.

Economists routinely argue that these alliances allow baseball teams, many of which seem to claim financial losses each year, to transfer profits and losses to the media company when it suits their purposes.

George Steinbrenner, the shipping magnate who purchased the New York Yankees from CBS in 1972, understands the power of strategic alliances that involve media interests. In fact, the alliance Steinbrenner formed in 1999 has drawn considerable attention in sports business and media circles.

Initially, confusion marked the announcement that the New York Yankees and the New Jersey Nets had merged to form YankeeNets. Analysts questioned why Steinbrenner would want to align his team's global brand, one with a rich tradition on and off the field, with the pitiful Nets, who only drew crowds by marketing its opponents' players.

Steinbrenner formed the alliance because he was looking ahead to the end of the 2000 baseball season, when the Yankees' longtime cable partner, the Madison Square Garden (MSG) Network, would have its contract expire. Steinbrenner, interested in securing programming content for his own Yankees regional sports network, believed the Nets could fill a seasonal void.

By establishing a sports channel that carried the games of multiple teams in the nation's largest TV market, media analysts predicted that the Yankees local television revenue, which equaled a MLB-high $56.7 million in 2001, could double within a few years.

In this strategic alliance, Steinbrenner would still have complete control of the Yankees and the Nets owners, Lewis Katz and Ray Chambers, continued to have complete autonomy over their team's business decisions. The two would own a combined 60 percent of the new network, and the rest would be owned by a series of investors including Goldman Sachs.

MSG paid the Yankees an additional $52 million for the right to broadcast games in 2001 but, by the 2002 season, YankeeNets debuted its Yankees Entertainment and Sports (YES) Network, which televised 125 Yankee games. Because the Nets' contract with Cablevision expired at the end of the 2001–2002 season, YES started its 75-game Nets schedule immediately after the final Yankee games of the season.

In part to secure more television programming and in part to ensure the long-term viability of the struggling Nets, the YankeeNets holding company purchased the NHL's New Jersey Devils from John McMullen in 2001. By acquiring the Devils, a team that won two Stanley Cups in the 1990s and had the second best record in the league during the decade, YankeeNets would now control three prominent New York franchises. This acquisition enabled YankeeNets to speak with a single voice when asking for what it believed would ensure the financial viability of the Nets and the Devils in New Jersey—a new arena.

Although the YankeeNets organization understood that getting a new arena would be difficult, both politically and financially, it positioned itself more favorably by developing a strategic alliance that afforded it added leverage in the negotiations.

The formation of YankeeNets—and the huge increases in revenue it anticipated—provided additional benefits. It afforded YankeeNets an opportunity to mitigate detrimental and potentially crippling sports industry developments, and trends, most notably labor strife and soaring player salaries. In short, YankeeNets' impressive revenue growth enables it to absorb any short-term losses created by strikes or lockouts, occasional losing seasons, and an increasing investment in player personnel.

The creation of YankeeNets and its structuring of numerous strategic alliances was originally undertaken in an effort to deliver economies of scale to the region's largest sports management company. However, the ultimate goal of the collective alliances was to create a new business, YES. As it turned out, in YES' first full year, the once-pitiful Nets advanced to the NBA Finals, and the Yankees, the supposed anchor of the alliance, was embroiled in a nasty lawsuit that prohibited the televising of its games on Cablevision. YES wanted Cablevision to provide Yankee games to all its customers, but Cablevision was reluctant to do so for economic reasons. So the two went the entire 2002 baseball season without each other. YES was forced to reduce the advertising rates it charged because the network's reach was reduced, and Cablevision simultaneously lost subscribers.

Beyond the creation of a new business, strategic alliances can be utilized to extend an organization's presence with the help of a higher profile partner.

The Poore Brothers company has to wish that its name could be more prominently featured on the TGI Friday's licensed snack chips. Debuting in late 2000, the license it was granted by TGI Friday's became the Poore Brothers best selling brand. Licensing arrangements such as this one are really thinly veiled alliances where each party hopes to improve its position with the assistance of the other. Although Poore Brothers sells its own branded product, it might not have been able to achieve the distribution enjoyed by TGI Friday's, given the restaurant's extensive brand recognition.

TGI Friday's is one of the most aggressive chain restaurants in the licensed supermarket food market. Two years earlier, Carlson Restaurants Worldwide, the restaurant's parent company, also granted a license to Anchor Foods, the leading manufacturer of breaded frozen appetizers in the world, to make its frozen snacks and dips.

Whether a player in the supermarket food market or professional sports, alliances can help increase market penetration and expand market development.

However, for major brands, licensing cannot be a one-way deal. Companies must not merely grant use of their corporate identities in exchange for licensing fees. Licensors have to protect their brands at all costs because if the licensee cuts corners in the manufacturing process or abuses the stipulated uses of the marks, it's the brand name that suffers.

For instance, in 1994, the NFL granted a league-high 454 licenses to companies to use the NFL marks on their various products. Less than a decade later, only about 250 companies were granted licenses in part because of the league's desire to better manage the brand by protecting the league's marks.

Not only does the licensor have to protect its own brand, but in a strategic alliance such as a licensing arrangement, the licensor must optimize the number of relationships to ensure product integrity and consistency by limiting the number of licenses and policing possible counterfeit or inappropriate uses of the license. Integrity and consistency are two attributes that enhance long-term product development and make one plus one equal three.

GREAT CHEMISTRY

Companies that seek business allies must have both a managerial ability to work together and the cooperative spirit to get things done. Chemistry is the result of positive, team-oriented, trust-filled relationships between key players. In sports, rarely is a championship team described without a reference to great chemistry among coaches and players.

Before a strategic alliance is formed, making sure that an appropriate amount of chemistry exists is vital, for not adequately doing so can lead to highly public fallout. Jen Davidson and Jean Racine were two female bobsledders who supposedly had a strong chance to win a gold medal in the 2002 Winter Olympics in Salt Lake City. They were competitive in a brand new sport, they were American, and they were good-looking.

Accordingly, their agent, Evan Morganstein, had little difficulty securing $500,000 in endorsements for the pair prior to the Games. Strategic alliances were formed with Kellogg's, Northwestern Mutual Insurance, General Motors, and Visa. Nike invested in Davidson, and Racine was sponsored by adidas.

They appeared on NBC commercials together. The two bobsledders, along with Olympic track star and two-time gold medalist Maurice Green, were designated to present President George W. Bush with a USOC blazer in the Oval Office. The following day they were on *The Today Show*, and later in the week they did a photo shoot for *Glamour* magazine.

Morganstein was also looking to shop their book rights. Little did he know that someone would want the book for the dirt and not for the glory. That's because less than two months later Davidson filed a grievance with the U.S. Bobsled and Skeleton Federation against Racine, who had dropped her as a partner one week before the Olympic trials, thus leaving Davidson completely out of the Olympics.

The pair's Web site, www.bobsledgirls.com, quickly degenerated to "under construction" status. Also left out in the cold were all the partners that worked so hard to plan campaigns, extensively using the two as marketing and promotion platforms. For these sponsors, the ugly break-up caused tremendous collateral damage. Despite the developments, Racine and Davidson continued to be featured on Crispix and Mini-Wheats boxes, creating high-profile opportunity cost for the companies that, had they known of the pending rift, would not have so prominently featured the bobsledders.

Although it might have been extremely difficult for sponsors to assess the inner dynamics between Racine and Davidson, the inability to do so left them vulnerable. When all was said and done, Racine and her new partner, Gea Johnson, placed fifth, failing to earn an Olympic medal.

Golfer Ian Woosnam gave his strategic alliance with his caddy every possible chance to succeed, but it never did. On the second tee in the final round of the 2001 British Open, Woosnam was tied for the lead heading into the second hole. That's when his caddy, Miles Byrne, told Woosnam that he was carrying an extra club in his bag. As a result, Woosnam was penalized two strokes and eventually forfeited approximately $340,000 in tournament winnings.

Woosnam indicated that not only was it the biggest mistake Byrne would ever make, but that he would be severely reprimanded—but not fired—for the error. Woosnam also said that, although he supposed he should have checked on the clubs himself, he believed doing so was what caddies get paid for.

Unfortunately for Byrne, two weeks later, he overslept and missed the tee-time for the final round of the Scandinavian Open. When he finally appeared, it was too late. Woosnam had another caddy with him and, after he finished his round, he terminated Byrne because he could no longer assume the risk associated with a caddy whose attention to detail was not up to Woosnam's standards.

Without proper chemistry, strategic alliances, whether between athletes or companies or both, cannot maximize their potential. The inability to strike the requisite level of chemistry between allies not only affects their ability to succeed, but also causes damage downstream to those organizations conducting business with those in the alliance.

BOTH SIDES EARN A "W"

If a strategic alliance is to be a win–win situation for both sides, the alliance's collective operations, risks, and rewards must be fairly apportioned. Allies must be willing to address new risks, be committed to flexibility and creativity, and be ready to transform the alliance structure.

The economic and cultural impact that professional sports franchises bring to communities is frequently debated, with local and regional governments skeptical about the benefits a city enjoys from having a team in its town. Although many corollaries exist when discussing the merits of college football to communities, properly structured alliances between municipalities and college football bowl games can reap dividends for both the participating universities and the host city, as well as local businesses associated with the tourism industry.

The Oahu Bowl, historically played in Honolulu, relocated to Seattle in 2001 and renamed itself the Seattle Bowl. At a time when many of the secondary bowls were struggling due to a lack of interest and, by extension, sponsorship revenue, the Seattle Bowl's alliance with college football for the formation of this revamped bowl game was successful, especially given the fact that the relocation was approved only eight months before the game.

In anticipation of the game and in an effort to fully leverage the game's exposure for the region, King County (WA) Executive Ron Sims signed a proclamation officially declaring December 21–28 Seattle Bowl Week in King County.

An announced crowd of 30,114 attended the inaugural Seattle Bowl on December 27, 2001, and an additional 1.8 million households nationwide watched the game between Stanford and Georgia Tech on ESPN. Played at Safeco Field, home of the Seattle Mariners, the Seattle Bowl succeeded in gaining national exposure for a region primarily known for Starbucks, rain by the buckets, and Ichiro.

The Seattle Chamber of Commerce and local vendors were pleased with this outcome, particularly considering that the game was played during a traditionally slow week for businesses relying on tourism to prosper. Hoteliers believed that whereas some of the hotels would be operating at 20 to 40 percent of capacity in the past, the bowl game could increase capacity between 15 and 50 percent, a sizable increase during an otherwise slow period.

The following January many were pleasantly surprised when bowl organizers said the event was profitable, no doubt thanks in part to a last-minute title sponsor, 989 Sports, which agreed to terms only five days before the game.

In addition to Seattle benefiting from the alliance, the participating schools also earned a win. Both schools earned $750,000 for their participation in the game. Although many universities actually lose money on bowl games because they are required to purchase large blocks of tickets and transport boosters and marching bands, they are willing to underwrite them because bowl games serve as both a recruiting platform and as a "thank you" for a job well done to those associated with the football program, namely players and their families.

This much-needed revenue and TV exposure would not have existed if the Oahu Bowl had simply folded. Rather, college football and bowl organizers each assumed risk and succeeded in transforming the alliance, ultimately to the mutual benefit of both the schools and the region.

Although the Seattle Bowl's relationship with the Pac-10 and the Atlantic Coast Conference (ACC) ended after the inaugural bowl, in May 2002 the Seattle Bowl was able to enter a new strategic alliance with the Mountain West Conference while maintaining the ACC. The fourth seed in the Mountain West is now scheduled to play the fifth or sixth choice from the ACC. The bowl's position of strength was further reinforced in July 2002, when the Seattle Bowl announced a five-year deal to play the game at the Seattle Seahawks' new stadium.

Anticipated win–win relationships are not relegated to regional alliances, as demonstrated by the NBA and AOL Time Warner.

As the economy continued to soften throughout 2001 and well into 2002, the NBA found itself in the midst of negotiating its new TV contract with existing rights holder NBC, as well as AOL Time Warner cable channels TNT and TBS. With TV ratings for the sport waning and the advertising dollars associated with these ratings also declining, the NBA had to consider a new business model in which future risk and return would be shared.

Given the size, success, and new media platforms historically enjoyed by AOL Time Warner, the NBA was eager to continue its relationship. So, too, was AOL Time Warner, which appreciated the NBA's brand strength and the credibility the league brought to it.

Rather than solely buying rights to air NBA games, AOL Time Warner offered to give the NBA an equity stake in a newly created channel instead, establishing a unique strategic alliance in the process. In exchange for its equity position, the NBA intended to allow the network to air several live NBA games a week. The new TV deal was to change the fundamental broadcast rights paradigm; what was once a transaction-based relationship would evolve into a potentially lucrative partnership for both entities.

The NBA viewed the anticipated launch of a new NBA channel as a good investment that could expand the NBA brand on TV while strengthening its ties with the biggest media company in the world. AOL Time Warner, for its part, anticipated that NBA games would attract new viewers to its family of online and broadcast properties. What neither fully appreciated was the increasing reluctance on behalf of cable operators to carry the new channel. Consequently, this alliance was tabled due to too few channels of distribution (i.e., cable operators) and the inability to craft a win–win–win relationship.

COMPATIBILITY

Successful strategic partnerships have compatible styles of operations and methods of management. Companies with similar goals, rewards, methods of operations, and corporate cultures tend to make better partners. No matter how compelling an alliance appears or how compatible the two entities seem to be, if the alliance's product is weak, failure is inevitable. The XFL has proven to be an extraordinary case study where a great alliance—at least on the surface—failed.

In 2000, NBC President Dick Ebersol shocked the sports world when he announced that NBC was entering a 50–50 partnership with Vince McMahon's WWF to launch a new professional football league, the XFL.

On paper, the alliance appeared reasonable. After all, NBC had relinquished its broadcast rights to the NFL two years earlier and was looking for an entertaining, "real" sport that, with in-game interviews of players and coaches, as well as on-field cameras, would mesh with the increasing popular reality TV shows, like *Survivor* and *Big Brother*. For the WWF, NBC was positioned to provide the automatic legitimacy that the XFL needed if the upstart league was to be taken seriously. Armed with a prime-time Saturday TV slot that began the week after the Super Bowl, in February 2001, and running through late April, the XFL had the best television exposure of any new sports league in history.

Unfortunately, the WWF deviated from its core competency. The WWF's primary strength rests in its ability to create and control the plot lines, develop characters, and deliver drama. However, with its stated intention of providing unscripted entertainment (i.e., "real" football), the WWF moved away from what it did best, and alienated critics and true football fans in the process. It was not as if the XFL didn't attempt to develop drama. In several games during the season, then Minnesota governor and former wrestler-turned-XFL-announcer Jesse Ventura tried to pick fights with New York Hitman coach Rusty Tillman. The problem was, Tillman wasn't getting paid to act—he was getting paid to coach—so he wasn't easily baited into an altercation.

Although it was believed that the WWF could deliver its target market of 12- to 24-year-old boys and young men to NBC, this demographic wasn't typically home on Saturday nights to watch the games.

NBC viewers were accustomed to watching NFL-quality football on Sundays, and hard core wrestling fans were accustomed to "pure" wrestling. A critical mistake was made in thinking the two fan bases were similar when, in fact, they proved to be quite different. Wrestling fans bring with them a willing suspension of disbelief. Pro football fans are realists. The wrestling crowd wrongly suspected that football fans wanted to hear the players vent, gloat, and mock. They didn't. Instead, these fans thought it bad form. The XFL, trying to be all things to all sports fans, succeeded in delivering a product that neither demographic base wanted to watch.

Additional attempts to lure the targeted fan base also fell short. Microphones in the huddles and all-access locker rooms during halftime weren't as compelling as they once seemed. Nor were the on-field live interviews with players following big plays.

The constant pomposity and arrogance about the league's self-proclaimed advantages over the NFL made many—including sponsors, advertisers, and industry observers, squeamish. One prominent Hall-of-Famer even suggested that the XFL spent so much time and so much money bashing the NFL, telling everyone how bad it is, that they forgot they had to play football.

TV ratings plunged and sponsors pulled out. On May 10, 2001, after just one season, and citing losses of $35 million each, the WWF and NBC (owned by GE), both public companies, officially pulled the plug on the XFL. Approximately a year later, *TV Guide* ranked the

XFL as the third worst TV show or programming in history behind only *The Jerry Springer Show* and *My Mother the Car.*

When NBC and the WWF aligned to create a new product, each misunderstood not only the compatibility of its respective organization's cultures, but each also miscalculated the demographic or cultural connection between the product and its customers. In 2002, NBC signaled that it had identified a more compatible football partner with whom it could structure a mutually beneficial alliance by acquiring the broadcast rights to the Arena Football League.

QUANTIFABLE OPPORTUNITY

If strategic alliances do not position each organization to materially and measurably improve their standing, whether measured in terms of sales, brand awareness, or shareholder value, the alliance might not prove worthwhile. Even in cases where an alliance appears to be able to deliver the requisite results, it cannot do so until or unless one of the allies is uniquely positioned with the know-how and reputation to take advantage of that opportunity.

For years, Sears maintained an alliance with college athletics, most notably by sponsoring the Sears Trophy, a $30,000 Waterford crystal football that is presented to the No. 1 college football team as determined by coaches and by awarding the winning school $20,000. However, in 2002, Sears—just days after the Sears Trophy was presented to Miami following its Rose Bowl championship game win over Nebraska—decided to discontinue the nine-year relationship.

Estimates placed Sears' financial commitment at between $10 million and $15 million per year on sponsorship and other marketing fees associated with its Sears Collegiate Champions Program. Although Sears believed the program had indeed increased brand awareness, it was unable to satisfactorily link its participation in the program to an increase in sales. Because the necessary quantifiable opportunity did not exist for Sears, it believed continuing to allocate dollars to the alliance no longer made sense.

Unlike Sears, which was unable to justify its ongoing involvement with college sports after quantifying its alliance with college sports, other companies have prospered.

A vivid example can be product placement that helps authenticate sports-themed movies. For example, the sports nutrition company, Met-Rx, was prominently displayed in the movie *Any Given Sunday*. *Any Given Sunday*, Oliver Stone's 1999 film about the underbelly of the world of professional football, was looking for companies to help add believability to the movie by giving it the same look and feel, particularly in the area of corporate sponsorship, as a professional football league—presumably the NFL.

In the script, the Miami Sharks emerging quarterback Willie Beamon films a commercial for a nutritional supplement. For less than the price of a billboard or even a magazine ad, Met-Rx became the product that Beamon pitched throughout the movie. Met-Rx fit well because not only did Warner Brothers believe that Met-Rx made an authentic partner because many athletes, former Dallas Cowboys QB Troy Aikman among them, used and endorsed its products, but also because Met-Rx felt that the movie's audience would be most likely to buy its products.

Met-Rx further capitalized on the strategic alliance by inserting reminders about the film in its Protein Plus Bars. Not only did sales of the bars increase by 33 percent while the movie was in theaters, but Warner Brothers apparently believed that the in-store promotions helped *Any Given Sunday* make its way back up the charts after an initial fall from the top.

Met-Rx executives noted that even though the movie rose to third place in the box office and then dropped down, the company kept running its promotion. After speaking with Warner Brothers, it became clear to Met-Rx that the entertainment giant would like to do more product placement with Met-Rx. Met-Rx executives believed the product placement worked because only that particular product from its whole product line witnessed an increase in sales during that period.

By quantifying its successful return on investment from the product placement in *Any Given Sunday* Met-Rx decided to return to the screen two years later with an appearance in *The Replacements*, another football-themed movie. Its ability to quantify the results of strategic alliances improves Met-Rx's competitive position and it allows it a framework for considering future alliances.

A CLEAR GAME PLAN

Proposed strategic alliances that boast specific, concrete objectives, time tables, lines of responsibility, and measurable results are best suited for potential success. Partnerships that are well thought out and articulated—in advance—will yield a game plan for long-term success.

Boxing has offered numerous infamous examples of strategic alliances over the years, including many of those involving legendary promoter Don King. Although many of boxing's alliances, especially those between fighters and their promoters, have only provided promoters a game plan for long-term success, other have helped all parties involved.

For example, HBO and Showtime switched from being pay-per-view (PPV) rivals to strategic partners in 2002. The premium cable networks negotiated a precedent-setting deal to split rights for a PPV telecast of the June 2002 heavyweight championship fight between World Boxing Council/International Boxing Federation champion Lennox Lewis, who had a contract with HBO, and challenger Mike Tyson, who had a contract with Showtime.

Before the deal could be signed, each network had to make sure the product they were jointly producing made sense for both parties. Issues dealing with the packaging and distributing of the PPV fight had to be resolved. This included the need to determine which network would actually telecast the fight, as well as how the PPV telecast would be branded and by whom it would be distributed. In the true spirit of cooperation, each network picked two broadcasters—HBO selected Jim Lampley and James Brown and Showtime hired Bobby Czyz and Jim Gray.

For HBO and Showtime, this alliance allowed both to participate in the marquee match, sharing expenses and revenue, and doing so with the clear objective of reinforcing their industry-leading brand names to boxing fans and promoters alike. In essence, the two networks enjoyed the sports marketing equivalent of "naming rights" to the top bout of 2002. The fight, in which Lennox Lewis soundly defeated Mike Tyson, drew 1.8 million PPV buys, making it not only the highest grossing bout of all time with $103 million in revenue, but also a strategic alliance that worked well for both networks.

When a company considers buying more "traditional" naming rights to a sports arena or stadium, it has historically considered what's included in the package. In addition to literally putting their names on the building, being allocated extensive advertising space in and around the athletic facility, and being given a luxury suite from which the company can conduct business development, these deals were originally fashioned as integrated sponsorship packages.

Naming rights deals have become increasingly complex in recent years and many, including Federal Express' alliance with the Washington Redskins, valued at $205 million over 20 years, have become primary marketing platforms for companies. In the process, successful naming rights arrangements have evolved and many are now strategic alliances, offering incremental revenue-generating and brand-building opportunities for both organizations.

This may be best exemplified in Atlanta where TBS and Royal Philips Electronics (Philips) have forged a strategic alliance to share and develop a diverse range of projects and properties. This alliance included naming rights to Atlanta's 20,000-seat sports and event facility, the Philips Arena, home of the NBA Hawks and NHL's Thrashers.

The 20-year alliance, which was hailed at the time as the most comprehensive naming-rights agreement ever negotiated, was valued in excess of $185 million.

According to officials with both organizations, the alliance was significant because they were combining vision and resources at a time when mastering the convergence of content, services, and high-speed access with the new generation of digital electronics devices was critical.

To optimize the alliance between TBS and Philips, two intercompany teams were formed to identify and develop opportunities for sharing resources between the two companies: a technology task force and a marketing and new media task force. These teams focus on development in a variety of areas, including e-commerce, enhanced TV, interactivity, new media, and promotional and merchandising opportunities.

Furthering their commitment, each company pledged to integrate the other's products into its business operations. The agreement includes a broad-based media package for Philips with Turner and Time Warner properties and a supplier arrangement for the use of Philips products, from broadcast equipment and consumer and business electronics, to consumer appliances and lighting products.

Moreover, Philips' technologies and products are featured throughout the arena. More than 1,000 Philips video monitors are used in the arena and the adjacent CNN Center, and all video components and lighting sources in public areas of the new facility are Philips Electronics products. In addition, Philips Electronics occupies a 3,000-square-foot retail showcase within the complex.

Philips is uniquely positioned given this extensive marketing alliance to not only develop new business opportunities given the organization's access to the Time Warner family of companies, but also is poised to create new business units or products in the process. AOL Time Warner receives significant revenue while reducing certain costs.

COMMITMENT AND SUPPORT

Success in business always seems to get back to vision and leadership. By demonstrating to colleagues and employees precisely why an alliance makes sense and warrants total dedication and effort, senior management must communicate and reinforce the critical elements of the alliance to ensure ongoing buy-in by all vested parties.

The strategic alliance between Philips and AOL Time Warner was discussed as a relationship predicated on a solid game plan. However, not all naming rights partnerships, which are great out-in-the-open examples of alliances, are as well devised, developed, and serviced.

For naming rights alliances to be successful, both organizations must determine the impact on each brand resulting from the alliance. As the stadium naming rights craze that started in earnest in the 1990s swept the nation, groups of fans seemingly protested every new corporate moniker and newspaper columnists bemoaned the corporatization of sports.

Although fans in Detroit wanted to keep the name of their ballpark, Tiger Stadium, Comerica purchased the right to attach its name to the stadium for 30 years at a cost of $66 million. Initially, some fans indicated that they wouldn't do business with Comerica Bank because the company's approach to naming rights was too in-the-face of the traditional fan. Over time, however, the outrage over corporately named arenas and stadiums such as the Target Center (Minneapolis), United Center (Chicago), and Pac Bell Park (San Francisco) faded. However, negative sentiment lingered in many sports towns where the connection of the teams to the community remained strong.

This was the case in Denver where the Broncos debuted their new football stadium in 2001. Leading up to its opening was a heated debate over whether naming rights should be sold to Mile High Stadium, one of the most storied venues in the NFL.

Some Denver citizens, including its mayor, Wellington Webb, said absolutely not, even though some proceeds of the sale of such rights would go toward reimbursing taxpayers for the money used to construct the stadium. Others didn't seem to mind as much, given that it was a new stadium and, with future Hall-of-Fame quarterback John Elway settling into retirement, a new era was beginning in Denver anyway; out with old and in with the new was these citizens' prevailing attitude.

After months of heated debate, the Metropolitan Football Stadium District decided to sell the rights to Denver-based mutual funds company Invesco. Even after Invesco paid $60 million for the right to call the stadium Invesco Field at Mile High for 20 years, the debate continued to rage. *The Denver Post* announced one week prior to the stadium's opening that it would refer to the stadium merely as "Mile High," refusing to honor the corporate name.

Fans, too, got into the act by filing a lawsuit months before the grand opening in hopes of voiding the deal. Regardless of whether Invesco believes "that all press is good press," what cannot be denied is that the company was forced to sustain months of negative press and mounting ill will. It might take the entire term of the naming rights agreement to determine if the alliance with the stadium was indeed mutually beneficial.

Ensuring a partner is financially solvent and has a sound business structure is also prudent when considering a strategic alliance. Due diligence is critical because once the deal is consummated, the two organizations become intertwined in the minds of many customers and shareholders. If one files for bankruptcy, you can assume the other's reputation will be influenced.

Internet investment firm CMGI paid $120 million in August 2000 for a 15-year naming rights alliance with the new New England Patriots stadium, scheduled to open for the 2002–2003 NFL season. At the time the deal was signed, CMGI's stock was trading at $43.90, down from its all-time high of $326.43 eight months earlier. One year after agreeing to the alliance and just one year before the debut of CMGI Field, the company's stock price was less than $2 a share. Although CMGI and the Patriots continued to state that the deal remained prudent for both organizations, each no doubt began questioning whether it would materialize as originally intended. About a month before the stadium was to open, CMGI was let out of its deal and the stadium was renamed Gillette Stadium.

A somewhat similar situation has already played itself out in St. Louis, where the NHL's Blues play in the Savvis Center even though Savvis asked out of its naming rights agreement. Just down the street from the Savvis Center, the St. Louis Rams changed the name of their stadium in 2001 to The Dome at America's Center after its former strategic ally, TWA, filed for bankruptcy and defaulted on its naming rights deal. Before the end of the year, the Rams announced a long-term strategic alliance with financial services firm Edward Jones for what would then be called the Edward Jones Dome.

Of course, fans still go to the games and no one believes that the Rams, a perennial contender in the NFL, will be immediately compromised on the field because of the association with TWA. Nonetheless, the Rams have compromised themselves because the more often a venue is forced to change its name the less value that name has for a presenting company, resulting in a probable decline in naming rights revenue for the team over time.

Then there was the home of MLB's Houston Astros, Enron Field. Because Enron had prepaid its naming rights fee through April 2002 for the ballpark that opened the prior year, there was little the team could do because their agreement with the failed energy company did not contain a "good citizen" clause. This forced the Astros to maintain the name of the stadium despite the marketing and community relations albatross the name created.

Once it became apparent that Enron was fully embroiled in a corporate scandal the likes of which had not been seen in American business, the Astros wanted to shed the ballpark's corporate name as soon as possible. After all, with so many local people affected by the company's deceit, who would want to go to a game at Enron Field?

Following rapid negotiations, the Astros were able to buy their way out of the alliance for $2.2 million and, due to quick work, were able to remove any semblance of Enron from the ballpark prior to opening day 2002. During the 2002 season Minute Maid, a Coca-Cola brand with corporate headquarters in Houston, acquired the stadium's naming and pouring rights for more than the original Enron deal, bringing to a close an extraordinarily awkward sports marketing crisis.

Comerica, Invesco, CMGI, Savvis, TWA, and Enron all intended to leverage their naming rights alliances to drive various aspects of their businesses. However, due to myriad reasons and circumstances, each's ability to increase market penetration and gain competitive advantages was comprised due to lower than anticipated levels of commitment and support.

For strategic alliances to be successful, senior management must also elicit buy-in by all vested parties, including employees or athletes. In 2001, some sports teams, including the New York Mets, began selling the exclusive right to be their teams' "official medical caregiver."

The Mets sold this designation to New York University Hospital for Joint Diseases (NYUHJD) after David Altchek, the Mets' team physician for 10 years, refused to bid on the account.

Turk Wendell, one of the Mets' pitchers at the time, summed up his concern over such an alliance—one apparently predicated on making money by posing a rhetorical question. He was curious if a team with a $90 million payroll was going to go with the highest bidder or someone it believed was the best possible doctor. No knock on those (NYU) doctors, commented Wendell, but why change doctors if you have a guy who knows the players and their (medical) histories, and the players like him?

The reason for the change, as articulated by Mets management, included, but was not limited to money. The team felt that the deal provided the organization with a stronger business relationship while still maintaining the high quality of care needed for Mets' players.

However, players were so concerned about the change—thinking it could compromise their health care—they contacted their union to express their dismay. Clearly, professional sports franchises would not knowingly sacrifice the quality of the health care provided to their athletes for a few extra dollars. The appearance that this might be occurring limits the team's ability to gain buy-in from arguably the most important party to the deal—the players.

Until this buy-in occurs, NYUHJD cannot fully capitalize on the relationship and leverage its connection to the team because one set of employees has not been made fully aware of the importance of the partnership.

CHAMPIONSHIP POINTS

Whether alliances are entered into to achieve economies of scale, increase market share, identify and develop new business, or for any other reason(s), they will not succeed unless the partners have:

■ Mutually understood and appreciated interests. Budding relationships like those enjoyed by 1-800-Flowers and Nike have worked because each partner's ally has brought with it complementary interests that extend the value of the alliance.

■ Mastered the new math. It does not require a heavyweight like George Steinbrenner to generate strong alliances that leverage assets and generate cash flow. Smaller organizations can do so provided they monitor the relationship and seek to uncover and exploit opportunities to build or extend new businesses.

- Demonstrated a fit. Organizations that cannot demonstrate adequate chemistry when structuring strategic alliances, frequently find themselves skating on thin ice. This applies to both the organization, in terms of culture, and extends to include the personalities of the individuals involved.
- Generated a pair of wins. Alliances cannot be successfully sustained if one party consistently derives greater value from it. If and when the structure of the alliance needs to be revisited, the parties to it must do so proactively to maintain the benefits created by the alliance.
- Gotten along. When compatible styles of operations and management exist, alliances can prove invaluable. When they are sorely lacking, the damage, both financial and in terms of brand value, cannot be quickly diminished.
- Measured the opportunity. The best intentioned alliances will not work until or unless those involved are able to articulate the tangible and intangible benefits of the partnership.
- Devised a clear game plan. Because strategic alliances will no doubt generate unintended consequences and issues, proper planning can mitigate these developments and help the alliance overcome any unforeseen shortcomings or vulnerabilities.
- Provided meaningful commitment and support. Strategic alliances are like any other important relationship; for them to work, each party must communicate its likes and dislikes, while consistently creating an atmosphere for buy-in.

The creation and implementation of well-thought-out strategic alliances can be a very powerful business tool that increases sales and builds shareholder value. However, a failure to fully comprehend all the intricacies associated with such business relationships all too often forces the organizations involved in the alliance to have to "play defense."

In traditional business, this includes having a strong game plan to handle crises.

7 CRISIS MANAGEMENT

The Point: By creating a comprehensive crisis management plan that addresses not only how to prepare for crises, but how best to deal with them as they are unfolding and beyond, an organization will be better able to manage the fallout when disaster strikes. The manner in which the sports industry has handled crises resulting from player indiscretions and league-wide decision making, as well as other matters beyond its control, sheds light on how businesses of all sizes should or shouldn't approach crisis management.

By the time "it" hits the "fan" it's too late. "It," in this case, is a crisis, and "fan" refers to sports fans—not the proverbial fan.

Before the era of televised sports and the 24-hour-a-day sports news programming that it spawned, sports crises and the fallout they caused received far less attention than they do today. For most sports fans (who remain the sports industry's ultimate customers), crises had been limited to long bathroom lines at the stadium or the inability to get a ticket for the big game.

Today's world of televised sports is known as much for its high-light reel and associated "play of the day" clips as it is for the over-riding spirit of athletic competition. More than 40 years ago ABC's legendary broadcaster Jim McKay "spanned the globe to bring you the constant variety of sport" during *Wide World of Sports*. Sports fans were treated to "the thrill of victory and the agony of defeat."

Today, fans are still treated to both the thrill and the agony of sports so brilliantly captured by *Wide World of Sports*, albeit more quickly. The immediacy and prevalence of all media, including sports on cable TV and via the Internet, has helped increase the enjoyment for most fans.

It has also vividly changed how the sports world deals with crises. Crises tend to be of two types—those that occur with no warning and those where ample warning exists. NASCAR and racing fans worldwide were immediately and extraordinarily affected by the crash that claimed the life of the sport's icon, Dale Earnhardt. MLB is seemingly in a perpetual crisis, a predictable one brought about by strained labor relations and ongoing economic woes. NASCAR's handling of its "breaking news" crisis differed from the way MLB handles its ongoing crises because, among other reasons, issues of timing, leadership, and organizational structure are different.

The critical distinction to be made between the two types of crises is that, like MLB's always simmering crises, its management not only knows about the pending crisis before it reaches the public, but is likely responsible for it due to its action or inaction. Conversely, and unbeknownst to NASCAR's management beforehand, millions of fans watched in horror on live television as Earnhardt's black #3 GM Goodwrench car struck the wall, killing him, on the final lap of the 2001 Daytona 500.

As vividly and unbelievably tragic as the Earnhardt crash was, it was not the first time large TV audiences were made aware of a disaster unfolding before their very eyes. This infamous distinction belongs to the 1972 Munich Olympics.

As the Vietnam War continued, unrest in the Middle East persisted, and race relations in America remained tense, the Olympics returned to Germany for the first time since Nazi Germany was home to the Games in 1936. Dubbed "The Olympics of Serenity," the Munich Games became a misnomer six days before they concluded when eight Arab terrorists stormed into the Olympic village donning track and field sweat suits, wearing ski masks, and carrying weapons in their athletic equipment bags. They broke into the apartment housing Israeli athletes, killing two of them and taking nine hostages in hopes of exchanging them for 200 jailed Palestinians and two prolific German terrorists.

At 6 a.m. on the morning of September 5, ABC announcer Jim McKay came on the air and said, "The Olympics of Serenity, have become the one thing the Germans didn't want them to be, the Olympics of terror."[1]

Throughout the day, McKay and ABC broadcast the day's only event by providing updates on the situation. After almost a full day of negotiations, the terrorists took the athletes by helicopter to a Munich airbase, where they hoped to fly them to the Middle East. However, after German sharpshooters shot three of the terrorists, the remaining terrorists killed all nine athlete hostages.

Eighteen hours after McKay first went on the air, the weary and emotionally drained announcer delivered the following statement, "We've just gotten the final word," McKay said. "You know, when I was a kid, my father used to say, 'Our greatest hopes and our worst fears are seldom realized.' Our worst fears have been realized tonight. They have now said that there were 11 hostages. Two were killed in their rooms yesterday morning. Nine were killed at the airport tonight. They're all gone."[2]

International Olympic Committee (IOC) President Avery Brundage had to take immediate action. The committee arranged for a makeshift memorial service at the Olympic stadium the next day, and Brundage announced that the games must continue. Thirty-four hours later, the Olympics continued, but not without some questioning whether the games should have been postponed indefinitely. Due to the events of September 5 and 6, the Olympics were forever changed. Among other changes, Olympic security dramatically increased and access to the athletes' village was—and continues to be—severely restricted.

Equally high-profile crises happen in the business world every day, devastating some organizations and inflicting no long-term damage on others.

Johnson & Johnson, for example, barely lost a step when an employee slipped cyanide into one of its strongest brands, Tylenol, killing seven people in 1982. The company quickly found the source of the tampering, recalled 31 million bottles of the painkiller at the cost of $100 million, and developed more tamper-resistant tablets and bottles. Along the way, Johnson & Johnson aired TV commercials explaining what happened, enabling the company to regain its market share within a year.

---

1.   Tomase, John, "Recalling the Olympics of Terror," *The Eagle-Tribune,* September 16, 2001.

2.   Ibid.

Jack in the Box, the fifth-largest hamburger chain in America, also handled a crisis well in 1993 when bacteria found in its burgers killed three children. At first, some franchise owners didn't realize the seriousness of the impact, but most of them understood it when sales dropped dramatically.

Jack in the Box didn't close all of its restaurants, a response that would have been similar to a sports league postponing its games. Instead, it sought to become the leader among fast food companies in food preparation. Jack in the Box convinced microbiologist David Theno to join the company and become vice president of quality assurance and product safety. Theno immediately began implementing a program. Within weeks, Jack in the Box restaurants had installed an entirely new cooking system. Hamburgers that were once tossed on the grill by human hands were now placed on the grill with the help of sanitized tongs.

Jack in the Box was required to compensate hundreds of people directly and indirectly affected by the bacteria as part of the company's agreeing to settle a class action lawsuit by paying $44.5 million. However, thanks to real changes in the organization, Jack in the Box—whose stock had dipped to around $3 a share in the wake of the incident—has consistently sold for more than $20 a share in recent years and was able to celebrate its 50th anniversary in 2001.

To minimize the potentially devastating effects on a company, its employees, and shareholders, organizations must be proactive in crisis management. Although certain readily identifiable circumstances lead to self-inflicted corporate crises, such as poor security or corrupt accounting practices, no one can predict with great confidence when a crisis will occur.

Senior management is paid to manage (potential) crises on a daily basis. Any event that materially influences a business's revenue and expenses, stock price, or competitive position will not only impact the financial bottom line, but will also measurably affect the organization's brand name.

THE "PLAYERS" IN A CRISIS

A crisis' severity is not only determined by the magnitude of the problem itself, but also by which—and to what extent—stakeholders are affected. The severity of a crisis can also be measured by how such stakeholders respond to what has occurred.

The stakeholders, or "players" might differ depending on the type of business or industry in which an organization operates. Although the media is no doubt a critical—and occasionally the most critical—stakeholder involved, others, such as attorneys, are also extremely important. Whether in sports or business, it is not uncommon to have to consider a crisis' impact on dozens of stakeholders.

A single crisis usually involves many players. Enron's fallout also meant a crisis for shareholders, as well as Arthur Andersen, among others. This is not unlike the demise of the Festina team in the 1998 Tour de France, which created a crisis for not only the team, but also the International Cycling Union (ICU), and Festina, the watch company that sponsored the team.

Days before the 1998 Tour de France began, a masseur for the Festina team was stopped at the Franco-Belgium border. In his car were more than 400 performance-enhancing products. Three days after the Tour de France began, the masseur said the drugs were intended for team use. Days later, the ICU suspended Festina director Bruno Roussel, who later said he supplied the drugs to the team and, in fact, five riders indeed used them. After another team, Dutch TVM, was also questioned, riders protested at the 12th stage and six days later, five more teams dropped out. The less rapidly and thoroughly a crisis is handled the greater the likelihood its fallout will engulf more stakeholders, such as the organizers of the Tour de France in the aforementioned example.

For a traditional business, the critical stakeholders, in addition to the news media, usually include senior management and employees, customers, competitors, and the public sector. In sports, especially the four major leagues, the news media is also very important. So too are the broadcast networks that televise the games and sponsors (because each are de facto financiers), the athletes and their unions, and fans. Depending on the situation at hand, other "players" might play a critical role, including teams and their employees, as well as local, state, and federal governments.

Once the impacted stakeholders have been identified, they must be quickly and correctly prioritized to ensure that they are kept adequately "in the loop." Any failure to do so to the satisfaction of stakeholders could harm an organization's long-term business relations with them. Regardless of how stakeholders are prioritized, it is critical to reach the primary ones before they hear about the crisis secondhand—probably from the media. Being proactive in reaching out to these stakeholders enables organizations to not only "tell their side of the story" first, but also demonstrates to key constituents that they are valued by the organization.

DEALING WITH THE CRISIS' PLAYERS

In instances in which the crisis has already occurred and is about to impact the organization's key stakeholders, a strategy is needed to minimize the disruption and financial damage. Developing such a strategy can be cumbersome and can require a tremendous amount of time and preparation. Nonetheless, this ounce of prevention will be well worth it when the crisis hits.

The strategy must involve identifying those functions and processes that are critical to the business. From here, it is necessary to design the operational and communications contingency plans to deal with the potential failure of one or more of the affected functions and processes. Simultaneously, consideration must be given to how key stakeholders will react when they find out that a crisis exists. Organizations with business continuity plans for responding to crises will be better positioned to minimize the inevitable business impact and financial damage.

10 RULES TO LIVE BY

Business strategists have identified 10 rules to live by when facing a crisis.[3] Following these rules, which have been both adhered to and ignored throughout sports and big business, has become even more important of late due to the immediacy of the media and its influence on consumers. The rules are as follows:

1. *Take charge*. This is not the same as accepting blame. It is, however, being responsible for addressing the crisis.
2. *Measure the crowd noise*. Know the difference between an embarrassing development and a full-blown crisis and measure your response accordingly. Understanding how your customers are going to react is key. The media is also going to want to know how you are going to proceed.

---

3. Adapted with permission from Hill and Knowlton's crisis practice.

3. *Feel the pain.* If you are not sympathizing for and empathizing with those affected, any rational arguments you put forth will not be heard. Before a company representative speaks the first word, he or she must make sure the organization knows who the key players in the recovery are, and that the important people on the staff are informed about what will be said.

4. *Be a stats geek.* Use research to understand what consumers are thinking about a particular crisis situation and what they think the company should do.

5. *Use a mouthpiece.* Third parties are becoming critically important as they are routinely viewed more favorably and with greater credibility than company spokespeople.

6. *Embrace the media.* Dealing forthrightly with the media yourself will be more effective than forcing them to gather information from other, possibly less accurate, sources. Make sure a full contingency plan is in place as consumers and strategic allies will want to know how you are going to handle the crisis in the media.

7. *Get ready for the on-court battle.* Expect litigation. Make sure you are proactively and forthrightly briefing legal counsel.

8. *Be cyber-savvy.* Information, and even more important, misinformation circulates on the Internet, via both e-mail and Web sites, at breakneck speeds. Be ready to address fallout arising from chat rooms, e-mail chains, and other online postings.

9. *Timing is everything.* You might do all the right things, but the perception of your company and how you manage the crisis is shaped in the first 24 hours.

10. *The best defense is a good offense.* Undertake the steps required to build your reputational assets before the crisis hits.

RULE #1: TAKE CHARGE

In 1997, Marv Albert, the TV voice of the New York Knicks and New York Rangers on the MSG Network and lead play-by-play man for NBA broadcasts on NBC, was charged with forcible sodomy and assault and battery. Prior to the trial, Albert categorically denied to his employers that he had anything to do with the woman who had alleged he had bitten her on the back and forced her to perform oral sex in a hotel room in February of that year.

Admitting to the charges early on and agreeing to an out-of-court settlement would have saved Albert and the television networks a lot of embarrassment. Even arranging a settlement before charges were pressed could have saved Albert and his working partners a tremendous amount of humiliation. However, Albert continued to deny, deny, deny and the broadcast networks stood by their man and let him broadcast. Then the firestorm hit.

In late September, two days of trial testimony revealed that Albert enjoyed three-way sex and had worn women's underwear. After a second woman came forward alleging similar activities with Albert in 1994, the broadcaster promptly issued a guilty plea. Within hours, NBC fired its lead NBA broadcaster and Albert resigned from the MSG Network. In the process, Albert's personal and professional credibility took a big hit.

However, just because the networks were partially shielded by the fact that most NBA fans wouldn't boycott broadcasts because of Albert, it didn't mean they escaped unscathed. Throughout the trial, *Time Magazine* revealed that Jay Leno had told 43 Albert jokes on *The Tonight Show* (yes, that's right, on NBC!) including this one: "Did you hear NBC gave Marv Albert the pink slip? Yeah, apparently he wore it home." Among other water cooler jokes: "Why did NBC initially stand behind Marv Albert? Because it was the safest place to be." New York newspaper headlines of "Menage a Marv" and "Marv Bites Back" merely compounded the problem.

Albert was rehired by MSG exactly a year after his last broadcast. He was then hired by Turner and eventually resumed his position as the lead voice of the NBA on NBC for the 2000–2001 season. At the end of the 2001–2002 basketball season, Albert was also named to the *Monday Night Football* radio broadcasts.

Taking responsibility—the basketball equivalent of taking the charge—and admitting fault won't make a crisis disappear; doing so is merely an acknowledgment that a crisis indeed exists. However, being candid and truthful with those who are most immediately and significantly affected avoids further damage. Had Albert told the woman he made a mistake that night, was sorry, and was perhaps willing to compensate her, this wouldn't have turned into the media circus it became. That, of course, still doesn't mean that Albert's actions were acceptable, just that the rest of the sports, business, and media industries would have been spared the gory details and much of the fallout arising from the incident's massive exposure.

RULE #2: MEASURE THE CROWD NOISE

Just days before NBA training camps opened for the 2000–2001 season, the NBA had a crisis on its hands when it found out that one of the league's up-and-coming star players, Allen Iverson of the Philadelphia 76ers, was going to release a rap single entitled, "40 Bars." Iverson, who used the rap name Jewelz, had previously been arrested for drug and firearms possession and, while in high school, was convicted on rioting charges and served four months in jail.

Although the song was scheduled to be released on an album in February, the lyrics found their way on to the Internet three months earlier. At the same time, radio stations were sent advance copies of the CD by Columbia Records, NBA Commissioner David Stern was being made aware of the crisis. The lyrics contained in the song were far different than those used by other NBA player/rappers Shaquille O'Neal and Kobe Bryant: "Come to me with faggot tendencies. You be sleeping where the maggots be," and "You man enough to pull a gun? Be man enough to squeeze it. Die if you don't believe it." The song concludes with the cocking of a gun and a gunshot.

Civil rights groups and the media were quick to respond. Fortunately, so too was Stern. Civil rights groups, some of which protested outside the First Union Center before a Philadelphia 76ers preseason game, demanded that Iverson apologize. Iverson then met with some of the groups to hear their concerns, but ultimately decided not to change the lyrics.

Stern reacted quickly. He arranged a meeting with Iverson and, after concluding the meeting, released a statement that explained that Iverson wouldn't be suspended or fined, but had to change the lyrics. Stern made clear that the lyrics not only affected the way people perceive Iverson, but also the way people might perceive the 76ers, as well as the NBA.

As the 76ers dominated the Eastern Conference, in large part due to Iverson's emergence as one of the NBA's top stars of 2001, the February release of the CD suddenly became late June. By the time late June arrived, Iverson had just finished his MVP season, leading his team to the NBA Finals. By the time training camp for the 2001–2002 season rolled around, Iverson made the announcement that allowed the NBA and the 76ers to breathe a sigh of relief. The CD was never going to be released.

Iverson said that due to the negativity behind the CD he just felt like it was not something he should pursue—or ask his teammates, children, or family to endure. In the end, Iverson considered the impact his CD would apparently have and decided he didn't have the passion for it anymore.

By measuring the response (i.e., the crowd noise) well, David Stern, NBA officials, and eventually even Allen Iverson realized that the statement he was hoping to make with his new rap CD wasn't worth the negative feedback that engulfed the stakeholders in this crisis.

RULE #3: FEEL THE PAIN

It is not possible to adequately deal with or move beyond a crisis without realizing—and appreciating—its impact on stakeholders, regardless of whether they were a party to the crisis or merely an innocent bystander to it.

Although the NFL had nothing to do with the terrorist attacks on New York and Washington, D.C. on September 11, 2001, it experienced its own crisis on a much smaller and far less consequential scale. The NFL and its commissioner, Paul Tagliabue, who once served in the office of the Secretary of Defense as a defense policy analyst on European and North Atlantic affairs, needed to decide if the league's games should be played the Sunday following the attacks.

MLB had already postponed some of its games (which would ultimately result in the playoffs and the World Series being pushed back and leading to the first November World Series in league history), but the league was wavering as to how to handle the continually and rapidly unfolding crisis. Numerous college football conferences vacillated about their playing status with many of the so-called "money conferences," those with lucrative TV contracts, initially suggesting that they would play.

The NFL also faced extraordinary logistical and financial issues. Given the NFL's scheduling differences, including the fact that teams only play once a week and some are granted "byes" from time to time, postponing the games was much more complicated. Without knowing how the events of September 11 would be resolved, Tagliabue called off the weekend games. He determined that it came down to the loss of life and the ability of players to absorb what the nation had been through. Tagliabue felt it was right to take a week to reflect and to help the friends, families, and people in the community who needed support.

Tagliabue was not immediately concerned about the potential revenue losses—a week's ticket revenue and compensation owed to the TV networks. Instead, he was only thinking about the others outside his corporation who were affected by the tragedy.

After considering multiple scheduling scenarios and their financial impact on important league stakeholders, Tagliabue, remarkably, kept the NFL season intact by postponing the Super Bowl one week. By more delicately balancing the interests of his constituents (including grief-stricken fans) than other sports leagues, Tagliabue demonstrated unparalleled crisis management acumen. His unprecedented savvy reinforced his standing as the sports world's top executive. *The Sporting News* named him the most powerful person in sports in 2001 and *The Sports Business Journal* selected Tagliabue as its 2001 Sports Executive of the Year.

Unfortunately, almost 40 years earlier, the brilliant 29-year career of NFL commissioner Pete Rozelle was slightly tarnished by his inability to see and feel the pain. Only two days after John F. Kennedy was assassinated in 1963, Rozelle announced that the NFL would play its seven-game schedule that week, whereas the rival American Football League canceled its four matchups.

Rozelle suggested at the time that everyone had a different way of paying respects and that he had done so by attending church that Sunday and imagined many of the people at the (Giants) game had as well. He didn't feel that playing the game was disrespectful—nor did he believe he had made a mistake. However, 30 years later, Rozelle admitted that it was indeed the worst decision of his career.

Tagliabue confronted the crisis caused by the September 11 attacks head on, taking the pulse of his crisis' stakeholders, including the American public, whose pain and grief were immeasurable, and delivering a measured response. In the process of demonstrating keen leadership that included "feeling the pain" of the American people, Tagliabue elevated his and the NFL's brand to new heights.

RULE #4: BE A STATS GEEK

Often, it is the company that must consider the rules discussed in this chapter when dealing with a crisis. However, when companies have strategic alliances with an organization experiencing a crisis, they, too, could be affected.

For example, when an athlete gets arrested, the athlete's agent might want to know how badly his or her client's public image has suffered and to what extent the arrest has hurt the agent's ability to recruit new clients. Additionally, those companies with whom the athlete has endorsement contracts would also immediately consider the merits of retaining him or her to represent the company to the public.

John Hancock Mutual Life Insurance was an official Olympic sponsor for many years, allocating tens of millions of dollars for the privilege to be associated with the Games. When it was determined that several Salt Lake City Olympic bid officials had bribed IOC officials to host the 2002 Olympic Games, the company threatened to withdraw its support.

David D'Alessandro, president of John Hancock, was a vocal critic of the Olympics who indicated his company had conducted three research surveys after the scandal, finding that many of the respondents no longer thought positively about the Olympics or its sponsors.

Compounding matters, the scandal emerged just as the Salt Lake Organizing Committee (SLOC) and the USOC were in the process of their $1.34 billion fundraising campaign to underwrite the cost of hosting the Games. While Olympic officials vociferously challenged John Hancock's findings, the issue remained highly visible in the mainstream press.

Because D'Alessandro didn't believe the IOC was acting quickly enough to resolve the scandal, Hancock's future investment in the Games was uncertain. However, the departure of 10 corrupt IOC members, who either were fired or were forced to resign, assuaged D'Alessandro's concerns about how the bidding process would be conducted. Consequently, Hancock re-signed a reported $50 million deal for what turned out to be a wildly successful 2002 games, as well as for the games in 2004 and 2006 and likely for the games in 2008 in Beijing.

John Hancock's response was a vivid reminder that crises have ripple effects that might impact other "players." It is important to understand—and swiftly address—the ramifications of crises to each and every company that yours is associated with.

Rule #5: Use a Mouthpiece

Commissioning public opinion polls sometimes works and sometimes doesn't. One reason companies conduct polling is to show the business world—and consumers—that what is being portrayed as the problem among the mass media really isn't as much of a issue (even if it is) as they are making it out to be. The third party, of course, technically conducts the poll, but the company itself determines which questions will be asked and in which spirit they will be posed.

The week after the 2001 winter meetings, public opinion of MLB Commissioner Bud Selig and team owners was low due to the MLB's surprise announcement that it would eliminate two teams due to poor financial health. This announcement was made just days after an exhilarating World Series was concluded and followed Selig's Congressional testimony, where he explained that baseball teams had amassed $232 million in operating losses in 2001.

Although much of public opinion indicated that eliminating two teams was disliked by fans and that these same fans believed Bud Selig was doing a poor job, MLB's survey revealed something different. The survey—conducted by Penn, Schoen, and Berland, which had been polling for MLB for more than 10 years—indicated that the sport's problem was a lack of competitive balance, which in fact was a significant issue facing MLB.

From 1995 through 2001, 219 of 224 playoff games were won by teams with the largest payrolls. The poll revealed that 75 percent of the fans believed that there was a problem with competitive balance in baseball and 77 percent of them were happy with Selig's attempts to improve competitive balance. Using statistics, the owners, in the new collective bargaining agreement negotiated in the summer of 2002, persuaded the players to agree to a luxury tax that was meant to slow down the spending of the higher payroll clubs. Management called this a competitive balance tax.

Of course, the poll included no questions about whether contraction helped combat the issue of competitive balance. There were no questions about whether fans believed that allowing teams to relocate would help competitive balance. No questions about the overall opinion fans had of Selig were asked.

Mouthpieces don't always work. It all depends on who receives the information and then who wants to listen to—and act on—the information. MLB's poll was intended to draw attention away from contraction and focus on improving competitive balance. For the most part, MLB did not accomplish this goal because of the relatively short list of media members that received the poll's results and the media's limited coverage of these results.

RULE #6: EMBRACE THE MEDIA

On September 10, 2000, Bobby Knight was fired from Indiana University after leading the school to three national championships and 24 NCAA tournament appearances in 29 years. At a time when far too many athletic programs stressed winning over matriculating student-athletes, Knight was known for graduating the majority of his players while contributing millions of dollars to the school's library.

Most of Knight's contributions to academia were overshadowed by a string of highly publicized incidents. To many, Knight was the sports industry's king of crises, a reputation he began to develop in 1979 when he struck a Puerto Rican policeman at the Pan Am Games. From the time he screamed and kicked his own player-son, Pat, at a game at Notre Dame in 1993, to the time he blasted an NCAA assistant for announcing that Knight wouldn't be at a press conference at which he eventually appeared, Knight was volatile. Throughout it all, he rarely indicated to the media that his behavior was anything less than acceptable.

The media was and remains critical to Knight's career because its job is to communicate with—especially in a time of crisis—important stakeholders who want to be kept abreast of Knight's actions and how these actions (or inaction) are portrayed in the media.

It is evident that Knight has not only failed to embrace the media, but has treated them as adversaries. Not surprisingly, this relationship with the media contributed to his losing his job at Indiana University, because the press was not willing to give him the benefit of the doubt about any of the crises he encountered. A good deal of media members believed that Knight truly didn't see the arrogant, insensitive bully that they had come to expect.

For this reason, many media members kept close tabs on Knight, monitoring his behavior in hopes of uncovering an outburst. After Knight was found to have choked former player Neil Reed and the university issued a "zero-tolerance policy"—meaning Knight's next indiscretion, however slight, would result in his firing—many in the media called for his dismissal.

Although Indiana officials certainly had their own issues with Knight, the media's constant and negative portrayal of him finally took its toll. A heated, albeit minor, exchange with an incoming Indiana freshman gave the university something it desperately needed: a violation of its zero-tolerance policy that enabled the school to fire Knight.

Embracing the media does not mean that it should be cow-towed to without reason, it simply means that a company should use the appropriate spokespeople to help combat the perception of the crisis to the rest of the organization's stakeholders. When Bobby Knight had a crisis, he appeared at press conferences, highly charged settings that did very little to improve his situation. He routinely over-looked one of the primary rules of crisis management: Identify and address what others deem to be a crisis or face tremendous scrutiny for failing to do so. Knight might not care about crisis management, but his new employer, Texas Tech, has to worry about it every time he steps out on the court or into a press conference.

RULE #7: GET READY FOR THE ON-COURT BATTLE

Ensuring that a legal team is thoroughly aware about any and all aspects of a crisis is very important because problems affecting (potential) customers might begin as complaints, but they can quickly turn into lawsuits.

Three fans complained about their seat location in the Tampa Bay Buccaneers new stadium, Raymond James Stadium, where the team moved for the 1998–1999 season. The three quickly retained a lawyer and were soon holding a news conference about their plight. The Buccaneers tried to have a circuit judge dismiss the case but, when that failed, the team filed a $1 million defamation suit—claiming that the fans' statements were false and unfair.

For the damage done to the team's reputation, the Buccaneers wanted $1 million from each fan, $5 million from the lawyer, and $5 million from the attorney's Tampa law firm. Ultimately, the team agreed to drop the case in June 2000.

Former Cleveland Browns owner Art Modell wasn't a popular man when he announced on November 6, 1995, that he was moving the team to Baltimore. Fans protested, calling the move unfair. Then, later that same day, they sued to keep the team in Cleveland. What began as a couple of plaintiffs quickly became thousands of season tickets holders who joined in the claim that insisted Modell violated his con-tract with them after leading them to believe that there was going to be another season in Cleveland. In April 2001, Modell settled out of court by paying $50 per season ticket held to each plaintiff.

Months later, and again in Ohio, the Cincinnati Bengals were compensating 1,750 season ticket holders. A Bengals fan, with the help of his lawyer, Janet Abaray, complained that he had paid for a specific location in the Bengals new stadium, but when he arrived at the first game, the seats weren't in the proper location, so he decided to sue the team.

Abaray then held a town meeting with other season ticket hold-ers who bought personal seat licenses, which merely gives fans the opportunity to buy season tickets, but had been assigned the wrong seats. As other ticket holders joined as plaintiffs, county commissioners advocated that the ticket holders should deal with the team directly rather than rely on the courts for relief.

The team admitted that the stadium was reconfigured *after* the seat assignments were made. In the settlement, ticket holders could upgrade their seats at no additional cost, keep their seats and pocket the difference in price, or relinquish their seats and receive a refund.

In a crisis that is sure to gain national attention, including those where season ticket holders sue professional sports teams, it is critical for organizations to retain legal counsel that not only understands the law as it applies to the case, but that are also extremely sensitive to sympathetic figures such as sports fans and the media that cover them.

RULE #8: BE CYBER SAVVY

Recall from Chapter 3 (with United and Untied.com) that negative news gets forwarded pretty quickly in the technological world of the Internet and via e-mail. Nike found out just how quickly with its Nike iD program.

In 1999, Nike capitalized on making a personal one-to-one relationship with its customers by debuting Nike iD. The ultimate in personal expression and individualism, the Nike iD program enabled customers at Nike.com to pay an additional $10 to special order shoes that contained a personalized message and color combination and arrived in the customer's mailbox in two to three weeks.

Since the mid-1980s, many customers who bought Nike shoes felt their purchase experience had become commodified. Although the customer couldn't completely design every aspect of the shoe, the Nike iD program attempted to prove that the company wasn't too big to care about the individual customer.

Making customers feel as if they were needed has always been a tenet of a good business and the one-to-one world helped make even larger companies create this perception. Nike had Nike iD just as Amazon.com has its personalized book lists based on past purchases.

Yet much to Nike's dismay, Jonah Peretti, a graduate student at MIT, capitalized on this branding opportunity by attempting to make his own brand statement. Peretti requested that the word *sweatshop* be emblazoned on his pair of Nikes.

What was intended to be a brand-building initiative ultimately became a major public relations challenge for the company as it faced swift and immediate fallout resulting from its selective allowance of personal expression. It is an example of how companies, even as prepared as Nike was with specific rules, could have difficulty in the one-to-one world. The following e-mail, one that became one of ESPN.com's most forwarded stories of 2001, magnified the problem as evidenced by these excerpts:[4]

From: Jonah H. Peretti
To: Personalize, NIKE iD
Subject: RE: Your NIKE iD order o16468000

Greetings,
My order was canceled, but my personal NIKE iD does not violate any of the criteria outlined in your message. The Personal iD on my custom ZOOM XC USA running shoes was the word "sweatshop." Sweatshop is not: 1) another's party's trademark, 2) the name of an athlete, 3) blank, or 4) profanity. I choose the iD because I wanted to remember the toil and labor of the children who made my shoes. Could you please ship them to me immediately.
Thanks and Happy New Year,
Jonah Peretti

From: Personalize, NIKE iD
To: Jonah H. Peretti
Subject: RE: Your NIKE iD order o16468000

Dear NIKE iD Customer,
Your NIKE iD order was canceled because the iD you have chosen contains, as stated in the previous e-mail correspondence, "inappropriate slang."
If you wish to reorder your NIKE iD product with a new personalization please visit us again at www.nike.com
Thank you,
NIKE iD

From: Jonah H. Peretti
To: Personalize, NIKE iD
Subject: RE: Your NIKE iD order o16468000

Dear NIKE iD,

---

4.   Farrey, Tom, "Just Don't Do It." ESPN.com. February 27, 2001.

Thank you for your quick response to my inquiry about my custom ZOOM XC USA running shoes. Although I commend you for your prompt customer service, I disagree with the claim that my personal iD was inappropriate slang. After consulting Webster's Dictionary, I discovered that "sweatshop" is in fact part of standard English, and not slang. The word means: "a shop or factory in which workers are employed for long hours at low wages and under unhealthy conditions," and its origin dates from 1892. So my personal iD does meet the criteria detailed in your first e-mail.

Your website advertises that the NIKE iD program is "about freedom to choose and freedom to express who you are." I share Nike's love of freedom and personal expression. The site also says that "If you want it done right ... build it yourself." I was thrilled to be able to build my own shoes, and my personal iD was offered as a small token of appreciation for the sweatshop workers poised to help me realize my vision. I hope that you will value my freedom of expression and reconsider your decision to reject my order.

Thank you,

Jonah Peretti

Although Nike did not reconsider Peretti's request, the company certainly learned the perils of the one-to-one world and how the e-mail and the Internet world can spread company ill will faster than ever before. Peretti's well-distributed e-mail, it turns out, has taught the company a valuable lesson in what experts call "viral" marketing, which thrives in an e-mail environment.

This didn't stop Nike from staying with the importance of creating individual shoes for the customer. In fact, the company never changed anything on its personalization rules because of the Peretti experience. Three years into the program, Nike had 23 shoes available for personalization and the program, which was once only available in the United States expanded to Europe and Japan.

Although it might not have admitted to changing its rules dealing with personalizing products, one has to believe that Nike has certainly become more cyber-savvy because of the Peretti's high-profile response.

RULE #9: TIMING IS EVERYTHING

On February 18, 2001, around 4:50 p.m., NASCAR was faced with the greatest crisis in its history after racing legend Dale Earnhardt, who had won 76 races and more than $41 million, crashed into a wall on the final turn of the Daytona 500.

By dissecting the timeline of events over the first three-and-a-half hours following what became the Associated Press sports story of the year, it quickly becomes clear just how important solid decision making is in the moments following a major crisis.

Earnhardt was extracted from the car and received immediate emergency care at the speedway following the crash, including on-site CPR. Within minutes, he had arrived at Halifax Medical Center, located just a few blocks away from International Speedway Boulevard, where a trauma team was waiting for him. At 5:16 p.m., Earnhardt was pronounced dead. By 6:50 p.m., official word had reached the speedway. Approximately 10 minutes later, NASCAR President Mike Helton, flanked by the medical center's doctor, Steve Bohannon, was briefing reporters.

Helton informed the media that he wasn't educated on everything and that all the answers wouldn't be known right away. Bohannon then explained everything he could from a medical standpoint. Helton and Bohannon didn't answer many questions, hoping not to fuel any fire surrounding safety standards.

At 7:40 p.m., the flag near the racetrack's finish line was lowered to half-mast. At 8 p.m., NASCAR announced that the post-Daytona 500 ceremony, set to take place Monday morning, was postponed indefinitely.

Over the following days, weeks, and months, many columnists criticized NASCAR for its safety standards and in the six months that followed the crash several conflicting reports surfaced about the actual cause of Earnhardt's death. Further, a separate controversy erupted over whether Earnhardt's seatbelt had broken or had been cut during extraction.

Still, important action was taken. On August 21, NASCAR released a 324-page report that included input from more than 50 experts. Three months later, NASCAR mandated that drivers in its top three divisions wear head and neck restraints.

What cannot be criticized was the timely and fluid manner in which NASCAR responded to one of the biggest sports tragedies of all time.

Because NASCAR handled the initial crisis well and measured the rest of its response over time, it averted what most certainly would have been even more scrutiny—scrutiny that could have harmed NASCAR just as it was gaining national notoriety.

Rule #10: The Best Defense Is a Good Offense

According to crisis management experts, the most effective crisis management occurs when potential crises are detected and dealt with quickly—before they can impact the organization's business. In those instances they never come to the attention of the organization's key stakeholders or the general public via the news media.[5]

The National Hot Rod Association (NHRA) is one of the few sports organizations that not only understands this in theory, but has put it to the test. The impact of the 1998 settlement between state attorneys general and the major U.S. tobacco companies rippled through the sports industry, most significantly impacting motorsports.

Forced to choose which sports sponsorship it would maintain, motorsports' biggest corporate partner, R.J. Reynolds' Winston cigarette brand, decided that maintaining its 31-year-old sports marketing relationship with NASCAR's Winston Cup was its top priority. Winston's decision, based in large part on NASCAR's enormous presence on network TV and its annual on-track attendance of approximately 4 million at its 35 national events, snuffed out another major motorsports league, the NHRA.

The comprehensive marketing partnership between Winston and the NHRA spanned 27 years and was valued at between $10 million and $15 million annually, making Winston the NHRA's most important sponsor. Replacing such a significant sponsor wasn't going to be easy at a time when the economy was soft and sponsorship dollars were few and far between.

A year before the official Winston/NASCAR announcement and because it believed it could lose Winston's support, the NHRA began contingency planning. On the one hand the NHRA could not undertake any initiatives that would undermine Winston's ongoing support, for doing so could prove costly and severely threaten the NHRA's viability.

On the other hand, having a tobacco company as a major NHRA sponsor limited its ability to broaden the sport's appeal to the next generation of fans. What the NHRA really wanted was a partner, one mutually vested and invested in the sport. This dynamic left the NHRA feeling ambivalent toward Winston, but allowed it to be proactive in advance of the announcement rather than be reactive as was

---

5.   http://www.crisisexperts.com/essence_main.htm.

the case with many sports leagues and properties that relied on tobacco money.

The NHRA began dealing with this potential funding crisis several years earlier when it committed to shoring up its management model by organizing itself in way that streamlined internal and external communications. With five vice presidents reporting directly to the NHRA president, the organization successfully crafted a managerial framework that enabled it to cohesively—and in a contained fashion—develop and implement a strategy for replacing Winston.

With its stated goal to grow the sport, the NHRA focused on extending the sport's coverage on TV and improving its racing facilities. In doing so the NHRA believed it would be able to leverage these developments during sponsor negotiations.

The NHRA's advance planning paid off, as it was able to articulate this vision to numerous would-be suitors, including the Coca-Cola Company's Powerade brand. Just as the negotiations were drawing to a close, the September 11 terrorist attacks occurred, leading many prominent sports spenders, including Coca-Cola, to circle their wagons.

Rather than panic and risk losing an ideal corporate partner, the NHRA quickly identified two steps it had to take to keep the sponsorship alive. First, it had to communicate to Powerade that not only wasn't the NHRA desperate to close the deal, but that it was more than willing to work with any new time table provided by Powerade. Second, and equally critical, the NHRA provided Powerade with timely and important new research detailing how and why the relationship should be quickly consummated.

These efforts were rewarded on December 3, 2001, when the NHRA announced that Powerade had agreed to a five-year worldwide exclusive agreement. NHRA called December 3 the most important day in the organization's history.

Although the NHRA might not have been able to live up to Winston's lofty expectations, it was able to provide Powerade with the highly coveted audiences, targeted youth programs, and incredible responsiveness it needed. Such a combination of attributes is rare in today's sports business world and enabled the NHRA to replenish the millions of dollars lost indirectly to the tobacco settlement.

In the end, the NHRA's reputational capital and brand name were greatly enhanced because of the way in which it handled this sponsor issue during a recession and following the September 11 attacks.

For the NHRA, it was a strong offense that kept it from having to play defense.

Not only did the NHRA correctly prepare for and navigate through a crisis that could have seriously impacted its long-term industry standing, it did so while taking into account the numerous stakeholders that contribute to or challenge its success.

MOVING ON

In addition to paying keen attention to the 10 rules just highlighted, it is mandatory for organizations to recognize the importance of knowing when and how to move on, and when to put the crisis behind them. However, in taking this positive step forward, organizations must be sure they appreciate the impact the crisis has had—and might continue to have—on the stakeholders associated with it. After all, as Kent State University learned, it is seldom as easy as relocating or simply changing the business's name when "moving on."

On May 4, 1970, Ohio National Guard members killed four students demonstrating over the United States' involvement in Vietnam. Although it was widely believed that the guardsmen were not in grave danger and, therefore, the fault was hardly that of the Kent State students, many believed the university would always be known first and foremost for the massacre.

In 1986, the university—in part because of the tragic event—removed the "State" from official stationery and letterhead. It was believed that one way to move on was to jettison a portion of the university's full name. Even during the 1999 basketball season, media notes handed out to the press covering games involving the Golden Flashes reminded members of the media to refer to the team as "Kent" instead of "Kent State." Sports information officials also made sure that the scoreboards in the arenas said Kent and not Kent State.

Ultimately, however, the alumni wanted the old name back. Most of them were proud of being Kent State students and Kent just sounded too foreign to many of them. So, in 2000, in time for the 30th anniversary of the school's ultimate crisis, the university reportedly paid an outside firm $300,000 to design a new logo and changed almost 100 on-campus signs back to read "Kent State."

In the same light, companies that have endured a significant crisis cannot just change their names in hopes that people will forget.

Recognizing the past, appreciating its role with important stakeholders, and moving on in an appropriate manner is more desirable than attempting to disguise or gloss over important crises.

CHAMPIONSHIP POINTS

Much has been learned about dealing with crises during the almost 30 years separating the 1972 Munich Olympics and the terrorist events of September 11, 2001. The manner, style, timeliness, and thoroughness of the response to a crisis have all evolved given technological advancements, particularly as they relate to the immediacy of the media in today's sports and business worlds.

Although the stakeholders, or "players," might differ depending on the type of business or industry in which an organization operates, it is important for executives to remember the following when faced with a crisis:

- Step up to the plate by rapidly acknowledging the situation and your desire to quickly and ethically resolve it.
- If you don't react unnecessarily to a crisis, you will not unnecessarily overreact to it. Measured responses help organizations avoid the bad rap associated with mishandling a crisis.
- Take your consumers' pulse about the situations by rapidly gathering any and all meaningful data that will help mitigate the crisis. The ability to accomplish this will allow an organization to run rings around the competition.
- Utilize an appropriate messenger, one with great credibility and believability, to help communicate how the crisis is being deftly handled. Select a mouthpiece that doesn't have laryngitis.
- Make the media your friend by disarming it when appropriate. Such an approach will enable the organization to save face with critical shareholders, including fans or customers and the media, and might result in the organization being given the benefit of the doubt when a crisis does occur. If more than one person is speaking on behalf of the company in a crisis, make sure they are saying the same thing. Specifically, tell those who shouldn't be talking to the media not to talk.
- Appreciate the role that will be played by the legal system both during and after a crisis. If the legal eagles fail to appreciate the stakeholders and their sympathizers, you will be courting disaster.

- Cyber-patrolling before, during, and after a crisis will help ensure that an organization is aware of—and prepared to deal with—the situation before it gets out of hand on the Internet. Redoubling online resources will help fend off long-term brand damage brought about by a crisis.
- Any failure to sympathize for, and empathize with, those affected by a crisis will limit how favorably stakeholders view your response, even if the response is tactically and legally sound. Don't let the competition lap you because you were asleep at the wheel during a crisis.
- Handling a crisis promptly, with great tact and demonstrable leadership, will help diffuse what could become a full-blown crisis. Professionally and publicly displaying crisis management acumen can reinforce your standing as the top player in your field.
- Go on the offensive by planning for crises. Effective contingency planning will help smoke the competition when an organization—or entire industry for that matter—faces turmoil.
- Consider how stakeholders will respond and react when you decide it is time to put a crisis behind you. Tactfully and purposefully moving on will help avoid compounding and extending the fallout from the initial crisis.

Recognizing, appreciating, and working with those entities impacted by an organization's response to a crisis has become a critically important element in today's business world.

Further, proactively dealing with crises has taken on new importance given the rapid emergence of new technologies and the 24-hour news cycle.

Effective crisis management has become increasingly vital throughout sports and business, particularly as each seeks to enter new markets.

8 PENETRATING NEW MARKETS

The Point: Business executives appreciate the daunting challenges associated with entering new markets, whether located in a neighboring town or distant continent. Despite realizing that the rules of the game can be quite different in new markets, sports-minded corporations, teams, leagues, and even athletes occasionally try to simply port their existing business strategies. They have done so with mixed results; results that provide valuable clues as to how best to penetrate desirable markets.

Selling products and services globally, or even to untapped local markets for that matter, can be a tricky proposition. However, successfully penetrating "foreign" markets can also provide greater credibility to your brand name and result in increased shareholder value, provided the intricacies associated with entering new markets are swiftly handled.

For those companies that choose to sell products or services abroad (however you define "abroad"), regulatory and distribution issues are prevalent. When a business moves from city to city or state to state, it must deal with the challenges of target marketing, nuances in buyer behavior, and assessing competitive environments. The dividends paid for successfully taking a business "abroad," however, are enormous and help cement a company's leadership position within its industry.

When Brian (an Olympic marathon runner) and Jennifer (a food science major) Maxwell founded the nutritional bar company Powerbar in 1986, they made the bars in their California kitchen and personally handed them out—one at a time—at running and other endurance events.

Once they decided to grow the business they recognized that they needed a game plan because it was unfeasible for them to personally attend every demographically appealing event in neighboring regions. Simultaneously, the Maxwells needed a comprehensive strategy and working capital.

With $250,000 in venture capital and a strategy focusing on their niche customer, avid runners, Powerbar set out to gain brand awareness and credibility by sponsoring races and placing free samples into post-race bags. The distribution strategy was predicated on getting the bars into nutritional stores across the country.

Soon, the making of the Powerbars involved line workers in Idaho and packaging people in North Carolina. Offices were eventually opened in Canada and Europe and, in 1999, sales reached more than $135 million, when Nestle, the world's largest food company, bought out the Maxwells.

By systematically expanding their products' distribution based on consumer preferences within specifically targeted markets, Powerbar's penetration into what it identified as new markets paid enormous dividends.

Although not all small business entrepreneurs are intent on expanding their business, many share a common dream to be as big and revered as possible.

Powerbar's success in penetrating new markets was achieved, in part, through methodical planning. The planning that enabled Powerbar to help create a $680 million industry now must be continued by Nestle, which is now being challenged by Clif Bar for the lead in the energy bar market. Other large companies, like Unilever—which acquired Slimfast—and Kellogg—which bought Kashi GoLean bars—certainly aren't compromised by lack of global distribution. Despite this competition—or perhaps because of it—Powerbar continues to reinforce its core identity and brand, most notably through community and grassroots marketing programs. They might be owned by Nestle but the look and feel of the "old" Powerbar remains.

Many small companies that don't thoroughly analyze the prevailing issues and concerns in new markets before setting out to conquer them find themselves facing community and public relations backlashes, as well financial setbacks. If you thought local, regional, and international business indiscretions and oversights were limited to small companies lacking adequate market research staffs, think again.

Even marketing powerhouse McDonald's has committed high-profile marketing gaffes. For example, it offended Muslims by printing the flags of the 24 nations competing in the 1994 World Cup on two million throw-away bags. The Saudi Arabian flag contains an important passage from the Koran and should not be discarded as trash according to the Muslim faith.

Nike, too, has had its setbacks. It shot a TV spot for hiking boots in Kenya using Samburu tribesmen. As one of the men speaks in his native Maa, the slogan "Just Do it" appears as a subtitle on the screen. Unfortunately, the translation wasn't quite correct. The tribesman, it turns out, was saying he didn't want the shoes.

In 1997, Nike faced a backlash when a logo on samples of a new Nike shoe looked like it had the word *Allah* written on them in Arabic. Nike insisted that the point of the design was to show the AIR logo up in flames, but the Council on American-Islamic Relations wanted an apology for the offensive design. Not only was it sacrilegious, but Muslims consider feet to be a naturally unclean part of the body. Although Nike said the shoes were prototypes, some "Air Allahs" still managed to find their way onto store shelves.

However, this miscue pales in comparison to the world-class blunders made by Reebok and Umbro. In 1996, Reebok actually named a women's running shoe after the mythical character Incubus, a demon who had sex with women while they were sleeping.

Reebok indicated that in-house marketers came up with the name. Its legal department checked to make sure no one else had patented it. Unbelievably, though, no one took the obvious step to check the word's meaning in the dictionary or independently confirm that it was a suitable name given the product's target market.

Webster's defines *incubus* as a spirit or demon thought in medieval times to lie on sleeping persons, especially on women, for the purpose of sexual intercourse. A second definition of the word is simply "nightmare."

In 1999, Umbro—which makes gear for England's national soccer team, as well as many other high-profile teams in Europe—named a running shoe Zyklon. But it was not until 2002, when the name actually appeared on the shoe, that people realized Zyklon was too similar to Zyklon B, the namesake of the poison gas that was used by the Nazis to kill Jews in concentration camps during World War II.

Jewish activist groups reacted quickly to Umbro's apparent lack of sensitivity. A company spokesperson called the relationship between the name and the poison gas "purely coincidental." But if Umbro was indeed unaware of the coincidence, all company executives had to do was simply enter the word in an Internet search and consider the first couple of references provided. The name was soon changed to Stealth Blanc.

These sports-oriented examples merely illustrate that attempting to market products and services outside a company's comfort zone can be costly in the event cultural norms and sensitivities are not carefully navigated. Companies need to understand the people to whom they are selling and precisely what the product and its attributes mean to these prospective customers.

In terms of using sports to penetrate untapped markets and build market share, perhaps there is no better company to analyze than Nike, itself constantly facing myriad challenges and threats as it increases its global business. Although Nike is an international conglomerate, its approach to penetrating foreign markets yields valuable insight for businesses of all sizes.

THE 800-POUND GORILLA

Phil Knight, while attending Stanford's Business School, was given the assignment to write a paper on small business. He chose to research and describe the industry that fascinated him the most—athletic shoes.

Working under the assumption that there was a market for track shoes that were both of higher quality and lower price than industry bellwether adidas, Knight envisioned a small company priding itself on its ability as a distributor. After graduating, Knight met with the Japanese shoe manufacturer Onitsuka, which manufactured the Tigers brand. Knight convinced Onitsuka that he could market the shoes profitably in the United States and, consequently, had samples of the shoes sent to him in Oregon.

When the samples arrived a year later, Knight contacted Bill Bowerman, his mentor and former track coach, about the prospect of providing his team with the Japanese footwear. Bowerman was thoroughly impressed with the shoes and suggested Knight secure a contractual agreement from the firm to guarantee the relationship. Bowerman believed he could help Knight market the shoe and suggested they form a partnership in which Knight handled the finances and day-to-day operations.

They each contributed $500 and started the business under the name Blue Ribbon Sports (BRS) which was run out of a storefront shop in Portland, Oregon, where Knight worked part-time selling shoes at local track meets. After shortages in working capital and cash flow from 1964 to 1966, BRS signed an agreement with Onitsuka giving it an exclusive, three-year contract to distribute Tiger track shoes in the United States.

In 1972, following numerous legal battles, distribution problems, and political infighting, the group known as BRS became Nike. In 1977, Nike began developing products in Taiwan and Korea, and by the time it was ready to enter China in 1980, Nike had achieved a 50 percent market share in the United States.

Based in Beaverton, Oregon, Nike—whose name was derived from the Greek goddess of victory—now boasts nearly $10 billion in annual revenue. Knight, who is still running the company, works with his 22,700 employees to maintain Nike's reputation as one of the most powerful organizations in sports. Nike has transformed itself from a regional shoe company of the 1970s to a global marketing powerhouse that today sells its products in 140 countries.

Nike's history, corporate culture, and commitment to innovation keep the firm competitive in its core operations. In particular, its corporate philosophy, characterized by its mission to "enhance people's lives through sports and fitness" and to "keep the magic of sport alive" motivate the company to penetrate new, particularly foreign, markets. Knight hinted in 1996 that Nike would indeed seek these increasingly important new markets when he suggested that sports had become the world's dominant form of entertainment.

Foreign markets were especially critical to Nike because, before too long, a majority of its employees and revenue would be generated abroad; presently 99 percent of its athletic footwear is made in Asia. Its status as a transnational company also serves Nike well in certain respects.

Transcending geographic boundaries during the production process limits a particular government's ability to intervene should a crisis emerge, as it did when Nike was believed to be exploiting its Southeast Asian factory workers by forcing them to work in deplorable circumstances. For example, Nike sold a shoe that was designed in Oregon and Tennessee. This same shoe had been developed by technicians in Taiwan and South Korea, as well as in Oregon. After receiving the required 52 different components from five different countries, the shoe was finally manufactured in South Korea and Indonesia. Such a vast production network made it difficult for the U.S. government to intervene.

Just because Nike escaped the wrath of the U.S. government, it by no means dodged a public relations and media backlash stemming from this controversy. Similarly, when small businesses operate out of several branches, for instance, don't expect that a customer service problem at one location will not resonate at headquarters. When a bank teller that works for a local, two-branch bank is rude to a customer, it is not uncommon for that customer to let the bank's president know that he or she plans on closing his or her checking account and transferring his or her CD to another institution. Patrons such as this routinely go one step further: They make everyone in their bridge club aware of the bank's shabby service.

When the 1998 U.S Olympic hockey team was eliminated after losing to Czechoslovakia, the players trashed the hotel where they were staying, embarrassing everyone associated with the team, including its official apparel provider, Nike. In this case, not treating the host city, Nagano, and the Olympics with their due respect caused great harm to the brands that attached themselves to the American team.

Because sports has become the dominant entertainment in the world, organizations that rely on it to help market goods and services must exert tremendous care whenever it is directly or indirectly on the global stage.

MARKETING ABROAD

For decades, firms were able to focus their marketing strategies within their home territory or region. Compared to the intricacies of conducting business abroad, it was relatively easy to devise and implement comprehensive business strategies within a company's core market. The business culture and standard operating procedures were predictable and reliable.

As foreign markets opened, American firms sought to take advantage of these rapidly expanding and potentially profitable markets. Simultaneously, cheaper transportation costs and improved communications made the concept of expanding across North America more palatable to smaller domestic businesses.

Marketing executives facing the daunting challenge associated with entering new markets were—and continue to be—forced to begin by answering three initial questions: Which markets should be approached? When should they be accessed? Precisely how will the marketing mission be accomplished?

The most important question of the three is how the firm should enter a new market. Five major factors exist when addressing the strategic challenge associated with this question. These are:[1]

- Regional or country characteristics
- Barriers and regulation
- Product characteristics
- Management objectives
- Market selection strategy

The first three of these are external to the company and the last two are internal decisions facing the firm.

REGIONAL OR COUNTRY CHARACTERISTICS

Regional and country characteristics consist of three attributes that a marketing manager should be aware of. The first is market size and growth. Depending on whether a market is mature or growing exponentially, a marketing manager would undertake different strategies.

If a company is intent on expanding to a different region, state, or country it must make sure there is adequate room for expansion. Alternatively, if the requisite room is not available it must devise a strategy for expanding the market by building a better mousetrap.

Unlike the cases of McDonald's, Nike, Reebok, and Umbro, a failure to expand beyond your core market might have little to do with cultural differences. It could simply be a case of brand hubris—you thought that because the Internet market was expanding you could easily go into "Yahoo! territory" and carve out market share.

Challenging a market leader isn't necessarily the problem. The problem comes if a firm moves in but doesn't properly analyze what

---

1. *Marketing Management* by Winer, Russell S. (pp. 449–454), Prentice Hall, 2000. © Adapted by permission of Pearson Education, Inc., Upper Saddle River, NJ.

it will take to compete alongside that local leader. In Hermosa Beach, California, for example, many residents were vocal about the need to protect local businesses from larger chain stores. These residents went as far as to suggest that national and regional chains, particularly restaurants and retailers, should not open for business along the beach as they would face a backlash if they chose to compete with long-standing local establishments in the small, closely knit beach community.

The expansion of professional sports into Tampa Bay is a compelling example of a regional mistake. Neither MLB's Devil Rays nor the NHL's Lightning have succeeded in Tampa because not only wasn't the market demand sufficiently demonstrated in advance of entering the market, but the competition for the entertainment dollar throughout the region threatened long-term viability. This, combined with other unfavorable factors, has resulted in each franchise losing millions of dollars per season.

The next aspect is the political and environmental risk. Is a firm willing to invest its resources in a potentially volatile country or region? Expanding into new markets frequently requires great human and financial resources, and expanding into less developed markets often requires even more of both.

The overseas shoe industry began in Japan and Korea, then extended to Taiwan and China and, eventually, to Indonesia. In October 2001, more than 100 Nike and Adidas employees and their families fled Indonesia—where about 30 percent of Nike shoes were manufactured—after the U.S. Department of State warned of attacks on U.S. citizens and facilities by radical Indonesian groups. A year later, Nike began to shift more of its business to Vietnam and Thailand.

The company still reported that major military or terrorist events in Asia could affect shoe and apparel distribution. To combat this, Nike has basic contingency plans so that the chain of supply is never fully compromised should events like these occur.

This is not unlike a local business that needs to prepare for a celebratory riot in the championship team's hometown. A local convenience store might benefit from the success of the Denver Broncos, but it might also be hurt by the team's success. In Denver, after the Broncos won their first championship in 1998, police had to use tear gas to calm the 30,000 fans in the downtown area that celebrated the victory by overturning cars, setting fires, and looting local stores.

Although it is understandable why many of these local businesses were unprepared to deal with the rowdy fans, what is unfortunate is that many of these same businesses did not adequately prepare for future disturbances by conducting contingency planning. When the Broncos won the Super Bowl the next season, every business on the affected Larimar Street should have had a plan in place. A riot did ensue for a second straight year, tear gas was again used, and $120,000 in damages was incurred.

When sports apparel and equipment companies want to sell overseas, they typically have to forge relationships with dealers and manufacturers. The companies can't just send product from their headquarters and hope that the merits of the product in America will help sell the product abroad. The company has to have personnel who personally meet with major stores in different countries and constantly check on how the product is being marketed, displayed, and positioned in general.

Some businesses succeed because of good customer service, but others prosper because they learn how best to sell their products in the context of the local business environment. Just because the targeted market is thousands of miles away doesn't mean that there shouldn't be the same concern for product placement. Thanks to solid communication and the right resources, Nike successfully sells its products worldwide. One of the keys to its success has been Nike's ability to ensure that its suppliers have similar backgrounds to those consumers targeted.

Nike has successfully built its brand image by networking with suppliers that are of the same cultural and ethnic background as the consumers it ultimately targets in these markets. Nike has also found that many consumers, including minorities, buy a particular brand of shoe based on how the company is perceived as treating them as valued customers.

When small companies migrate from niche to broader markets, such as when Powerbar moved from having a presence in nutritional stores to also having shelf space in supermarkets, they must ensure that they remain in close communication with their supplier base. If the supplier doesn't know how to position the product in new markets, it could be detrimental to the brand's growth.

In sports, the "supplier" can be a team like the NBA's Houston Rockets, and the "product" can be a newly drafted player, such as 7'6" Chinese center Yao Ming, the first pick in the 2002 NBA draft. The Rockets, which had been interested in marketing its product to

Chinese-Americans in the greater Houston area for years, had been largely unsuccessful in reaching this target market. The team's on-court performance was not helping, as the Rockets compiled the second-worst attendance in the NBA for the 2001–2002 season.

As soon as Yao Ming entered the team's picture, a Chinese business purchased 100 season tickets and promised to purchase thousands more for big games. However, the team knew it had to take this (and other emerging business opportunities) a step further. The team had to educate its employees about the Chinese culture: How do the Chinese expect to be treated at the arena? Is this different than the expectations of other basketball fans? What elements of the game-day experience are most important to them? In short, any failure to recognize the wants and needs of this expanding target market will be detrimental to the brand's (Rockets') growth. After identifying a dozen potential Chinese sponsors, the Rockets signed a six-year, $6 million deal with the Chinese beer company Yanjing before the season.

The Rockets could easily have talked to the sports marketers at Nike, which not only sponsored Yao Ming and his team in China—the Shanghai Sharks—but continue to have him serve as a company endorser.

Finally, the economic and market infrastructure of a country might help a firm decide if it wants to alter its operating procedures to adapt to a certain country's methods of operation.

Building a presence in a new market also requires forging a credible connection between the company's product and the company's targeted consumers in those markets.

Nike has always used sports and sports personalities to frame the company's personality and commitment to sports fans and enthusiasts. From individual track and field legends Alberto Salazar, Joan Benoit, and Carl Lewis in the early 1980s to its current licensing agreements with sports teams and universities including the Dallas Cowboys, as well as the University of Michigan and Duke University, Nike has integrated sports into every aspect of its operations. When it set out to increase its rapidly expanding global market share, Nike undertook the same fundamental approach, this time concentrating its efforts in soccer and golf.

Although soccer and golf are only responsible for about 10 percent of Nike's revenue, their importance to Nike cannot be overstated. Over the last few years each of these sports has outpaced all others in terms of growth.

Because the revenue growth in its established categories of running, basketball, football, and baseball has slowed as they became mature business segments, Nike turned much of its attention to a sport and an athlete that possess significant global appeal.

Local businesses moving into neighboring markets best establish credibility through word of mouth. The smaller the distance between the new market and the home base, the faster the word—good or bad—tends to spread. Word of mouth by customers is actually much more credible than getting the lowdown from paid athlete endorsers.

BARRIERS AND REGULATIONS

Trade barriers and government regulations are the second set of factors that must be considered when entering new markets. Many countries limit the ability of foreign companies to operate freely. On the other hand, import tariffs can be very costly for companies trying to sell goods in a particular country. It becomes a double-edged sword for companies that seek to take advantage of a growing foreign market. They can enter a country and risk incurring the costs associated with different business and political climates and cultures, or they can simply export to those countries, paying hefty tariffs in the process.

For the 2002 Salt Lake City Olympics, 10 primary sponsors, including Eastman Kodak, John Hancock, and Visa, paid at least $50 million for their "official sponsor" status.

Although allocating even more resources for the 2008 Olympics in Beijing might indeed prove worthwhile to these and other sponsors, most agree involvement in the Beijing Games to be far more risky. Many companies view the 2008 Games as a tremendous platform for communicating their marketing messages to largely untapped markets. Yet many of these same sponsors remain concerned about China's ability to host the Olympics, especially given that nation's poor record on human rights and the negative impact this could have on those companies that have attached themselves to the Games via sponsorship.

Analyzing the costs and benefits of the aforementioned options in an effort to find an optimal balance is typically quite difficult. This analysis has become increasingly more challenging now that many transnationals, literally and figuratively, have people looking over their shoulders.

When Jim Keady, a St. John's University assistant soccer coach who was writing a master's research paper on Nike's labor practices, left the school because he refused to wear Nike shoes, as required by the school's athletic contract, he decided to work for a month in a Nike shoe factory in Indonesia.

Armed with a cameraman, an interpreter, and a Web site (www.nikewages.org), Keady set out to tell the world about his—and Nike's—exploits. Keady did so by documenting the life of Indonesian workers by putting himself "in their shoes," living as they did, in August 2001.

In one of his interviews, one worker told Keady that in one area of the factory there were 350 people forced to use three toilets, two of which were broken. In this factory, a bad mistake could mean hours of public embarrassment in front of fellow workers.

Keady's crusade was just beginning. He went on a speaking tour and talked about sweatshops to students at colleges and universities including the University of Notre Dame and the University of Connecticut. His personal involvement, going beyond principle and into action, made Nike factory-bashing a compelling story for news networks like ABC, CBS, and NBC. *Real Sports* on HBO and ESPN's *Outside the Lines* showed footage taped by Keady.

Keady's $11 million lawsuit against Nike and St. John's was dismissed by a U.S. Court of Appeals, but his story is important to tell to merely demonstrate how easy it is to chip away at a brand that stretches around the world. The bigger a company becomes and the more it expands, the more vulnerable the brand becomes. A mom-and-pop company executive knows everything that transpires and can micromanage the brand. Nike can never have enough executives to make sure that every factory is running smoothly at all times or enough security so that people like Keady don't film conditions—even if they are possibly violating human rights.

Small businesses are not immune from such controversies. Whether it is the local throw-away newspaper that makes mention of a dry cleaner's employment of illegal immigrants or publishes a short story chronicling a restaurant's lapses in cleanliness, small businesses must be attuned to issues that could diminish their good name.

Global companies like Nestle, which bought Powerbar, have gone through the same international scrutiny regarding their trade practices. Visit any Internet search engine and type in "Nestle and baby milk" and you'll notice a similar abundance of protest sites. Critics say Nestle has a blatant disregard for both a World Health Organization study, which estimates that that 1.5 million infants die around the world every year because they are not breastfed, and a 20-year-old code, which restricts how breast milk substitutes can be marketed.

Critics claim to target Nestle because it went out of its way to advertise infant formula to mothers by giving out free samples and sending direct mail. Nestle has also given free milk to maternity hospitals in Third World countries to persuade new parents to use their brand after leaving the hospital.

One critic went so far as to say that not until Nestle's deceptive public relations machinery was rendered ineffectual would the company address its entrenched disregard for the way it markets its products.

Nestle's Jim Keady was Syed Aamar Raza, a former Nestle sales employee who, after hearing of the death of a four-month-old bottle-fed baby, made it his crusade to denounce Nestle's marketing tactics, including the bribing of doctors.

Although Nike and Nestle might firmly believe that their marketing strategies and corporate policies are sound, a vocal minority will always seek to keep the public pressure on those companies they perceive as recklessly pursuing profits at the expense of human lives.

Human rights and marketing mistakes allegedly committed by Nike and Nestle vividly demonstrate how distance from headquarters doesn't release the company from its responsibilities. It also demonstrates that it is more prudent to spend time and resources preventing potential damage to the brand than it is to repair the damaged brand after the fact.

Over the years, Nike has responded to human rights activists complaining about its sweatshops. In 1998, it set forward its code of conduct and in October 2001 it issued its first corporate responsibility report, which detailed the company's efforts to monitor health, safety, wages, benefits, and management requirements.

In 1996, *The New York Times* published a few op-ed pieces accusing Nike of exploiting cheap Asian labor. Phil Knight responded by writing a rebuttal commentary stating that Nike paid double the minimum wage in countries where its products were being produced. In 1998, Mark Kasky, an activist in California, sued Nike contending that Knight's commentary, as well as a host of other Nike releases to the media, violated the state's laws against false advertising. In 2002, the California Supreme Court ruled that Knight's comments counted as commercial speech and if any of his statements were wrong, Nike could lose the profits it made in California based on these statements. Companies and their high-profile leaders and spokespeople must remain vigilant when hoping to publicly "right" what many perceive to be a "wrong." Any perceived reaction or, worse yet, overreaction, may merely compound the problem.

During this same period, Nike demonstrated that it fully appreciated the importance of giving back to the community.

In 1999, it sponsored a Playzone project that refurbished playgrounds in Southeast Asia and also launched a series of shoes in the region. A pair of shoes in what Nike termed its "play" series could be bought for as low as $3. Knight also said that by the end of 2001, Nike would not utilize any footwear factory that did not provide for after-hours education. Although this is an encouraging development, Nike will have to demonstrate this commitment over time to fully recover from the controversy and resuscitate its image.

Businesses that enter new markets should view corporate philanthropy as an ongoing responsibility it has to the community. Business people should be aware, however, that there is a fine line between "giving back" to a community in an effort to be well regarded and being perceived as attempting to "buy" their way into a new market by trying to curry favor with potential customers.

Companies must decide for themselves what the acceptable trade-offs are between profitability and brand management. Occasionally, as was the case with Nike, the tangible bottom line can be enhanced while the brand's name—an extraordinarily important intangible—can be weakened.

PRODUCT CHARACTERISTICS

The final external factor regarding how to enter a new market concerns product characteristics. Depending on the product, it might be beneficial to have a local business either license the rights or manufacture the product. Products that could benefit from this situation are the less expensive products and those that are not as technically involved, such as soft drinks, clothes, and athletic shoes and apparel. More expensive goods, such as automobiles and computers, are usually exported.

It is also important to appreciate how people in different regions or of different ethnicities expect the product to be packaged or sold to them. For example, the San Francisco Giants gift shop at Pac Bell Park has to make sure it has plenty of plastic gift bags bearing the Giants logo. That's because people coming from Japan to see Japanese outfielder Tsuyoshi Shinjo are expected to bring back Giants gifts in the store's "official" bag. Not having the bag to bring the gift back in is inadequate because part of the gift-giving process is demonstrating that you went to the official store to make the purchase. If there are five Shinjo jerseys bought, the customer must have five bags to authenticate the purchase.

Nike understands the value of such customer experiences and relationships and utilizes soccer, the most popular sport in the world, as its "packaging" to help it authenticate its presence and penetrate certain global markets.

In vintage Nike fashion, it entered into the largest soccer sponsorship of all time: a marketing deal with England's Manchester United—one of sport's leading global brands—valued at nearly $430 million over 13 years. The Manchester United deal was not Nike's initial foray into international soccer. Nike signed its first major deal with InterMilan in 1994; this was followed a few years later when it agreed to a 10-year deal with the Brazilian National Soccer Team valued at $200 million.

Simply throwing hundreds of millions of dollars at a decidedly non-American sport would not guarantee success. Lacking an established and historical standing in the sport, many soccer fans and industry leaders viewed Nike's entry into the $2.5 billion soccer business as anything but delicate. Rather, Nike was thought to be attempting to buy into the sport's most coveted circles.

This frequently happens to businesses that venture into new areas in a heavy-handed fashion. However, as long as the company is genuine and its high-profile entrance into, and commitment to, a market is demonstrated over time, consumers will be inclined to give the company the benefit of the doubt.

Although some fans were undoubtedly dismayed to see the Nike swoosh on their team's jerseys at least the company sought to establish a long-term relationship with soccer fans. Conversely, local businesses that appear to only be interested in the customer's dollar—and not a long-term relationship—are undoubtedly harmed by their heavy-handed approach.

How do many consumers respond to that new neighborhood business when it sticks that "we're open for business" flyer on your car windshield? A common reaction is annoyance, especially when you only realize the flyer is on your windshield after you've closed the door and buckled your seatbelt. Not only is the announcement viewed as an inconvenience, but the flyers often litter the parking lot as well. This is hardly the way to make a great first impression.

By attaching itself to the soccer's leading global brands, as well as dedicating millions of dollars to product development and marketing, Nike increased its soccer revenue more than tenfold to $450 million in the seven years following the InterMilan deal, and hopes to double that revenue within a five-year span. This revenue increase is particularly impressive given the fact that the costs associated with playing soccer are minuscule relative to golf.

This rapid market penetration contributed to Adidas' decision to pay $70 million for a 10 percent stake in Germany's top soccer team, Bayern Munich.

In addition to its landmark deals with several of soccer's leading brand names, Nike has also attached itself—albeit indirectly—to the most popular sporting event in the world, soccer's World Cup.

The Fédération Internationale de Football Association (FIFA) has been soccer's governing body for almost 100 years and oversees the World Cup. FIFA had 15 corporate partners for the 2002 World Cup played in Japan and Korea, including MasterCard and adidas.

These corporate partners invest heavily in their relationship with the World Cup as an estimated 60 billion people watch at least some of the tournament. Because the World Cup is the world's most popular sporting event, it provides corporations an extraordinary opportunity to enhance their global profiles and increase brand awareness.

Adidas leveraged its official partner status by targeting those attending the games as well as those watching the worldwide TV broadcasts. Nike, which was not among the official corporate partners, was relegated to engaging in other marketing activities. Nike reportedly spent $155 million to promote the World Cup in 42 countries after spending only $5 million in 1994. By comparison, Adidas reportedly spent about $40 million. The World Cup final, which pitted the victorious Brazil (outfitted by Nike) against Germany (outfitted by Adidas), provided Nike yet another great—and global—marketing platform.

Nike has also recognized that an important part of its continued revenue growth will be a function of how it contributes to and underwrites the sport domestically. Nike is helping U.S. Soccer, the governing body that oversees amateur soccer, by funding teen development squads. Further, as part of its Manchester United sponsorship, Nike is paying about $1.4 million per year to help start a grassroots soccer program in England.

Nike believes that helping prepare American and British stars for global soccer markets will help reinforce its commitment and sense of belonging to the worldwide soccer community.

The amount of money pouring into soccer and golf (see the next section) forced Nike to curtail much of its domestic sponsorship spending at the professional sports league level.

MANAGEMENT OBJECTIVES AND MARKET SELECTION STRATEGY

The last two factors involved in penetrating new markets, management's objectives and market selection strategy, are both internal to the firm. Management's objectives rely heavily on the commitment of the firm to expand. If a firm does not want to take on the financial burden or risk, it might consider a joint venture with a company in the desired new market. If a firm is willing to take on the risk of entering a foreign market on its own and invest the necessary capital to establish itself, it can reap all of the rewards from its investment.

The final issue of market entry is that of market selection. With different types of risk associated with each market, a firm must determine the amount of risk it is willing to take. Firms that want to enter countries that have significant business risk might consider partnerships to minimize the downside. Although the risks might be different on the local level, for instance when a business considers expanding from Winston-Salem, North Carolina, to Chapel Hill, the same considerations must be made. Furthermore, if a firm wants to enter multiple new markets simultaneously, it might have to consider lower cost and lower risk markets so it will have the resources to implement a wider range of marketing programs.

Either way, a firm must decide how risk averse it is, analyze the risk of each potential company, and then allocate the resources needed for each foreign investment.

For Nike, this meant "joint venturing" with Tiger Woods. Hiring Woods as a global spokesman for the company enabled Nike to more easily penetrate foreign markets with the help of one of the most recognizable and decidedly international athletes in the world. Having each region of the world covered by a representative to whom local customers and suppliers can relate is very important. Woods delivers this "connection" through his ethnicity, global media exposure, and travel to tournaments on all corners of the globe. In essence, he is that believable, local salesman sought after by all companies.

In 2000, Nike renewed Woods' endorsement deal for another five years at an estimated $100 million. Even though golf doesn't garner the same global attention and fervor as soccer, Woods—himself a global brand—helps propel the brand into other foreign markets by virtue of his ability to authenticate all things Nike. Prior to Woods, Nike was seen as an athletic brand that offered golf-related products. However, their golf shoes were never taken seriously. With Woods, the company quickly became one of the sport's standard bearers; essentially a golf company all its own, supported by a world-class brand called Nike. To the extent Woods can extend his higher end consumer appeal to the global masses, Nike will thrive and continue to build global market share.

Not coincidentally, Tiger Woods switched from playing Titleist balls to the newly designed and manufactured Nike ball. Shortly after Woods made the change, and following his absolutely brilliant 2000 season in which he seemed to win every PGA event, Nike's share of the $1 billion golf market increased from 1 to 4 percent. This led total revenue for Nike Golf to increase 50 percent to $300 million. To Nike's delight, this revenue increase occurred while the percentage of Woods' golf product sold fell from 60 to about 15 percent.[2] He was indeed successful in branding the company's entire product line. The broad appeal of Nike Golf products allowed the company to nearly triple the number of retail stores stocking it.

How quickly will Nike carve out its fair share of this $2.5 billion annual market, particularly now that Woods has begun playing Nike's irons? Who said there could never be another Michael Jordan?

Although Nike golf also has David Duval as an endorser, the brand truly rests with Woods, which makes it tough on Nike, given that Woods hasn't immediately switched to their irons. Companies finding themselves in similar situations often must make sure that their brand messenger or conduit never becomes bigger than the product. Should the organization's "go-between," such as Woods, leave or lose credibility, the company would have a tough time maintaining the customers who bought in because of the relationship forged between the customers and the messenger.

---

2.   Dworkin, Andy, "Nike Mulls Over Tiger's Draw." *Portland Oregonian*, July 25, 2000, p. C1. The Oregonian © 2001 Oregonian Publishing Co. All rights reserved. Reprinted with permission.

Every year the local high school baseball team might have a bake sale. Besides the players' parents, the neighbors of some of the players on the team are usually the best customers because they have a communal relationship with the seller. If the baked goods being sold are mediocre, it's more likely that once the player-next-door is no longer a member of the team, the neighbor will be less likely to buy from team members with whom they are not familiar. These neighbors might instead prefer to wait for another community-driven event brought to them by familiar messengers: Girl Scout cookie season.

Familiarity is among the advantages athletes like Woods provide to global companies. He travels worldwide with great exposure and notoriety, making us feel as if we know him—as if he is our neighbor, not unlike those scruffy high school ballplayers or pigtailed little girls. Companies like Nike are able to take this phenomenon one step further: Unlike the neighborhood kids who grow up and head off to college, Woods' long-term contract with Nike ensures that he'll be hanging around the neighborhood for a very, very long time.

The local business can find its Tiger Woods by establishing relationships with noncompeting businesses in the area. This can take the form of a cross-promotion with another local business that has broad local appeal. Whatever the specific approach, a company must also realize that it can work to have numerous Tiger Woods in many regions; that is, people that have instant credibility in the business in that particular region. After all, rumor has it that there are more than a few Girl Scout troops.

EMERGING MARKETS

Once a firm commits to enter a new market, it enters a new phase marked by additional factors that make decision making increasingly complex. These factors, each of which has a significant impact on the marketing strategy, include technology, legal and ethical constraints, economic forces, customers, resource limitations, cultural and demographic influences, competition, and political forces.[3]

3. *Marketing Management* by Winer, Russell S. (pp. 441-445), Prentice Hall, 2000. © Adapted by permission of Pearson Education, Inc., Upper Saddle River, NJ.

Because technological infrastructures vary greatly from market to market, marketers are frequently forced to treat each country separately, realizing that inequities impact their strategic initiatives.

An example of this is vividly provided by Wal-Mart, whose supply chain management system in the United States has helped the company become successful. With each of its stores and distribution centers technologically connected, Wal-Mart is able to streamline inventory and become very cost-effective. Because this infrastructure is not available in all countries, Wal-Mart must analyze and decide which foreign markets could best suit its technological capabilities and needs. In addition to potential technological concerns, labor and transportation matters also routinely influence new market penetration.

Ethical constraints are also an issue for international marketers. It is very easy for a firm to exploit a foreign country given that market's working conditions. In foreign markets, certain actions could be seen as ethical, whereas those same actions might be deemed unacceptable by American standards. Therefore, it is critical to strike a balance between domestic and global business practices when utilizing resources from foreign markets.

Economic forces also cause problems for those marketing abroad. The financial problems of Southeast Asia in the late 1990s, for example, had a drastic impact on firms too reliant on that region. Accordingly, it remains crucial that a firm hedges its risk by conducting market research before allocating resources to a new market.

Many service-oriented businesses, such as delis and drug stores, routinely open in cities after a major defense contract is awarded to a large manufacturer. However, by incorrectly assessing the true economic impact of the new contract to the local community, small businesses might not accurately assess the demand for the products and services they hope to offer.

A hotel chain might also open a new franchise in town to take part in the anticipated economic revitalization linked to the construction of a new sports stadium. However, without properly analyzing how business will fare on nonevent nights, or by not fully appreciating the sheer number of events likely to be held at the new stadium and their impact on tourism, the hotel chain's management might just be setting itself up to fail.

The fourth force is the customer. In each country, customers put different values on different product attributes. It is up to the marketer to determine what these values are and then, by extension, how best to position their product to reach intended target markets.

For example, former Los Angeles Lakers star Magic Johnson has built a successful $500 million business—but not just because he brings national chains, like Starbucks, Loews movie theaters, and TGI Friday's, into inner-city neighborhoods. He goes one step further. Johnson has succeeded in positioning himself as the local "face" of these businesses, leading customers to believe that they have a local, high-profile advocate in their midst.

Before Johnson opened his first theater in 1994, he—at the last minute—told the manager that there had to be a strawberry drink among his fountain offerings because he believed many of his customers preferred the flavor. On the same point, his two TGI Friday's restaurants might have more fried foods than other Friday's franchises. His Starbucks might provide an ethnic favorite like a cobbler or pie. In short, he has succeeded, in part, because he has customized his product to meet customer preferences.

Natural, financial, and human resource limitations are also prevalent when marketing in a new area. For instance, if a firm entering a new market requires a certain skill set for its employees that cannot be satisfied in the local area due to language barriers or training costs, it could become cost-prohibitive for a company to conduct business in the region.

Many bobblehead dolls and sports figurines are made in China. Often, distributors that work in the United States are communicating with a manager overseas; a foreign manager who often conveys instructions to people who quite possibly have never seen much of the particular player whose likeness they are expected to reproduce.

When comic book mogul Todd McFarlane entered the sports action figure business, he immediately experienced trouble when attempting to have his product manufactured abroad.

For those making the figurines in China to have a better idea of how to scale the small water bottles that came attached to the figurines of hockey goalies, someone in McFarlane's company sent a water bottle to be mocked up. Soon, hundreds of the toys came back with small water bottles, except they all inadvertently had a Bell Helmets logo on them. This error was made because the particular water bottle that was sent had a Bell Helmets logo on it and it was incorrectly assumed that the logo was an essential marking on the toy. As it turns out, Bell Helmets has no relationship with the NHL, forcing the company to destroy the replica bottles.

The impact of cultural influences cannot be overstated. International marketers must carefully and with great tact adapt products, services, and, if need be, its own company culture to the local market culture if success is to be attained.

The competitive environment also presents challenges for international marketers. This competition comes not only from other firms trying to enter a new market, but also from local firms as well. Local firms routinely receive preferential treatment from local governments, resulting in a competitive advantage. Moreover, because government policies differ from country to country, firms must complete thorough due diligence to ensure that their core competencies will not and cannot be compromised by local political forces and relationships.

A different and ever-changing political environment also requires the undivided attention of marketers and frequently forces them to alter their strategy on a moment's notice. One recent example of this is the continued changes in the economic policies in India brought about by its government. This government interaction has forced many international firms to rethink their presence throughout the region, with many simply choosing to forgo business there entirely.

This framework for conducting international business applies quite well to the sports apparel industry. Until about 20 years ago, none of the major American companies, Nike included, had a significant presence in foreign markets. Even 10 years ago, less than a third of Reebok's and Nike's revenue was generated abroad. By 2001, those percentages grew to more than 40 percent for each company. Analysts now believe a majority of Nike's revenue will be generated abroad within a few years.

Conducting business abroad today, whether in the next city, county, country, or continent, brings with it significant challenges. Failing to understand the differences in market segments—whether consumer, supplier, or government-related—can devastate a company financially and harm its brand.

Successfully penetrating new markets requires tremendous planning, buttressed by finesse and tact. Focusing on the wants and needs of diverse customers, often against a backdrop of logistical and political uncertainties, remains one of business' largest challenges.

CHAMPIONSHIP POINTS

Nike's global strategy, one heavily supported by athletes and sports teams, allows businesses of all sizes to appreciate the attention to detail required when entering new markets.

Executives, whether working for transnationals like Nike or local mom-and-pops, recognize that to compete successfully abroad, they must do the following:

- Never "pull an Incubus." Allocate the necessary time and resources to understanding the market you hope to penetrate. This does not mean that a company should push the limits of "paralysis by analysis," simply that adequate preparation will pay huge dividends.

- Study the rulebook. Realize that the rules of the game can be quite different in new markets. Simply shifting an existing strategy probably won't get the job done abroad.

- Know the dominant entertainment in their world. Whether a company is the 800-pound gorilla or the struggling sole proprietorship, it must recognize the appropriate platforms from which it can grow its business.

- Appreciate the nuances of "foreign" markets. Companies of all sizes must exert tremendous care whenever directly or indirectly on the global stage. Initiatives outside of a company's core territory can lead to high-profile failures that will limit its ability to enter a market in the future.

- Understand that allocating responsibility to different regions ultimately won't deflect attention—positive or negative—from the home office.

- Be your own Jim Keady. Take charge of addressing business challenges before others do it for you. In the long run, it will not only be cheaper, but will also lead to better brand management.

- Get involved in the community. Investing time and money in the communities in which the new markets are located favorably positions companies as good corporate citizens.

- Realize that expanding abroad by sending shipments or simply buying ad space in a new market might convince a company that it has arrived in a new market. However, not until a company establishes the requisite relationships and creates the proper infrastructure for close contacts between the company and its new local suppliers will customers know it exists.

■ Seek credible product and brand messengers, individuals who lend the organization not just recognizability, but also the all-important credibility needed to establish and reinforce important business relationships.

Businesses desiring to sell products and services beyond their home markets often find it to be an insurmountable challenge. However, those organizations that succeed in doing so often establish a recognizable, global brand name in the process, much to the delight of shareholders.

The ability to successfully penetrate new markets—or grow the business in general—is but one, albeit critical, component in the brand-building process.

9 BUILDING A BRAND

The Point: Establishing, building, and extending a brand, regardless of whether the brand in question is a traditional business or one linked to sports, requires ongoing, hands-on management and leadership at every turn. Brand building visionaries protect their brand at all costs, even if doing so requires micromanagement. A company's reputation and integrity with consumers takes years to develop but only minutes to undermine as evidenced throughout the sports world.

Finding a universally accepted definition of the word *brand* and the associated process known as *branding* has been about as hard as coming to a consensus among sports fans about the best team of all time. You can argue all you want about the great dynasties fielded by the Yankees, Boston Celtics, San Francisco 49ers, and Montreal Canadiens, but, like great sports teams, the notion of brands and branding has meant different things to different people.

Over the last decade, numerous academicians and practitioners have undertaken the daunting task of getting their hands around the increasingly important practice of branding. They have done so at a time when business has been moving at the speed of light. One day, bellwether brands are rock solid, the next day they are on the ropes, facing a federal investigation or hoping to avert bankruptcy following a freefall in their market capitalization.

Successful branding efforts attract attention to an organization and help paint the company's picture for the consumer, inspiring loyalty to the company's products and services in the process. Once branded, these well-positioned brands command a premium price among customers and increase shareholder value.

The inherent value of branding is often realized when analyzing the decision-making process of consumers, particularly when they are considering the merits of largely indistinguishable products. Chesebrough-Ponds, the maker of Q-tips, provides a compelling example of this marketing phenomenon. Despite the fact that competing products, such as the generic supermarket chain variety, are quite similar, many consumers prefer to pay a little extra for the Q-tip name and the quality the brand name implies.

Catchy or creative brand names and logos also contribute to brand value, especially for fledgling companies hoping to compete with larger, well-regarded brands. Karen and Kevin Push walked into Bad Ass Coffee Co., whose motto is "Coffee with an Attitude" in Kona, Hawaii, because they were initially amused by the name. Days later, the two bought the store and went on to become the company's first franchisees. Today there are about 20 Bad Ass franchises and, although the name certainly helps get customers in the door, Bad Ass executives know that they won't keep them if their products or customer service are inferior.

In the sports world, a fashionable logo for a minor league team without a large national fan base—like the Carolina Mudcats or the Rancho Cucamonga Quakes—helps the team earn additional money through merchandise sales. Although only a single part of the branding equation, great logos, whether attached to companies or sports teams, significantly impact brand value. Like other branding elements, a compelling logo alone will not help an organization develop and reinforce its brand if the products or services it offers are lacking. For major sports brands, such as professional sports franchises, to foster loyalty among fans they must consistently deliver a compelling entertainment experience that fans feel vested in. Such is the case with the Yankees, Cowboys, and Lakers, among others.

FutureBrand, a company that assists in valuing brands, determined the value of each domestic professional sports franchise and brand by calculating the revenue and profit stream generated by the brand and the strength or degree of risk of the brand in its market in relation to competitors.

Specifically, FutureBrand considered a team's popularity, fan base, and factors that affected fan interest, size of media market, winning percentage, stadium operations, and the growth of the particular sport. This criteria, when taken as a group, suggests that great brands combine a committed customer base with a solid product supported by savvy marketing.

According to the study (see Table 9-1), the Yankees brand alone, which includes the blue and white interlocking "NY" and the team name itself, was worth $334 million in 2002, placing the team's brand in the same value category as Bose or Four Seasons Hotels.[1]

TABLE 9-1   Top-Ranked Sports Brand Values

RANK	SPORTS FRANCHISE	VALUE (US $M)
1	New York Yankees	334
2	Dallas Cowboys	300
3	Los Angeles Lakers	272
4	New York Knicks	236
5	Washington Redskins	191
6	New York Giants	167
7	Chicago Bulls	156
8	New York Rangers	155
9	Green Bay Packers	153
10	Detroit Red Wings	152

The Cowboys brand was second at $300 million, followed by the Lakers at $272 million. Not surprisingly, all three teams have won at least three championships over the past 10 years. If and when any of these teams are sold, their brand value will make up a significant part of the sales price.

There is much to be learned from observing America's greatest brands, including the aforementioned sports franchises that recognize that they, like the leagues in which they play, have become valuable brand names.

---

1. Rovell, Darren. "What's in a name? For Yankees, about $334 million." ESPN.com, July 10, 2002.

THE BRANDING PROCESS

Despite the trials and tribulations of some of the truly great old-school brands, like Coca-Cola, as well as those created during the new economy, such as Google.com, several consistent attributes of brands and the branding process have gelled. Consequently, an activity once relegated to consumer product companies hawking packaged goods, branding now applies to every aspect of business, including employees and executives who seek to establish and maintain their own brand names.

Branding is critically important to businesses, both large and small, because it contributes to business success. Consider the neighborhood toy store that is forced to compete with a recently opened franchise giant such as Toys R' Us. Toys R' Us orders greater quantities of each product than the single, local toy store and therefore can sell the identical product for less. It might also boast a greater variety of products. However, the local store can keep its customer base if has branded itself well. Branding attributes that enable some businesses to be successful include a comfortable atmosphere and shopping experience, friendly local characters behind the counter that everyone seems to know, and a long-standing presence in, and commitment to, the community.

According to *The Evolving Nature of Branding: Consumer and Managerial Considerations,* six stages of brand evolution exist.[2] These stages have not only been an integral part of the most valuable brands in the world, but they also continue to influence these brands' mind share, stock price, and, in the case of sports, corporate and everyday fan bases. Most organizations, including sports teams and leagues, aspire to stage five of the following branding process.

Stage one consists of unbranded goods that are typically treated as commodities. Rarely a part of developed economies, producers make little effort to distinguish or brand their goods with the result that the customer's perception of the good is utilitarian. In this stage commodities are fungible, interchangeable goods that customers are unable to distinguish between. When was the last time you cared about what brand of ice you were buying?

---

2.   de Chernatony, L., and McEnally, M. © *The 1999 Academy of Marketing Science*. The Academy of Marketing Science.

In the second stage, the "brand as reference" stage, the brand name is often that of the producer or manufacturer. The name is used for identification; any advertising support focuses on rational attributes (i.e., "gets clothes cleaner"). Over time, the name becomes the guarantee of quality or consistency, such as Gold Medal Flour. When a brand has reached this stage, a consumer might decide to purchase the known brand (Q-tip) over the identical supermarket variety, believing that the brand name is of better quality.

In stage three, the "brand as personality" stage, the brand name might "stand alone," with its marketing support focusing on emotional appeal or product benefits. An example of this would be that "Caring mothers use Ivory Soap." This stage in the branding process begins to link the product with customer attributes, providing an added dimension to the purchasing process.

In the fourth stage, the consumer now "owns" the brand. This is known as the "brand as icon" stage, in which the brand taps into higher order values of society and its advertising assumes a close relationship with consumers. Often established internationally, the use of symbolic brand language is prevalent. The legendary Marlboro Man falls neatly into this category. Local businesses reach this stage when the community readily recognizes its logos, mascots, or taglines with no further reference to the company.

"Brand as company," the fifth branding stage, is highlighted by brands that have a complex identity, and consumers tend to assess this identity very carefully. Because consumers are actively involved in the brand-creation process, the company needs to focus on its consumer base and utilize an integrated communication strategy to embrace them. For instance, customers at IKEA participate in all stages of the planning and purchase process. They are willing to be involved in the product design process by designing their own kitchen cabinets from modular units or choosing fabrics for the furniture they are purchasing. They further participate in the process by transporting and assembling their own product.

Few companies have sought and entered the sixth stage, the "brand as policy" stage, which is defined by a strong alignment of the company with ethical, social, and political causes. "Spokes-companies," such as Benetton—which says it believes that "all human beings are born free and equal in dignity and rights"—are essentially owned by customers who are committed to the company's philosophy. Many consumers purchase the products of brands such as Ben

& Jerry's or the Body Shop because they agree with and support the political and social positions taken by these companies.

For a corporation to successfully brand itself and fall into the "brand as icon" or "brand as company" category, it must consistently and over time deliver and reinforce the marketing message and product attributes. Successful branding takes time and long-term commitment. Establishing a brand requires investment spending, including both the allocation of financial and human resources. It also helps to have a visionary leader at the helm.

ESTABLISHING A BRAND

Great brands don't appear overnight; they evolve over time through a combination of timely and insightful decision making, as well as through great, visionary leadership that has the ability to turn potential problems into opportunities.

In 1903, William Davidson and Arthur Harley, 21 and 20 years old, respectively, went into the motorcycle business. Their first motorcycle had a mere two-horsepower engine and was made from scrap metal—including a carburetor made out of a tomato can. The two, along with a friend, consistently tinkered with the product design. By year's end they had sold a grand total of three motorcycles. Through road races and motorcycle contests, the Harley-Davidson name quickly became well known. The entrepreneurs learned much from these events that helped shape the brand, especially that motorcycle riders preferred the thundering noise associated with the bikes, which has since become a hallmark of Harley-Davidson motorcycles.

By the company's 10th anniversary, 200 Harley dealers had opened nationwide and exports to Japan were well underway. Seven years later, Harley-Davidson was the largest motorcycle manufacturer in the world. The brand established and then subsequently reinforced itself throughout business and industry, as evidenced by its motorcycles being used by both police and the military, especially during both World Wars.

By 1947, the Harley-Davidson brand had become synonymous with rebellion and toughness. Those wanting to communicate these traits simply wore the Harley-Davidson jacket, prominently displaying the now familiar orange and black logo. For the next half-century, the Harleys never stopped evolving. The organization always paid keen attention to new technology and widened its customer base by creating low-end $4,400 bikes and high-end $20,000-plus custom-made models for corporate executives. However, it wasn't always a free ride. Harley CEO Jeff Blaustein saw the company nearly collapse twice during his 26-year Harley-Davidson career.

Since going public in 1986, the company's share price rose 15,000 percent through 2001, partly because it intensified fandom by establishing the Harley Owners Group (H.O.G.), which has more than 650,000 members who meet at organized motorcycle get-togethers and tours around the country. These events encourage prospective new riders to give a Harley a test drive by offering riding lessons through its "Rider's Edge" program. *Forbes* named the company the 2001 Company of the Year after it announced record revenue for the 16th straight year.

Although not every great global brand starts off with a tomato can for a carburetor, most indeed recognize the inherent value in, and believe in the marketability of, their evolving—if not entirely unproven—product.

The NBA was created in the summer of 1948 as a 17-team product resulting from the mergers of the Basketball Association of America and the National Basketball League. At best, the NBA was at stage two of the branding process, an upstart league elbowing for position against other, more established sports leagues of all types. Unlike MLB, which was approaching its 50th anniversary, the NHL, which had been in existence for more than three decades, and the NFL, which was coming to the end of its second decade of play, the fledgling NBA was a generic product in search of an identity.

Not only did these established leagues have a tremendous head start in securing the hearts, minds, and wallets of sports fans, they were doing so while cashing in on the evolving importance of the media. By the mid-1930s, baseball was America's sport, its popularity evidenced by the fact that it sold the presenting radio broadcast rights to the World Series to the Ford Motor Company for $400,000.

Similarly, NFL Commissioner Pete Rozelle knew that popularity of his sport was linked to television. Rozelle signed a two-year, $4.7 million contract with CBS in 1962. The NBA was clearly in the NFL's shadows, as television contracts from 1952 to 1962 with Dumont Broadcasting and NBC didn't garner much attention or produce much revenue.

It was evident to the NBA by the mid-1970s that it was no longer competing with other upstart basketball leagues. Rather, it was battling the already established sports leagues for the almighty TV dollar.

The NBA became a virtual hoops monopoly in 1976 by purchasing the rights to four teams from the American Basketball Association, its main competitor. Somewhat unwittingly, it also transitioned itself from "brand as reference" to "brand as personality." Many have said that today's major professional sports leagues don't mesh with the business world because they are monopolies. Because monopolistic power is not set in stone, had the NBA failed to evolve into a great brand, another challenger could have emerged to take a piece of basketball's pie. Although positioned to begin marketing a consistent message that included the publicizing of its teams and star athletes, the NBA still found itself locked in a battle for fan support with baseball and football, which were providing sports fans with memorable World Series and Super Bowls throughout the decade.

On the way to the top, many brands falter. In the face of failure, or perhaps even consistent mediocrity, brands that make it are those that learn to evolve and find meaningful solutions to pressing problems. Many companies that relied on selling products nationwide over the phone or through mail order faced such a moment as a result of the explosive popularity of the Internet. For many of those organizations that failed to allocate the resources necessary to establish an adequate presence on the World Wide Web, surviving in the digital economy became a major challenge.

The NBA's struggle for legitimacy in the early 1980s caused the league to hemorrhage financially, leading it to amass between $80 million and $90 million in deferred payments owed to players and other creditors. In addition to major financial difficulties brought about by rising player salaries and increased travel costs due to league expansion, the NBA was plagued by drug problems and waning credibility—prohibiting it from reaching "brand as icon" status. The NBA's fan base, both corporate and individual, was unwilling to fully embrace the league, for doing so might harm their own reputations and brand names.

The NBA's television partner, CBS, thought so little of the NBA in the early 1980s that game six of the 1980 NBA Finals, when Magic Johnson scored 40 points and Jamaal Wilkes added 37 to lead the Lakers over the Philadelphia 76ers, was shown on tape delay. Game six of Larry Bird's first Finals was similarly tape delayed, so as not to conflict with CBS' broadcasting of *Magnum P.I.*, *Ladies and Gentleman*, and *Bob Newhart*. A year later, game six between Larry Bird's

Boston Celtics and the 76ers was preempted by a rerun of *Dallas*, which was followed by *Nurse*.

It was at this critical juncture in the league's evolution that it not only needed—but also required—a visionary leader who understood the inherent value in brand building.

BRAND-BUILDING VISIONARIES

For any brand to become a good and eventually a great one, it needs more than just a brand steward, it needs a brand visionary. The NBA's visionary has been, and continues to be, Commissioner David Stern.

The NBA has established itself over the last 18 years as a premiere brand under Stern's noteworthy leadership. He previously served as the league's general counsel and executive vice president, which helped him comprehend the NBA's standing in the sports and business industries, as well as the challenges it faced.

Thanks to Stern's vision and skills as a consensus builder, the NBA rebounded and began to gain marketing and financial momentum. This momentum was a direct result of two major developments in 1983 in which Stern, then legal counsel to the NBA, was instrumental. The league implemented a salary cap and established professional sports' first leaguewide drug policy. Had the NBA failed to establish an acceptable level of financial stability and credibility, neither sponsors nor fans would have supported the league by purchasing advertising time or game tickets. This marked the beginning of Stern's keen ability to develop and manage the NBA brand. His brand-building and management acumen was so widely heralded that *The Sporting News* named him the sixth most powerful person in sports during the 20th century.

Further, by leveraging the NBA's emerging talent—its brand messengers—most notably Magic Johnson, Larry Bird, and, years later, Michael Jordan, and by expanding television audiences, Stern was successful in quadrupling league revenue.

Stern and the NBA were also immeasurably helped by the fact that all but one of the NBA Finals played during his first decade as commissioner included at least one of these stars. Further, from 1980–2002, 22 of 23 NBA Finals matchups featured at least one team in the country's four most populous cities—New York, Los Angeles, Chicago, or Houston. This enabled the NBA to become and remain a sport with personality and success linked to, and reinforced by, a mere handful of superstars and the large markets in which they played.

Some might argue that the NBA was lucky and that its brand was created and subsequently strengthened by fortuitous developments beyond its control—such as having the most desirable teams make it to the finals, the league's showcase that exposed the sport to the greatest amount of (potential) fans.

However, even skeptics who subscribe to this line of thinking must recognize that "good luck" doesn't necessarily or automatically translate to successful brand building. Rather, brand managers who put their brand in position "to get lucky" and know how to capitalize off that luck establish and extend the most revered brands.

A red Swingline stapler appeared in the movie *Office Space*. Although the 1999 film, which later became a "cult classic," bombed at the box office, it was very successful when it came out on video. The stapler was among the prized possessions of one of the movie's main characters, Milton, who spent too much time making sure none of his coworkers would steal it. As the movie gained momentum as a cult classic, people started calling the company asking for the red staplers. However, the stapler's color was the brainchild of the movie's prop manager and not the company. Consequently, Swingline didn't have any red staplers for sale. The company, rather than shrugging off the situation as bad luck, began making red staplers available and also made them easy to locate by featuring them on the company's Web site.

The NBA and Stern swiftly extended the NBA's brand awareness by creating its own "red stapler," when the league undertook creative marketing and management initiatives that made consumers recognize and remember the NBA. Exciting made-for-TV events like the All-Star Game, Slam Dunk contest, and the NBA draft helped build marketing momentum and contributed legitimacy to the league's first great advertising campaign, which included the brilliant tagline, "The NBA. . .It's 'Fan'tastic!'" He also allocated money and resources to grassroots, public-service-oriented programs, especially those with a "stay-in-school" theme. Stern believed it was never too early to begin cultivating the next generation of fans.

During the years the marketing and advertising campaigns ran—accentuated by the play of Johnson, Bird, and Jordan—average game attendance increased 44 percent to just over 16,000.

From that point forward, Stern continued to craft the NBA's brand image, shaping fans beliefs and positive attitudes about the league. He worked hard to parlay this emerging image into brand equity, creating tremendous goodwill that added to the overall value of the league in the minds of fans and sponsors alike. Once achieved, Stern reinforced the positioning of the brand and leveraged it to make all those associated with sports, especially the broadcast TV networks, brand loyal to the NBA. He did this by adding additional NBA-themed programming, increasing the number and quality of foreign players in the NBA, and implementing a fully integrated merchandising strategy.

Stern's stewardship has been instrumental in establishing, maintaining, and extending important and lucrative league relationships on a global basis. The NBA has accomplished its lofty position by successfully marketing an ever-evolving brand to worldwide corporate partners while creating internal media outlets that protect the brand by furthering its positive perception, particularly NBA Entertainment and NBA.com. Stern understands, perhaps better than any sports executive, that how he and his staff continue to refine and position the brand will determine its long-term viability. However, the more powerful and visible a brand such as the NBA is, the more its image can be tarnished by a collection of seemingly minor indiscretions, breaches in integrity, or lapses in judgment. In some instances, it is a case of the bigger they are, the harder they fall.

The Product's Role in Branding

It's often easy to forget that those who work for your brand, ranging from retail clerks and office administrators to board members, are also representatives of it. In sports, it is often the case that prominent star players are as much a part of the product—if not more—as any league or team employee.

Johnson and Bird were the league's initial product managers and global messengers, serving as the NBA's ambassadors by consistently demonstrating on national TV just how exciting and entertaining the league could be.

As important as Magic's Lakers winning the five championships (1980, 1982, 1985, 1987, and 1988) and Bird's Celtics winning three (1981, 1984, and 1986) were during the decade, these incredible accomplishments were somehow overshadowed by a development that occurred during Stern's first full year as commissioner.

The Chicago Bulls selected North Carolina's Michael Jordan with the third pick in the 1984 draft (behind Sam Bowie and Hakeem Olajuwon). The red-sneaker-wearing, tongue-wagging, and frequently airborne Jordan initially supplemented, but then quickly surpassed, the achievements of Bird and Johnson. Collectively, these three enabled the NBA to emerge from the 1980s as "brand as icon," rivaling the extraordinary success of the NFL and MLB.

Not only don't "regular" businesses have a traditional (employee/player) draft; some also lack the opportunity to always attract the smartest, most qualified candidates. Clearly this is not the case with the NBA, where all the world's best basketball players swarm to the league. However, in much the same way there are great products that fail because of any combination of factors including lack of foresight, inadequate distribution channels, and the inability to adapt to change, the NBA became the power it did because it successfully leveraged Jordan by providing the ideal platform for the league's greatest product.

For more than a decade, Michael Jordan was the NBA and the NBA was Michael Jordan. Whatever the reasons, he became interchangeable with the league—as much a part of the brand as the omnipresent swoosh is to Nike. He also quickly came to transcend sports, entertainment, race, and big business, leading even sociologists to weigh in on the role of Jordan in American society.

Because of his unique ability to transcend sports, Jordan was able to assist the NBA in transforming itself into such a great global brand. To some, seeing Jordan wasn't about seeing basketball. Rather, it was about watching the personification of grace, beauty, and physical domination. In essence, Jordan's product attributes rivaled those associated with other great global brands.

Could there exist a better advocate for the NBA than Jordan? Stern, in his wildest dreams, could not have concocted a more universally appealing figure to assist in extending the NBA brand. Stern systematically established the NBA brand name while Jordan instantaneously extended it.

People who previously had a "take it or leave it" attitude about sports—and basketball in particular—were tuning in to watch games. They were showing up at arenas all over the country. In fact, thousands of once-apathetic fans showed up in droves, genuinely hoping to see Jordan shine even if it meant a loss for the home team.

Jordan demonstrated that great brands can transcend the actual product being marketed and attract a larger customer base in the process. In Jordan's case it wasn't about the game anymore, it was about the grace, the dunks, the beauty—Jordan was as much an art form as he was an athlete.

Mention was made in Chapter 8 about how it can be detrimental if and when the messenger overshadows the product. In rare cases, like Jordan's relationship with the NBA, having a messenger who transcends the product—in this case professional basketball—can actually be beneficial, provided the messenger is also the product.

Seattle Supersonics owner Howard Schultz's company, Starbucks, presents a vivid business example of this branding experience.

To some, the ubiquitous coffee chain is their favorite destination—but not necessarily because of its mocha frappuchinos or double lattes. Some Starbucks customers frequent the coffee chain because of its environment—the comfortable chairs, the music (they sell their own collection of it), and at some locations, computers with high-speed Internet access. Thanks to this atmosphere, Starbucks became one of the interview rooms of choice for office-less dot-com executives interviewing future employees in the late 1990s. Students set up shop at Starbucks to study in much the way families visit McDonald's to bring their kids to the Playlands or PlayPlaces that adjoined thousands of the fast food restaurants nationwide.

Stern knew that the more he allowed Jordan the limelight, the better both he and the league looked. In essence, Stern continued to build the brand and increase revenue by simply yielding the floor to Jordan. As a savvy brand manager, Stern knew how and when to let the NBA's branding process evolve with the help of the world's most popular athlete.

From the time Jordan won NBA Rookie of the Year honors for the 1984–1985 season, until the end of the 1980s, overall NBA attendance rose nearly 50 percent and the Bulls became the NBA's most popular road team. In the Windy City, the Bulls alone sold out more games in an 18-month period from 1987–1988 than they had in their entire 22-year history. Simultaneously, the NBA's gross revenues nearly doubled to $300 million, in large part due to the game's explosive growth on network and cable TV.

When David Stern became commissioner in 1984, TV rights netted the league approximately $20 million annually. Due to the growing interest in the NBA from fans and advertisers, the networks began to shower the league with money. Five years later, NBC outbid longtime partner CBS by paying $150 million a year for the next four years.

In early 2002, the NBA negotiated its new TV contract, one that even in tough economic times, slightly surpassed its previous four-year, $2.64 billion deal by signing new TV partners, ESPN/ABC and AOL Time Warner to a six-year, $4.6 billion deal through the 2007-08 season. (For additional details on this strategic alliance, please see Chapter 6.)

(Micro) Managing the Brand

Just as positive product attributes, such as the NBA's Johnson, Bird, and Jordan, help strengthen brands, detrimental product attributes can play an equally important, although negative role, in shaping an organization's brand.

Every time an NBA player is cited for what otherwise would have been a private transgression, the NBA's brand is at stake. It's something that the league is growing accustomed to, having cut its teeth on Dennis Rodman, Allen Iverson, and a tumultuous 2002 offseason that included the murder of league veteran Bison Dele and former New Jersey Nets center Jayson Williams being named a prime murder suspect in a separate case.

To counterbalance brand bruisers such as the tattoo-laden Rodman, the NBA's entertainment arm produces its own "virgin" content. In the past, producers with the TV show *Inside Stuff*, an NBA Entertainment production, have been told that any player who has had trouble with the law in recent weeks cannot be featured on the show.

The NBA even created an education program designed to acquaint first-year players with the social and financial issues they will face once they enter the league. The Rookie Orientation Program acquaints players with issues ranging from sexual harassment, sexually transmitted diseases, and anger management, to personal financial issues including taxation, investing, and saving for the future. This program is in place to protect the brand from those rookies that don't yet know or appreciate the importance of it.

Throughout corporate training programs, a strong emphasis must similarly be placed on assessing the appropriate amount and degree of internal, as well as external brand management.

Attempting to control or otherwise micromanage the brand has sometimes landed the NBA in hot water. For instance, thanks to the fine art of airbrushing, rapper Allen Iverson appeared sans earrings, necklace, and tattoos, in the holiday edition of the 1999–2000 version of *Hoop Magazine*, an official league publication.

Perceived by many in mainstream America as a menace, Iverson's attitude and lifestyle was unlikely at the time to play in Peoria or on Madison Avenue for that matter. When advertisers see Iverson's tattoos and cornrows and learn of his ever-increasing police record, many organizations, including the NBA, feel as though he is simply too controversial or risky to prominently associate with their brands. Although one of the NBA's tasks is to manufacture stars, often by sanitizing their image and attempting to polish their reputations, it must be careful when doing so, so as not to alienate a portion of the fan base that relishes these players' incredible skill, regardless of the marketing baggage they possess.

For his part, Iverson responded by stating that he is who he is and that nobody can change that. He was also curious to know who gave the NBA the authority to attempt to remake his image. In essence, Iverson was concerned that others were inappropriately, and without his permission, repositioning his personal brand.

League officials said it shouldn't have happened and that the league would promote Iverson for who he is. A previous editor of the magazine spoke about the "Allen Iverson rule," which was a movement to keep him off the cover since 1996.

Because brand building is all about creating a positive and lasting impression with customers, occasionally, as was the case with Iverson, the NBA felt compelled to covertly manage its brand. Attempting to polish the image of a high-profile employee without his or her knowledge contributes to making the brand in part something that it's not, which ultimately harms the brand in the eyes of many potential and existing customers.

Reebok, which paid Iverson as an endorser, stayed with him despite the controversial lyrics on his rap album, because the company believed he was the perfect spokesman for rebellious, urban youth. Somewhat to the chagrin of the NBA, by 2001 *Time* magazine was hailing Iverson as "America's Greatest Athlete." This chagrin was front and center again in July 2002 when Iverson was once again arrested, this time on no fewer than 14 felony and misdemeanor charges stemming from an altercation in which he brandished a gun.

Although all of these charges were dropped two months later, Iverson had reinforced his rebellious nature.

The challenge for businesses, whether preserving or building their brand, is to encourage individualism among employees, while managing their employees to make sure that their individualism doesn't compromise the organization's bond with the customer.

Forget Joltin' Joe DiMaggio; that phrase you're hearing from corporate America is, "Where have you gone, Michael Jordan?"

BRAND CONSTITUENTS

Brand constituents are stakeholders that have a vested interest in the positioning, managing, and extending of the brand. These constituents have traditionally been customers and shareholders. In the case of the NBA, its owners and individual players are among those that just happen to play both roles.

For businesses of all sizes, employees are extremely important brand constituents. A store can appear to be the best and most convenient one in the town, but if customer service is lacking, no one is going to return. When a customer walks into a business establishment and the bell rings, a brand builder realizes the importance of his or her employee's responsiveness, as well as his or her willingness and ability to help the customer.

The Dallas Mavericks main maverick, team owner Mark Cuban, has been an unbelievable brand manager. Cuban, realizing that his team's brand value remains largely in the hands of his employees—the players—treats them extraordinarily well, paying close attention to any and all requests. Although attempts at giving his players electronic gadgets, personal shoppers, and nutritionists have failed due to league salary cap constraints, any visiting NBA player will tell you that the American Airlines Center, where the Dallas Mavericks play, has the best amenities of any arena in the league.

Thanks in large part to his employees' high morale and his "winning is everything" attitude, the Dallas Mavericks (whose recent record of futility is only surpassed by the Los Angeles Clippers), made the playoffs in the 2000–2001 season for the first time in 11 years.

Cuban subscribes to the notion that his employees are critical to presenting a professional and successful brand. Further, he believes that his players not only determine his team's brand, but also measurably impact the overriding NBA brand.

Brand managers who also take a turn at being an employee gain respect among those constituents who determine the brand's fate. In the process, these managers also gain valuable insight from customers about their likes and dislikes about the product offering. Many also emerge from the process as critically important brand constituents of their own. In fact, Cuban himself has assumed the role of a major brand constituent of the NBA—and of David Stern in particular.

By regularly and publicly voicing his opinion on the NBA brand and its direction, Cuban has drawn both praise and criticism for his efforts. Highlighting issues dealing with game operations, officiating, travel, and the overall marketing of the game, Cuban called upon Stern to develop a culture of excellence that works to control the NBA's destiny rather than being at the whim of media cycles.

Nonetheless, Cuban was fined $505,000 for his indiscretions, including four fines for criticizing officials, and one $100,000 fine for sitting on the baseline for a game against the Minnesota Timberwolves.

Cuban almost matched his 2001–2002 fine total in one fell swoop when he was fined $500,000 by the league the next season for telling a reporter that Ed Rush, the NBA's head of officials, "couldn't manage a Dairy Queen." The league obviously didn't appreciate that Cuban displayed his disgust of officiating in a public forum, but Cuban insisted that he went through the league and that they only listen when the world knows about it. Cuban accepted a tongue-and-cheek challenge from Dairy Queen to manage one of its restaurants for a few hours. With the sports media congregated outside a Texas Dairy Queen, Cuban took the opportunity to discuss the need for reform in the NBA with the media after his shift had ended.

Cuban matched his NBA fines with donations to charities, including a cancer fund, because Dallas Mavericks head coach Don Nelson spent the 2000–2001 season battling the disease and his wife spent much of the following season also stricken by it. After the World Trade Center bombing on September 11, 2001, Cuban was among the first to donate following the tragedy, giving $1 million to New York City. His leadership by example highlighted his commitment to public service and enabled him to reinforce his standing as a good corporate citizen. Philanthropic involvement such as this, especially when it is undertaken with no expectation of reciprocation, contributes to a brand's value.

Is Cuban a brand builder or brand meddler? Although he clearly cares as much about the game as Stern and superstar Michael Jordan, his new-guard methods of guerrilla communication squarely place the onus of managing a collective, leaguewide message on the NBA league office. Should the league not handle the situation to the satisfaction of its constituents, its brand name could suffer.

Granted Mark Cuban is not your run-of-the-mill brand constituent. Nonetheless, his keen interest in protecting and improving all aspects of the NBA brand are important to note. This is especially the case because he is a high-profile constituent whose opinion carries as much weight as consumer advocacy groups or disgruntled patrons would with any other business. Learning how to identify and diffuse the issues raised by potentially harmful constituents is critical for any brand seeking acclaim, regardless of its size and whether the acclaim it seeks is local or on a global scale.

MAINTAINING THE MESSAGE

Failing to consistently and, over time, deliver and reinforce the marketing message and product attributes, or, worse yet, providing mixed marketing messages, routinely diminishes brands. This is not to say that marketing and advertising campaigns must remain static; merely that the inherent message contained within these branding vehicles communicates and reinforces the message.

Any disruption or inconsistency in the branding process undermines an organization's ability to establish its brand. Such disruptions or inconsistencies consist of any development that breaks the branding chain.

For example, the branding process can be detrimentally influenced when a competing product is present. Alternatively, the branding process can also be negatively impacted in the event the core brand and its attributes are not consistently presented. An example of this is the omission of the brand in any brand-building opportunity. Because the NBA was all about Jordan, failing to include him in NBC's promotion of upcoming Bulls games would result in a missed opportunity to reinforce the NBA's brand and its close association with Jordan. Similarly, should McDonald's, one of the companies Jordan endorsed, not feature him in a promotional campaign targeting sports fans, it would be missing a golden opportunity to connect its brand to Jordan's.

Because the brand resides within the hearts and minds of (prospective) customers, any confusion in the marketplace will assuredly impact the value of the organization in the consumers' mind. For example, avid NBA fans, loyal purchasers of Nike footwear and apparel, and especially Nike, would be dismayed to learn that Michael Jordan was promoting Reebok. In an effort to ensure that its customers do not become confused, most corporations require athletes to avoid such conflicts of interest by agreeing to exclusively endorse a specific product or product line for a defined period of time in exchange for certain consideration.

Similarly, it is critical that when sports leagues rely on athletes to assist in the branding process, this symbiotic relationship not be interrupted. Should an interruption take place, a league must confront numerous public and private challenges; challenges that impact marketing, financial, and human resources—and threaten the integrity of the brand.

For example, the reputation and standing of the league in the marketplace and among key industry stakeholders will be affected. Those impacted by any branding inconsistency or interruption include, but are not limited to, (potential) customers at all levels of the buying process (i.e., TV networks, sponsors, and fans), competitors, other sports marketing channels, athletes, and employees.

By the time Jordan retired for the second time at the end of the 1997–1998 season, the NBA was also dealing with the lockout of its players, which postponed the start of the season from November to January. This combination, along with the increasing ticket prices seen throughout much of pro sports, alienated fans and was reflected in a decline in attendance.

More ominous than fewer fans in attendance was the decline in the sport's TV ratings. With roughly 75 percent of the NBA's TV revenue generated during the championship series, the NBA was hit hard as ratings fell to levels not witnessed since the Bulls won their first title in 1991. Overall, the NBA, NBC, and TNT had to adjust to six to eight million fewer households watching league games, and presumably buying less league merchandise. In addition to reduced viewership, and due to the emergence of such urban brands as FUBU and the prevalence of nonlicensed "knock-off" NBA products, gross retail sales of NBA-licensed products plummeted more than 50 percent between 1995 and 1999, and totaled $1 billion by 1999.

Most industry observers believed that the only way to resurrect the sagging fortunes of the NBA was to anoint a new Jordan, a process that never fully took hold following his first retirement after the 1992–1993 season. However, the question of just which player that would or should be consumed the media, sponsors, advertisers, and fans.

For years, the NBA didn't have to aggressively market its teams or the majority of its 350 players. The battle of Magic versus Larry gave way to Isiah Thomas' run with the Bad Boy Detroit Pistons (remember Bill Laimbeer?), which led to Michael Jordan and his run of six titles in eight years. In the wake of Jordan's departure, which player or players would emerge as the marketing face of the NBA?

In Los Angeles, Kobe Bryant and Shaquille O'Neal were beginning to gel, winning two championships during Jordan's absence— and a third during Jordan's return beginning with the 2001-02 season. Because they were both comparable in star power, however, neither emerged as the dominant face of the NBA.

Allen Iverson led Philadelphia to the finals in 2001, but his positioning as an unsavory character all but eliminated his ascension. Grant Hill of the Orlando Magic and Kevin Garnett of the Minnesota Timberwolves had the requisite talent, but Hill was frequently injured and Garnett wasn't playing for a high-profile, successful team; in fact, the Timberwolves have yet to make it past the first round of the playoffs.

Attention quickly turned to the Toronto Raptors' Vince Carter. However, he was stuck playing for a low-revenue team in Canada, which saw its other franchise, the Vancouver Grizzlies, relocate to Memphis, Tennessee, following tens of millions of dollars in losses. Unable or unwilling to find his way across the border to a major U.S. TV market, Carter signed a long-term contract in 2001 to remain in Toronto.

It was clear that the NBA would be led into the 21st century with a group of stars, each boasting his own considerable strengths and weaknesses, guiding its brand. Then along came the "savior."

After a few years as a part-owner of the Washington Wizards, Jordan announced his return as a player for the Wizards in late September 2001. Ticket sales in Washington and around the league rebounded; local TV ratings increased as both diehard and casual fans tuned in to satisfy their curiosities.

Did his "back to the future" coronation help or hurt the NBA brand? Struggling for three years to find the right formula for long-term branding success in the post-Jordan era, the NBA and league stakeholders were ambivalent about his return at the age of 38. Yes, short-term revenue from a variety of sources, including money made as fans crossed through turnstiles and bought the latest Jordan-inspired merchandise, would increase.

However, Jordan's return also posed a real problem because the league's ability to redefine itself once and for all following Jordan's retirement was threatened. His return cast a long shadow over the emerging stars, relegating them to second-class citizens and mitigating their ability to help market the league going forward. Jordan's return surely helped in the short run, but it had little or no impact on the new TV contract.

There was, however, a significant intangible linked to Jordan's return. Could he somehow slow what corporate America believed to be the urbanization of the NBA? Stemming the tide of an increasingly in-your-face sport, dominated by a group portrayed by sports agents and unions as largely misunderstood and vilified by much of middle America, remains important to the NBA if it hopes to sell its product (i.e., solid and sustainable TV ratings) to mainstream audiences for years to come.

In short, Jordan's return was anything but a financial and branding slam dunk for the league. Perhaps Jordan broke the branding chain, or maybe he simply disrupted a branding process gone astray.

Companies must make sure they are not overpromoting their old mainstay product or service, merely hoping to resurrect the results of yesteryear. Allocating time and resources to resuscitate a former success story might only serve to hinder the organization's ability to succeed long term because doing so might confuse the customer and be a drain on human and financial resources. For instance, automobile manufacturers must decide when a certain once-popular car model or feature no longer warrants the same degree of marketing or promotional support.

It is important for organizations attempting to brand themselves that they identify and swiftly address developments that impact the branding chain; a failure to do so not only confuses customers, it can wreak havoc on the brand's identity.

GOING GLOBAL

Once a brand has firmly established itself, it can begin contemplating the moves required, including establishing the proper relationships and networks, to take the brand global.

In 1864, Gerard A. Heineken purchased an old brewery in the Netherlands. Four years later, he opened another in Amsterdam, which was followed in 1874 with a brewery in Rotterdam. For the first time, and with great success, he leased his first brewery to produce Heineken abroad (in Belgium) in 1878.

Heineken thrived because it correctly believed that global expansion could best be accomplished by forming joint ventures, acquiring existing breweries rather than importing the beer straight from the Netherlands, and licensing the brand.

In 1931, a joint venture was formed in Singapore and, by 1960, Heineken owned or had an interest in breweries in 24 countries beyond the Netherlands. The beer with the green bottle and the red star grew to become the world's third largest selling beer thanks to the relationships the brand established with breweries around the globe. However, had Heineken not devoted the resources to ensuring that the breweries abroad were brewing enough—and the required quality—beer, the story of its global expansion might not have been so extraordinary.

In the early 1980s, the NBA was a domestic TV property. However, by the end of the decade, the game could be seen in more than 50 foreign countries, and, by 2001, the NBA was broadcast in more than 200 countries, reaching 750 million households worldwide. The NBA is now broadcast from Albania to Zimbabwe and at least 200 countries in between.

It is understood that the game of basketball is among the world's most popular sports. Its success as an Olympic sport allows children from all over the world to watch it and aspire to play it. The NBA also fostered internationalization by getting its best players to play on the country's dream team when the amateur-only rule was lifted before the 1992 Barcelona Olympics. Further, it played overseas exhibitions in France, Spain, Italy, and Germany. Playing teams from other countries also allowed the NBA to scout future players.

The league learned, as many companies have, that modifying the product to appeal to certain markets would help its popularity. For the NBA this meant drafting more and more foreign players and marketing their presence. Spain watched the Memphis Grizzlies Pao Gasol, and in Yugoslavia the attention focused on the Sacramento Kings "Peja" Stojakovic. Germans rooted for the Dallas Mavericks Dirk Nowitzki and Greeks followed the Phoenix Suns Iakovos Tsakalidis. In the 2002 NBA draft, five of the first 16 players were foreign, including the top overall pick Chinese center, Yao Ming.

In the summer of 2002, the United States team, filled with American NBA players, lost to Spain, Yugoslavia, and Argentina and didn't medal in the World Basketball Championships in Indianapolis. Prior to the tournament, the United States was 53–0 when using NBA players.

The NFL plays preseason games in foreign markets such as Ireland, Japan, and Mexico and plays NFL Europe games in Germany, Scotland, the Netherlands, and Spain, yet there is not one native from any of those countries on an NFL roster. Having foreign players in the league affords the NBA a true connection to international fans. So, too, did having the world's most recognizable personal brand, Michael Jordan, playing in the NBA. Jordan's global appeal, when combined with the distinctly international flavor the NBA now offers, led David Stern to comment during his 2002 State of the League address that the possibility existed that the NBA would have a branded presence (in the form of a franchise) internationally, either in Mexico or Europe by the end of the decade.

BRAND EXTENSIONS

Although a consensus generally exists about the definition of brands and their contribution to a company's bottom line, the pressing question now becomes how best to use the brand to increase shareholder value.

Leading brands frequently attempt to take advantage of their brand strength by extending the core brand into other areas. This can be a perilous path for (sports) marketers. In fact, a great way to harm a brand is to attach its name to everything because brand extensions, or subbranding, often harm core brands by siphoning market share away from the core brand rather than taking market share away from competitors. For instance, a compelling case can be made that purchasers of Miller Lite and Diet 7-Up were wooed from their core brands more so than those of its competitors, Budweiser and Pepsi.

The NBA's brand extension of the WNBA in 1995 hasn't been entirely beneficial for the NBA. Perhaps financial losses of its current magnitude were perceived from the outset, but would the NBA have entered the market if it knew that coverage of its championship series would, in year five, be relegated to page four or five on the sports page? Or that a mere 1,000 people would sign up to purchase season tickets for the proposed WNBA expansion team in Chicago?

It seems that the only time the WNBA garners page one attention is when one of its players, Lisa Harrison, wins the Playboy.com poll as the "WNBA's Sexiest Babe." Or if one of its teams folds—as the Miami Sol, Orlando Miracle, and Portland Fire did in 2002.

Control over a premier brand's affiliate brands is also essential, as evidenced by the NBA's decision to start the National Development Basketball League (NBDL) from scratch. The NBA is striving to make the NBDL a family-friendly form of affordable entertainment that offers fans an acceptable quality of play.

The NBDL, which began in the fall of 2001 as a regional league throughout several Southern states, affords the NBA the opportunity to not only streamline costs due to shorter travel distances and other efficiencies, but also allows the NBA to concentrate its marketing efforts of the NBDL throughout a manageable geographic region.

As a brand affiliate, the NBDL also enables the NBA to cultivate players, coaches (the Greenville Groove became the first men's professional sports franchise to hire a female coach), referees, front office executives, and fans.

The NBDL's geographic concentration enabled it to sign a cable TV deal with Fox Sports Net South for the broadcasting of 19 games across the regional network's seven-state coverage area. This regional programming buttresses the three-year broadcast contract the NBDL has with ESPN and ESPN2, which is significant because it provides a national platform for advertisers.

If and when the league is successful in the South, the NBA will establish other regional leagues around the country, possibly setting up a true national championship whereby NBDL franchises from the West, Midwest, East, and South compete for league honors.

Before the NBDL can succeed, it must demonstrate—like all brand extensions—that it is able to stand on its own. The NBDL can use the NBA as a crutch to generate publicity for the new league and persuade customers to sample the product. However, if the NBDL, like other brand extensions, isn't a sound product on its own, it won't survive.

The NBA, like any organization, must continue to manage its brands and, when appropriate, control its message. It has to do so expertly, professionally, and ethically, and must do so with its entire stable of constituents in mind.

Should any business, including the NBA, fail to adequately manage its global brand, it will be unable to effectively reach domestic and international customers of all ages. Further, the organization's ability to do so will be comprised if those with whom it has important relationships, particularly sponsors and advertisers in the case of the NBA, believe the company is delivering an unclear message that limits their ability to sell products and services to global audiences.

CHAMPIONSHIP POINTS

Establishing, building, and extending a brand, such as the NBA, requires ongoing, hands-on management and leadership at every turn. When attempting to create a great brand, organizations must do the following:

- Appreciate that great brands, like the Yankees, deliver the rare combination of a compelling name, logo, customer service, employee commitment, and quality of product or service, among other marketable attributes.
- Retain a brand management visionary, a near-mercenary who intimately understands brand building and the organization's objectives and goals.
- Identify internal brand leaders (your David Stern) and messengers (your Michael Jordan).
- Recognize the breadth of stakeholders that impact the brand, ranging from employees (athletes) to distributors (TV networks) to those involved in a product's aftermarket.
- Realize branding opportunities and seize them as Swingline did.
- Commit to providing stellar customer service, listening intently to every (potential) customer regardless of his or her current spending and loyalty to the company.
- Allocate human and financial resources to customer development. Look at your potential workforce as seriously as basketball teams look at the NBA draft. Failing to cultivate and replenish customers leads to a decline in market share and, by extension, brand value.

- Consistently invest in the core brand. It's less expensive and more effective to investment spend to protect a brand name than it is to allocate time and resources to rehabilitate a damaged one.
- Expand the brand to international markets after first allocating the necessary human and financial resources to greatly reduce the probability of harming it on a global basis.
- Protect the brand at all costs, even if doing so requires measured micromanagement of it. A company's reputation and integrity with consumers takes years to develop but only minutes to undermine.
- Manage its message in every place it is seen or heard.

Great organizations, even those that have risen to become global brands, are required to periodically reinvent or reposition themselves. This generally occurs after successful branding efforts have led the business into new industry segments or following regulatory or other industry-altering developments that mandate the business revitalize its operations.

10 REPOSITIONING A BUSINESS

The Point: All organizations, inside and outside of sports, deal with the ebbs and flows of the business cycle. Executives must be prepared to deal with the pressing issues that will determine the extent to which they can continue to thrive—or even just stay alive—during times of uncertainty. Great business leaders invest in and protect the organization on an ongoing basis, and realize that if they consistently refine the business they might not be faced with having to totally reposition it.

We've all been there before, or at the very least, thought our businesses (and careers) were there. "There" is teetering on the brink, needing a makeover of some sort to revitalize the organization in an effort to improve employee morale, instill confidence in vendors, and protect the company's stock price.

Businesses of all sizes, regardless of the industry they are in or the products or services they sell, encounter downturns that require them to reposition or reinvent themselves. This need to reposition can result from changes in economic conditions, consumer preferences, legislation, the competitive landscape, or a myriad other reasons such as management complacency.

Nike chairman Phil Knight believes that the footwear industry cycle lasts about seven years, and forces Nike to periodically reinvent itself and reawaken customers with new product lines supported by creative marketing and advertising campaigns.

Back in the 1980s, Nike relinquished its industry lead to Reebok after Nike decided that it would not immediately follow Reebok's entrance into the aerobic shoe market—a market driven by consumers' desire for fashionable, stylish shoes. Nike's unwillingness to develop an aerobic shoe enabled Reebok to overtake Nike by marketing to women who ultimately were responsible for 75 percent of company sales.

A decade later, consumers preferred performance to style and fashion. Nike, with its superstar spokespeople and glitzy ad campaigns, reemerged as the industry leader by positioning itself as the manufacturer of authentic shoes worn by athletes.

By 2000, both Nike and Reebok found themselves competing with new or rejuvenated industry players, including And 1, Puma, and Pony; upstarts that set out to carve market share away from the industry behemoths.

And 1 did so by tapping into the inner-city communities, marketing to hard-core hoopsters with smaller disposable incomes. It was long thought that those living in the inner city didn't have the money to spend on expensive basketball shoes. However, as it has turned out, many spend their disposable incomes on basketball-related items, including shoes.

And 1 gained an edge by hiring controversial New York Knicks forward Latrell Sprewell, infamous for choking then Golden State Warriors coach P. J. Carlesimo. Further, the company didn't hesitate going after Rafer Alston, the streetballer who didn't even start in the NBA, but was well known as an inner-city playground legend. In 2002, And 1 even named a shoe after Alston—the "Skip to My Lou's." For And 1, Alston authenticated its product and provided the company a "real" marketing platform. Soon, Nike came up with its Freestyle campaign to show that it too was "true to the street," and Reebok signed Allen Iverson to a lifetime contract to authenticate its urban line.

Puma, founded in 1924, and primarily known worldwide for its connection to soccer, as well as track and field, was also making inroads in the United States—at least on the apparel side of things, as it became the jersey provider to 13 NFL teams. The company lucked out when the St. Louis Rams and Tennessee Titans, both outfitted by Puma, played each other in the 1999 Super Bowl. Unlike And 1, Puma decided to rely on the association fans had with their favorite teams to help position the company as an industry player. Two years later, Puma's NFL plan went down the drain when Reebok agreed to a 10-year, $250 million deal to outfit all the league's teams. This development led Puma to return its focus to soccer.

After more than a decade of inactivity, the Pony brand was bought by a company called The Firm. Hoping to revive the Pony brand name following the footwear and apparel company's bankruptcy, The Firm announced in 2001 that it would take an "antimarketing" approach to attract its targeted audience of young hipsters. To accomplish this, Pony outfitted rock bands, including Limp Bizkit and KoRn, in an effort to market its footwear and apparel as "cool" and "hip" among its core audience. Nike signed saxophonist Mike Phillips to wear its Jordan brand and Reebok signed artists including Scarface and Shakira.

Pony returned to the sports world in 2002 by introducing an "antimarketing" campaign utilizing rebellious sports legends, individuals whose athletic prowess was worthy of the hall of fame, but due to being blackballed or banned from their respective sports, they were never enshrined. The campaign included Jack Tatum of the Oakland Raiders and Pete Rose of the Cincinnati Reds, who was banned from baseball in 1989 for gambling on sporting events.

How will Nike and Reebok respond to these changes in the competitive landscape, as well as ongoing shifts in consumer preferences? How would a merchant who owns a single shoe store in the local shopping mall reawaken his customers after NikeTown becomes an anchor tenant?

Whereas Nike was able to regain it market leadership position, Atari was not. Atari, the once-dominant producer of video game consoles (the industry's version of hardware), not only lost market share but also eventually went out of business due to its inability to adapt to, and take advantage of, the latest technological innovations.

Atari dominated the early video game marketplace. The Atari VCS 2600 launched in December 1977, selling for $200 to $250. In five years, the brand—which was acquired by Warner Communications for $28 million in 1976—had generated $5 billion in sales. Atari was able to hold off early challengers like Colecovision and Intellivision thanks to the success of games (the industry's version of software) like Pong and Pac-Man, as well as the very first video games licensed from major motion pictures, *E.T.* and *Raiders of the Lost Ark*.

However, when the video game market temporarily declined— Atari reportedly lost $2 million a day throughout 1983—it became apparent that the company had not positioned itself for future success by recognizing the industry's business cycle and allocating resources appropriately to ensure that any downturn would be minimal.

Eventually, Atari was overtaken by a Japanese company called Nintendo, which developed Atari's popular Donkey Kong game and was creating games like Super Mario Brothers and the Legend of Zelda. Another competitor, Sega—armed with its key property Sonic the Hedgehog—also entered the market in the mid-1980s to challenge Atari.

However, it turned out that Nintendo and Sega would only be battling each other. In 1989, when Nintendo debuted its handheld device, known as Gameboy, Atari responded with its Atari Lynx, the first handheld video game system to be in color. For a variety of reasons, including the fact that to a new generation of kids the Atari brand name meant little, sales of the Lynx were minimal.

Four years later, after being acquired by Time Warner, Atari outpaced another newcomer (the Sony Playstation) to the market when it introduced the Jaguar, the world's first 64-bit computer system. Still lacking an authentic brand in the eyes of its critical demographic, sales of the Jaguar lagged and the video game system proved to be the last Atari ever produced.

In the 1990s, Nintendo and Sega continued to battle for the top position, matching each other's technological progress and selling consoles by turning proprietary games into franchises. Both did so by turning properties, including Super Mario Brothers and Sonic the Hedgehog, into TV shows or licensing the games' key images to stuffed animal and clothing manufacturers.

The video game business remains one of the most volatile in the world. Companies want to produce both the console (hardware) and the games (software). But the console is usually such a money loser that the games have to sell very well for today's companies to show a net gain.

In 2001, Sega announced it was dropping out of the console business and would just make games due to cost concerns. Today, Nintendo and Sony are now being challenged by Microsoft, which entered the video game console and games business in 2001 with the launch of its state-of-the-art system, the Xbox.

In professional sports, business cycles are also significantly impacted by the manner in which sports leagues are organized and run. Similarities might exist between sports and more traditional businesses, but the structure of professional sports serves to change both the depth and the length of industry cycles.

Sports also maintains a cherished spot in American culture. The connection that generations of fans have made with sports is passionate and runs far deeper than any other industry. Consequently, it enjoys a cultural distinctiveness and, more often than not, gives sports the upper hand in negotiations, often resulting in teams' ability to optimize their business cycles.

Turnarounds in the NFL can happen more quickly than in the other major sports leagues because the league has a hard salary cap, which provides the NFL with greater parity among its teams. In fact, from 1998 to 2002, seven different teams made it to the Super Bowl.

Just because sports enjoys a virtual monopoly in the market, this does not mean that business principles from the sports world are not transferable to customary business settings. Because industry leadership positions often change more frequently in the NFL than in the traditional business world (imagine if the software industry had a reverse-order entry draft for software engineers whereby the least competitive firms had their pick of the top graduates every year), considering how an NFL team approaches and deals with its business cycle is a worthwhile activity. When discussing the concept of repositioning a business against the favorable backdrop enjoyed by sports, there might be no better example than the Dallas Cowboys.

In recent years, the team has been the butt of one of the oldest and most recycled sports jokes: What do you call 53 men sitting around watching the Super Bowl on TV? That's right, none other than the Dallas Cowboys.

Dubbed "America's Team," the Cowboys have been required to turn their business around twice over the last 15 years. Presently in the midst of what the team hopes will be its second turnaround, the Cowboys' budding revitalization is being met with great scrutiny and, at times, even greater success.

REPOSITIONING

The majority of companies that have turned themselves around in one fashion or another have revised their strategy. There are several areas that the company must analyze to create a new or revised strategic framework. It must analyze its own business, its current strategy, its management, and the market it is in.

Apple has been rightly dubbed the comeback kid of the business world. In 1976, Steve Jobs and Steve Wozniak, two high school buddies, created Apple in a garage, just like Hewlett and Packard decades earlier. By 1982, Apple had reached $1 billion in sales, yet the pioneer of personal computers was unable to remain the industry leader. Ten years after Jobs left Apple in 1985, the company was in serious trouble. In September 1995, the company announced that its line of notebook computers could literally catch on fire. Over the following four months, Apple's CFO, its head of marketing, and four senior vice presidents resigned.

When Dell and Gateway entered the personal computer market, Apple was written off by many industry observers. However, in 1997, Jobs returned and helped reinvent Apple by using the Apple name to help the company with initiatives that the competition wasn't aggressively pursuing.

He debuted the iMac and Powerbook, inexpensive and efficient laptops and readied Apple for the 21st century by debuting the iBook (electronic book), iPod (a digital music player), and the iPhoto (a photo editing product used for digital camera images). By strategically analyzing—and then devising a game plan to exploit the weaknesses of the new industry leaders—Apple has succeeded in reestablishing its dormant brand name even though it was forced to reduce the prices of these innovative products in the process.

A company in distress should first look internally by analyzing its own business. This includes analyzing its strengths, weaknesses, and strategic barriers that have caused the firm to succeed in the past but currently cause it to flounder.

The initial analysis will provide the backbone necessary to redefine the strategy. What are the company's core competencies? Is it positioned incorrectly? What does it do to keep its employees motivated? Can it survive? These are just some of the questions that managers of these downtrodden firms must answer if they want to get their organizations back on track.

Next, a company should examine its current market. It cannot be complacent and simply concern itself with how it is positioned with customers and suppliers. It must also look outward to see if the environment around it is changing.

For Jones, this included the NBA's Mavericks, a regional competitor for the entertainment dollar. In fact, the year Jones acquired the Cowboys, the Mavericks had their first losing season in six years, a development that, if it became a trend (which it did), could provide

Jones an opportunity to market his team to basketball fans in search of a winner.

Another key aspect that must be evaluated is the company's management and culture. These areas of the business can often become stale and stagnant. Entrenched in the past, these areas must constantly be evaluated to enable change. Corporate culture is often the single biggest factor that inhibits change. The organization does not want to change the way the business has been operating, especially if there are no visible problems. The appropriate management structure and management personnel will deliver the leadership necessary to implement change and a turnaround in an organization.

This is especially the case in small businesses that have grown accustomed to relying on the same way of doing business day after day, despite changes in the local business climate that must be addressed. When a Starbucks enters the neighborhood retail village, the owner of the decades-old donut store had better be quick to assess and respond to changing market conditions. After all, glazed donuts and coffee served in styrofoam cups might not satisfy a customer base that now wants an "experience" when picking up that cup of joe. Simply urging customers to support the little guy won't do it for most, especially if the product offering isn't compelling.

With a new leader like Jones taking over, the pain associated with the changes that needed to occur was dulled as he held less of an attachment to the team and what he perceived as its antiquated operations. Although he cared deeply about the team and its rich tradition, his primary interest in the Cowboys history was directly linked to what he could learn from it, as he hoped not to repeat mistakes made by previous management.

Reevaluating the company's management does not end after examining the structure. It is also necessary to view the management tools that are in place, or not in place, within the organization. These tools include, but are by no means limited to, appropriate and constructive supervision, as well as the opportunity for employees to raise objections. Without these tools in place, management will not operate effectively.

Repositioning with an Attitude

The Cowboys, perhaps as much as any team in sports, draws incredible attention to itself due to the flamboyant nature of its owner, Jerry Jones.

The general public frequently perceives sports owners, like many ultrasuccessful businessmen, as cocky and egocentric. Although some of this perception is undeserved, there exists a fine line between confidence and arrogance. Executives that cross the line face the wrath of shareholders, and sports franchise owners are forced to read about their approach to business in the local paper's letters to the editor.

Yankees owner George Steinbrenner and Jones finished first and second, respectively, out of a list of 14 owners, in a 2001 poll in which more than 15,000 people were asked to name the least favorable owners in professional sports. Steinbrenner's and Jones' flamboyance and history of success have drawn their fair share of detractors.

Each owner's flashy management style and approach to ownership has riled fans from coast to coast, but it has also occasionally provided fodder for these fans when such reviled owners talk out of turn.

When Jones, who is the only owner who can be found on the sidelines during every game, announced at the beginning of the 2001 season that the Cowboys would win 10 games, it was seen by some as another ridiculous prediction by a man who is so into himself and his product that he can't see the forest through the trees. The "forest" in this case was another losing season, obscured by the "trees"—Jones' grandiose view of his team.

Jones has always believed he was better at putting a team together than anyone else. This supreme confidence resulted in part from his tremendous turnaround of the Cowboys nearly 15 years ago.

Leadership and Senior Management

In February 1989, a syndicate led by Jones purchased the Cowboys for $140 million; $95 million for the team and another $45 million for the stadium lease. In exchange for his 53 percent share of the team, Jones put up $90 million of his own money and borrowed the remainder against his personal assets.

As part of deal, Jones did not acquire Texas Stadium, but rather the operating rights to it. He received the benefits of stadium ownership without incurring the negative tax consequences. Jones agreed to pay the city a modest fixed lease and assumed the stadium's operating expenses, totaling about $5 million a year. In exchange, he received 100 percent of the revenue from parking, concessions, merchandise, stadium advertising, and luxury suite sales.

Jones began overhauling the organization by first ousting former leadership. Getting rid of an organization's roots isn't always easy, well received, or without controversy, but Jones had the commitment from his minority owners. Jones, like Oakland Raiders owner Al Davis, wanted to be as hands-on as possible—and he wasn't shy about these intentions.

He fired legendary coach Tom Landry the very day he acquired the team that won just three of 16 games in 1988. How much of a legend was Landry? He played fullback and defensive back for the Texas Longhorns in the late 1940s, and he became the third winningest coach in the history of the NFL while serving as the Cowboys only coach. In fact, from 1966 to 1985, Landry led the team to 20 consecutive winning seasons.

Although it was said that Jones' predecessor, H. R. "Bum" Bright, was also ready to dismiss Landry had Bright not sold the team, Jones rubbed many the wrong way, including many league and team officials who believed Jones had preordained Jimmy Johnson as the team's new coach.

Jones didn't care about how people perceived what he was doing with his new investment. He fired the heads of many departments, including public relations director Doug Todd. Of those remaining, many resigned, including GM Tex Schramm, head of player personnel Gil Brandt, and vice president Joe Bailey.

Jones understood that he would face tremendous pressure given these management changes, especially because Landry and Schramm had been with the team since the 1960s. However, in the three seasons leading up to Jones' purchase, the franchise had posted three consecutive losing seasons for the first time since 1964.

Jones believed that he could turn the Cowboys around by devoting all of his time, energy, and resourcefulness to the team. He set out to accomplish this by overhauling his executive staff and team roster, and by containing organizational costs. Combining his commitment to the team with his desire to capitalize on the brand name of the Cowboys, Jones quickly made sweeping—and excruciatingly difficult—changes throughout the organization.

It is not uncommon for new team owners to "clean house" on their purchase. Some do it because of chronic organizational ineptness. Other new owners make wholesale changes to let fans, the media, and even other franchise owners know that things will be different; not necessarily better, but at least different.

In many respects the immediate and pronounced changes brought to the organizations by the likes of Jones are no different than most new ownership who immediately seek to assuage shareholder concerns by taking a broom to the executive suite. However, this sweeping must be undertaken carefully and with customers in mind.

This is witnessed on the local level when the neighborhood tavern changes ownership and the first thing the new management team does is bring in its own bartender, a guy that might have worked well at its other location but has no roots in the local community. In this instance, the barflies (shareholders) are merely hoping to commiserate with a bartender (executive) they have known for years. Often, such patrons are willing to change their buying habits by following their bartender down the street to his or her new afternoon gig.

When Jones made the immediate and highly public changes in his senior management, most notably the firing of Landry, they were met with great criticism. Many believed Jones had trampled on the sanctity of America's Team, and others thought the changes were necessary believing that the game "had passed" Landry by. Regardless, it was evident that Jones did not fully understand or comprehend the extent to which the Cowboys were not just loved, but revered. He appeared heavy-handed, lacking an appreciation for the tradition and legacy of the team.

Recent mergers and acquisitions throughout the world of big business have demonstrated that Jones was not alone in misunderstanding the business culture or environment in which newly acquired or merged businesses operate.

Quaker Oats bought Snapple for $1.7 billion in 1994. The drink company had experienced major growth propelled in part by its wide range of spokespeople, including shock jock Howard Stern, talk radio commentator Rush Limbaugh, and Wendy, "the Snapple lady" with the heavy Long Island accent who actually answered phones at company headquarters.

However, when Quaker Oats completed its acquisition, it swiftly removed all three. Stern bashed the brand, sales plummeted, and shelf space in supermarkets became harder to protect. When Triarc Cos. bought the brand three years later for $300 million it moved quickly to rehabilitate the brand by running ads on Stern's radio show and bringing back Wendy. This back-to-the-future approach helped as sales slowly recovered.

It can be argued that Quaker Oats instituted the changes because it wanted to communicate an "under new management" message, but telling people that, especially when a brand is strong, doesn't necessarily enhance it.

Think about your favorite restaurant. You're a "regular" who is far more familiar with the waitresses than you are with the management. One day, a new owner takes over. As long as the food is good and the dining experience is the same you might not notice the transition. Now suppose the new management comes in and hangs one of those "Under New Management" signs in the window. Your first impression, instead of not noticing, might now be this: Was there something wrong that I didn't notice? Why did the old managers leave? Were there rats in the kitchen?

Jones risked hanging up the sign, but his reasons behind the change were better reasoned than those of Quaker Oats.

After weathering the intense scrutiny associated with these high-profile dismissals, Jones turned his attention to restructuring the team on the field. Because the team finished with a 3–13 record, the Cowboys received the top pick in the 1989 NFL draft. Jones and his new head coach, former University of Miami coach Jimmy Johnson had two choices: They could trade the pick and acquire numerous additional draft picks or players or keep the pick and use it to select the draft's consensus top prospect, UCLA quarterback Troy Aikman.

Many of a company's employees have become part of the team because they were at the right place at the right time. They knew someone who worked in the firm, or maybe they came out of college when a hiring boom was taking place. Perhaps they simply went to the right college—the one where the organization heavily recruits new talent or where the company CEO is a member of the board of trustees.

You might contend that no company can discover every incredible prospect like scouts and draft analysts arguably do, but selecting the right talent at the right time is still as paramount to an NFL team as it is in the business world.

Knowing that eager, dedicated employees are the backbone to the organization, Jones built his core of athletes by focusing on young, draft-eligible talent. Jones selected Aikman because he felt that, in addition to his extraordinary talent, picking Aikman would demonstrate to fans that Jones indeed was committed to putting a winning team on the field—regardless of cost. Aikman's six-year contract for $11 million was the largest contract a rookie had ever received, Jones was determined to send a clear message that he would rejuvenate America's Team.

Has your company ever had the chance to hire someone like Troy Aikman—someone you thought was "the franchise"? Did you make the right choice or blow it, squandering precious time and resources on employees that never panned out? Just how sure was Jones that Aikman was the ideal fit for the Cowboys? He signed him four days *before* the draft. The Cleveland Browns signed their No. 1 pick in 1999 prior to the draft and the Houston Texans came to terms with their No. 1 pick, David Carr, before the 2002 draft. In 1989, such developments were not only rare, but were considered fairly risky.

Jones strongly believed that stability and continuity in ownership and coaching were two of the three key ingredients to success in the NFL, the third being a superstar quarterback and a supporting cast for the future.

Whether he realized it or not, Jones was evoking the key elements of any successful business, namely competent management, strong leadership, and great employees.

He realized that although Aikman was going to be the team's leader, the quarterback could not—by himself—solve all the team's problems and recognized that Aikman's on-field leadership needed to be complemented by a compelling supporting cast if he was to rebuild the organization.

Accordingly, Jones overhauled his player personnel. He rapidly jettisoned high-priced and underachieving veterans for hungry, cost-effective younger players. Believing that he and his coaching staff were superior at identifying talent, Jones set out to systematically overhaul the team by acquiring additional draft picks, future players that he believed would contribute to multiple Super Bowl victories.

Jones' approach to building the franchise from within by leveraging senior management's collective eye for talent was validated when the Cowboys pulled off one of the most lopsided trades in the history of professional sports. On October 12, 1989, the Cowboys traded

Herschel Walker and two third-round draft picks to the Minnesota Vikings for five players and seven draft picks, including Minnesota's first- and second-round selections from 1990 through 1992. Outstanding players that joined the Cowboys as a direct result of the trade included running back Emmitt Smith and defensive tackle Russell Maryland.

The added maneuverability given the team through the additional draft picks enabled the Cowboys to trade some of these picks during future NFL drafts, yielding the team even more draft picks—in fact, a club record 17 in 1991. Further, in Jones' first four years, the Cowboys made 45 trades.

In addition to drafting Aikman, the lopsided Herschel Walker trade gave the Cowboys the depth and breadth of employees needed to complement management and leadership.

INTERNAL CHANGES AND MARKETING

With management, leadership, and players in place, Jones turned his attention to the ongoing management and marketing of the team.

Like any company, the Cowboys were now in a position to scrutinize and adjust their strategy. They reevaluated their objectives, cost strategy, target customers, quality programs, and how they would handle future planning to sustain growth.

Jones undertook programs to cut costs while improving the team's connection to fans. The Cowboys had 109 nonathlete employees on the payroll, compared to the Cincinnati Bengals' 28. He gutted much of middle management and plowed the savings into sales and marketing programs designed to increase lagging attendance and secure sponsors.

He even relocated the team's training camp to Texas from California in an effort to generate fan interest. More than 100,000 fans attended workouts, and more than 400 media credentials were issued in three weeks time.

He complemented these moves by reducing certain ticket costs in an effort to demonstrate his commitment to fans and show them that he understood the long-term value in keeping his product affordable to "everyday" fans.

Further belt tightening was evident as Jones forced outside vendors, including those who printed tickets and programs, arranged
training room supplies, and insurance, to begin bidding for the Cowboys account. Rather than simply staying with vendors because of
their long-standing relationship with the team, the Cowboys sent a
clear message that Jones was going to run a tight financial ship as he
struggled to turn a profit.

Such belt tightening would not be limited to those servicing the
team. Employee use of complimentary game tickets and company
cars were also included in the excesses that Jones quickly reined in.
In short, Jones was hell-bent on putting a stop to what he viewed as
abusive practices. His critics said that he was almost too profit motivated, not giving employees bonuses when they deserved them and
not treating former employees, especially championship Cowboys
players, with the respect many felt they deserved.

The cutbacks might have seemed like a cheap and unnecessary
move to those on the outside, but during a company's reorganization,
the primary opinions that matter are those of company shareholders
and employees. Businesses must communicate that financial constraints are for the good of the organization and that budget cuts will
contribute to reestablishing a successful company if morale and
motivation are to be maintained.

Making sure that employees feel involved in the company's
progress during periods of change is critical. Look no further than
the quality of service from employee-owned organizations such as
regional supermarkets like Publix (126,000 employees) and Hy-Vee
(46,000 employees).

At Publix, workers benefit by receiving stock. Hy-Vee gives its
workers a share in profits through a trust fund and also distributes
bonuses and commissions based on each store's individual performance.

Because of their cleanliness, courtesy, checkouts, and prices,
both Publix and Hy-Vee were chosen among the best places to work
in the United States by *Fortune* magazine and *Consumer Reports*,
respectively. Employees, regardless of industry, will perform better
and be more dedicated to the cause when they are included in the
process.

When St. Louis Rams quarterback Kurt Warner was cut from the
Green Bay Packers in 1994, he went back home to Cedar Rapids,
Iowa, where he worked at Hy-Vee stocking the shelves at minimum
wage ($5.50 an hour). From there he went on to star in the Arena

Football League before heading off to play in the NFL Europe and, eventually, in the NFL where he earned MVP honors in Super Bowl XXXVI.

Jones' restructuring of his executive and coaching staffs, his commitment to reduce waste within the organization, revamp the player roster, and capitalize on anticipated trends in TV revenue (the revenue distributed to each team based on an 84 percent increase in the league's new TV contracts provided Jones added financial latitude) enabled him to turn the franchise around.

He made himself the top decision maker and gave his sons Stephen (executive vice president and director of player personnel) and Jerry Jr. (chief marketing officer) top positions in the front office. Nepotism, which is rampant throughout sports, poses problems in many organizations, particularly if those given positions lack experience and the respect of their colleagues.

Fortunately for Jones, the other members of the Cowboys "family" accepted his sons. Plus, as with any organization, including the Pittsburgh Steelers, which have been run by the Rooney family for three generations, there's nothing wrong with nepotism if the heirs are qualified.

By 1990, the Cowboys had improved their record to 7-9. This was followed a year later by an 11-5 season, including a playoff victory. In 1992, in only Jones' fourth year as owner, the Cowboys posted a 13-3 record and beat the Buffalo Bills in Super Bowl XXVII, his first of three championships in the decade.

Not surprisingly, the Cowboys financial situation improved dramatically as evidenced by a 32 percent increase in estimated franchise value between 1990 and 1994. In 1994, *Financial World* magazine proclaimed the Cowboys the most valuable team in the NFL, worth an estimated $238 million. In 2001, the team was valued by *Forbes* magazine at $743 million, slightly behind the Washington Redskins. One difference: The Redskins' owner, Daniel Snyder, paid $800 million for his team.

THE SECOND COMING?

Jones is well aware that businesses, including NFL teams, are cyclical and that seldom does one organization get to the top and stay there. Throughout the later part of the 1990s and early 2000s the Cowboys struggled on the field, leading to intense criticism of Jones and his approach to resurrecting the floundering team.

Jones was repeatedly bashed during this period for his approach to taking credit and assessing blame. Like any business that gains momentum and demonstrates a track record of success, tension arises as to whom should be credited with the turnaround. In the case of the Cowboys, Jones believed he deserved much of the credit because he oversaw all major decisions, yet his two coaches during that period—Jimmy Johnson and Barry Switzer—also believed they were due significant recognition.

The team's record was 10–6 in 1998, 8–8 in 1999, and 5–11 in 2000, 2001, and 2002. For some teams, a five-year record of 33–47 would have not only been an improvement, it would have been acceptable. For the Cowboys it demonstrates that when you have previously succeeded in turning around an organization, the expectations are higher and you have to be ready to do so even quicker the second time. Corporate shareholders and sports fans alike expect it and won't typically settle for less, often regardless of the factors that might have contributed to the downturn.

Drug use, coaching changes, and injuries took their toll on the Cowboys quicker than any owner would have expected. Defensive tackle Leon Lett was suspended for most of 1997 with drug problems, a crisis that also enveloped wide receiver Michael Irvin.

Head coaching changes also prevailed, with Chan Gailey replacing Barry Switzer in 1998 and, again, in 2000 as Dave Campo replaced Gailey. Irvin had to retire after the 2000 season due to a neck injury. Fullback Daryl Johnston and quarterback Aikman were also forced to retire because of injuries.

Jones needed to rebuild again. Just like 1989, he was forced to play a rookie quarterback in 2001, Quincy Carter, a second-round pick from Georgia who was, by all accounts, no Troy Aikman. Seventy of the 87 players listed on the team's training camp roster had three years of NFL experience or less.

For the first time since the 1988 and 1989 seasons, the Cowboys posted double-digit losses in consecutive seasons. Jones said he would rebuild again through great drafts. To accomplish this he first had to recall—and demonstrate that he learned from—the mistakes he made the first time around.

In the sports world, employee problems, management changes, and staff attrition are measured by wins and losses. In the traditional business world, these developments would have negatively impacted a company's share price, hindering its ability to compete in the market.

Following this initial decade, one in which the Cowboys dominated on the field, Jones was quick to point out that he had made mistakes along the way. In fact, he ranked his top three management errors during this period.

The first was not paying adequate attention to players' off-field behavior. Jones allowed the issue of player indiscretions to sneak up on him because he was too content with the team's on-field results and was reluctant to address the issue head on. Eventually he mandated that players stay away from the team's most popular hangout and cut a player who didn't obey his directive.

Jones had far greater difficulty curtailing his players' drug use and this shortcoming continued to be a drag on the team's reputation, so much so that when one of Jones' star players, Mark Tuinei, died of a drug overdose in 1999, few were surprised.

Many executives overlook serious personnel problems in their organizations, hoping that they will somehow resolve themselves. However, unfocused or undisciplined employees routinely undermine a company's success. A failure to address such shortcomings, whether they are small nuisances such as a secretary being perpetually late for work, or major, such as an executive involved in sexual harassment, can lead to the demise of the entire company. This is especially true with organizations that are routinely in the public eye like professional sports teams. There are very few companies and industries that are subjected to weekly—if not daily—media accounts about the way a particular organization is handling its business affairs.

Owners and managers should always realize that customers usually have a choice of where to shop. Sometimes the difference is the employees that a store keeps. Owners and managers that insist on a dress code or prohibit long hair or earrings understand that personal appearance, and the perceived improved service that comes with it, is important to certain customers.

Although a certain employee's personal or professional troubles won't necessarily tarnish the company's image in the eyes of the consumer, it must be realized that an employee's lack of focus in the workplace, whatever the reason, can undermine the company's morale, products, and profitability.

Jones' second biggest regret during his first 10 years as owner was retaining Coach Barry Switzer following the 1995 season. A strained relationship with his highest profile employee fueled debate about his leadership acumen and shifted far too much of the focus away from the product on the field. As much as an executive regrets the need to make necessary high-profile changes in senior management, it must be done. Any short-term fallout caused will pale in comparison to leaving the wrong person in charge of a critical part of the organization's business.

His final regret, one that Jones says continues to haunt him, was his first set of decisions regarding the replacement of senior management, decisions compounded by the fact that he made them immediately on his acquisition of the team.

The integrity of the brand is on the line every day, but because of the power of the media, any time a group of journalists are gathered in one place for a press conference everything must run smoothly. This applies to all businesses, including those that are rivals to the Cowboys.

Awkward media relations are prevalent throughout the business world and are not limited to situations dealing with the termination of an employee or senior manager. Three weeks after the 1999-2000 NFL season, the Chicago Bears called for a gathering of the media where they promised to introduce their new head coach, Dave McGinnis. However, 90 minutes after the press conference was supposed to start, the Bears cancelled it because they had announced the deal without it being finalized and McGinnis left the building. The Bears then had to admit that a final deal wasn't done and negotiations appeared to be in limbo.

The widely circulated Associated Press article led by reminding readers of the team's intent—that the Bears wanted Dave McGinnis to bring the black and blue back to their defense. However, following the highly public incident, what the team received instead was a red face on one of the most embarrassing days in Bears' history. The following Monday, they announced Dick Jauron as their new head coach.

Who was partly responsible for the botched press conference? None other than team president Michael McCaskey, a former Harvard Business School professor and author of a 1982 book called *The Executive Challenge: Managing Change and Ambiguity*.

As long as a mistake is recognized and is not repeated, it can be dismissed as a one-time blunder without becoming a chronic management concern. Jones, by spelling out his mistakes, obviously has recognized them and it allows him to proceed with confidence into his second revitalization of the brand.

Media relations is even important to the small businessman. Simply knowing that everything is "on the record" once a journalist presents himself or herself is very important. That's because whatever the company representative says could be construed as a statement representative of the ideals and values of the business itself. Good owners and managers instruct their staff about who should— and who should not—talk to the media before the situation arises.

One mistake Jones didn't publicly admit to was hiring several "yes" men coaches so that he could ultimately maintain all the power. By hiring Bill Parcells after the 2002 season and giving him some guaranteed authority, Jones was willing to relinquish some of his power. This was an important change not enjoyed by Parcells' recent predecessors and one that could have been a contributing factor to the previous coaches' downfall.

APPLYING THE SAME PRINCIPLES AND PASSIONS

Jones wants people to recognize that, even though he had success with the team in the early '90s, he was capable of adjusting and using the same principles and passion to succeed a decade later.

It took several years, but the 2002 NFL Draft—which included University of Texas safety Roy Williams, University of Pittsburgh wide receiver Antonio Bryant, and University of Colorado center Andre Gurode—combined with the Parcells hiring, could ultimately mark the beginning of Jones' second turnaround in Dallas.

The business of sports and team ownership continued to evolve in the dozen years since Jones bought the Cowboys. Money from TV, sponsorship, and luxury boxes had poured in, making the team one of the most valuable in all of sports. However, as the Cowboys struggled on the field, Jones realized what Nike's Knight meant about the need to reinvent his business.

Accordingly, he identified a handful of marketing initiatives that he believed could help him market the team and reposition it in the eyes of consumers. He planned on leveraging the team's brand to enhance his franchise value by tweaking the same principles and passions he relied on a decade earlier.

This time around, however, the stakes and the opportunities were much larger. He wanted to make sure that faithful Cowboys fans would have the best of everything; from a new stadium to a title-contending team. In short, he wants to broaden the Cowboy experience and, in the process, allow fans of all walks of life to be a part of America's Team.

GAINING PUBLIC SECTOR BUY-IN

Jones believes that a new stadium with a neighboring entertainment complex would be an extension of the Cowboys "personality."

This massive undertaking is currently being pitched to cities throughout the greater Dallas-Fort Worth area and would not only include the stadium, but would also include hundreds of acres of retail and entertainment space, as well as office space, residential housing, and even a Cowboys Hall of Fame.

In an effort to draw tourists year-round to this Cowboys' branded experience, Jones believes he needs significant public financing if the project is to be completed by the end of the decade.

Although corporations of all sizes periodically receive government subsidies or other incentives such as tax breaks, nowhere is the topic of corporate welfare as hotly debated as it is throughout sports.

Two primary reasons exist for why billionaire owners have succeeded in securing subsidies—usually in the form of taxpayer-financed stadiums. Sports leagues control the supply of, and demand for, teams. Essentially, leagues can manufacture demand by restricting the number of franchises available. Next, teams routinely control the timing of when the stadium discussion takes place. By threatening to relocate or even go out of business, teams have the ability to dictate the terms and timing to municipalities because they are more agile than their public-sector adversaries.

Although having a brand that is strong enough and positioned favorably enough to leverage public dollars takes many years to accomplish, many heavy hitters throughout the business world have done so successfully.

Consider the Boeing Corporation, for example. In 2001, Boeing, which had its headquarters in Seattle, announced it was going to move its headquarters to Chicago, which won a bid of Olympic (city bidding) proportions over Denver and Dallas.

Based on an economic impact study commissioned by the city and conducted by Arthur Andersen, it was estimated that Boeing, which generated $51.3 billion in revenue in 2000 and would qualify as Illinois' biggest company, would have an estimated $4.5 billion economic impact on the city.

This was not unlike those economic impact studies routinely commissioned by sports teams to convince voters to support a stadium financing bill. As is regularly the case with public sector financing of stadiums, economists were quick to point out that Boeing would have a marginal economic impact and many of the economic benefits that would be generated would be reaped by Boeing and its employees more than the city itself.

Boeing, like the majority of its counterparts in professional sports, prevailed and was eligible for up to $41 million in state incentives and $23 million in city donations, including money to build the corporation's hangar at Midway Airport.

Unfortunately, exactly one week after Boeing moved into its Chicago headquarters, terrorists attacked the World Trade Center and the Pentagon. This development, when combined with the lack of demand in the aircraft industry, led Boeing to announce plans to reduce its workforce by as much as 30 percent, or 30,000 workers. Toward the end of 2002, the company said it was still on target, having cut more than 24,000 jobs nationwide.

Sports fans can relate to this as they wait years and years to finally get a team only to learn that it will be a longer road to success than originally thought.

As for Jones, following the terrorist attacks, he took a slightly less in-your-face approach and demonstrated finesse in his media dealings and public relations.

When asked about stadium project delays in light of the terrorist attacks, Jones was quick to put his professional interests in perspective relative to world events. He noted that the world had become a different place and that the timing was inappropriate to consider the specifics of any proposed stadium deal. Nonetheless, Jones will revisit the issue of public sector buy-in as early as appropriate in an effort to further improve the team, the fan experience, and by extension, the franchise's value.

SEEKING OUT NEW BUSINESS OPPORTUNITIES

Fear of damaging the Cowboys brand by extending its reach was never a concern for Jerry Jones. Every time he undertook a new marketing program he did so by first ensuring that his risks had been mitigated and then by determining that the marketing opportunity would add value to his core brand.

In 1995, Jones entered into a 10-year contract between Texas Stadium and Pepsi for a reported $40 million. This arrangement angered the NFL, which had a leaguewide agreement with Coke that gave the company exclusive rights to NFL marks, including all the teams. Jones countered by reminding the NFL that the deal he struck included the stadium, and not the Cowboys directly. Despite the NFL's tremendous backlash and litigation between Jones and the league, Jones agreed to similar arrangements with Nike and American Express.

Strong corporate leaders understand Jones' basic premise that strategies that are well reasoned, communicated, and implemented build shareholder value. These leaders are also aware that vigilant brand management is required when rebuilding an organization.

In 2002, Jones debuted his second football team, the Dallas Desperados, which play in the Arena Football League (AFL). To more closely link the AFL team to the Cowboys, Jones incorporated the Cowboys famous star logo into that of the Desperados.

Brand extensions, whether attached to a sports team or packaged goods conglomerate, can also be utilized to develop the next generation of management. Jones had the entire Cowboys staff involved in the launch of the Desperados and is paying keen attention to the team's management because some of those employees might work out so well that he will want them to work directly for the Cowboys. For example, many believe Jones' son, Jerry Jones, Jr., the Desperados president and GM will eventually take on an even higher profile role with his father's team.

Jones has extended this managerial training ground beyond the front office. He hired Cowboys special teams coach Joe Avezzano, once believed to be a leading candidate to be the Cowboys head coach, to be the Desperados head coach.

League surveys have indicated that a majority percentage of AFL fans are already NFL fans, whereas only about half of NFL fans are

AFL fans. This customer dynamic will enable both teams to leverage the strengths of their committed fan bases. For instance, NFL fans that say they can't afford to attend a Cowboys game will be able to attend affordable, family-friendly professional football. Although the Cowboys' average ticket price hovers around $50, a Desperados fan could purchase a seven-game season ticket package for a total of $35.

Fans bought their tickets and gear. In their first season, the Desperados were among the leaders in home attendance—more than 12,000 fans per game—and the team advanced to the quarterfinals in the playoffs. Thanks to the team's performance and its leveraging the Cowboys retail outlets, the Desperados outsold the most of the 16-team league in terms of merchandise sales.

Jones continues to seek out additional subbrands. He has made it known that he wants to buy five or six additional franchises in another arena football league and scatter them around Texas and Mexico in the next several years. His research shows that he has reason to do it; according to Jones, the Cowboys are followed and favored by a significant percentage of Hispanics throughout the regions.

Jones never stops thinking about the next opportunity to extend the brand as evidenced by his 2001 opening of the Cowboys golf course. Jones believes the course will become as important a part of his daily business activities as Texas Stadium. He thinks the golf course will become popular because duffers won't be able to complete a round of golf without running into some ex-Cowboy, current team member, or somebody involved with the Cowboy organization.

PERSUADING CUSTOMERS TO SPREAD THE WORD

Few companies have succeeded in building their names and logos into fashion statements. Because the Cowboys, along with the Yankees, Lakers, Detroit Red Wings, and Notre Dame, are consistently among the most popular teams as measured by the sale of licensed apparel, they have succeeded in doing just that. Because they have, the Cowboys have created an incredibly unique and lucrative brand building opportunity through which everybody wearing Cowboys merchandise is essentially paying Jones for the opportunity to market his team.

As long as a company has the necessary marketing acumen and the resources to support it, it can take advantage of merchandising its name, provided it is committed to exercising control over everything that has its brand name attached to it.

Jones realized the value of managing his own merchandise operation. He took advantage of a provision in the NFL's new 10-year, $250 million apparel deal with Reebok by removing the Cowboys from the NFL's leaguewide merchandise deal. The Cowboys were the only team choosing to design and market their own merchandise. According to Jones, the decision boiled down to the issue of expertise. Jones thinks he can market and sell the Dallas Cowboys better than anyone else and is a staunch believer that the Cowboys can promote the apparel, and the apparel can promote the team.

This philosophy was on full display in July 2002 when the Cowboys announced that the J. C. Penney Co. would become the team's official apparel retailer throughout Texas, as well as New Mexico, Louisiana, Arkansas, and Oklahoma. Historically, this five-state region has accounted for more than half of the team's apparel sales in the United States.

However, this vision and strategy regarding the sale of merchandise was not new to Jones; in fact his perspective on marketing merchandise dates back nearly a decade.

In 1994, Jones worked hard to convince the league to allow him to debut a double star jersey for the traditional Thanksgiving game. Thanks to the approval and hard-core sales push, the Cowboys sold more than 130,000 of the jerseys in a single week. Today, such specialty commemorative jerseys are commonplace, and generate significant incremental revenue.

Creating additional, and sometimes subtle, opportunities to make contact with an organization's customers by offering them something unique and of value can help drive sales.

In the 1960s, former New York Jets owner Leon Hess wanted to devise a way to thank the customers of his east coast gas station chain. After establishing a relationship with a toy manufacturer, Hess started selling miniature Hess trucks at his stations. Over the years, additional products, such as Hess fire engines, buses, and vans, were offered. By 2001, a Hess helicopter, motorcycle, and cruiser were available.

Although Hess intended to use the toys as vehicles to brand the company, he also restricted output, which resulted in the products becoming valuable collectibles. In fact, several hundred Hess vehicles are typically up for bid at any given time on eBay and some pieces from 1964 have sold for more than $2,000. Dealers have even emerged who sell replacement Hess toy truck parts.

It's great advertising that reminds customers not only to come back every year to buy the latest model, but also to make it their service station of choice on a year-round basis.

Jones also undertook a transportation-related marketing and branding program. Toward the end of the 2001 season, the Cowboys announced that they would create a specialty license plate bearing the Cowboys blue star. Although regional universities had previously undertaken the same initiative, the Cowboys program had a twist— $25 of the additional license registration fee of $35 would be given back to the city of Irving, where the Cowboys play. The proceeds could then be used to either fund stadium renovation or construction.

This quasi-merchandising program provides the Cowboys with two great benefits: It subtly markets the team statewide, and provides a facilities improvement fund that is dedicated to enhancing the fan experience.

Hess and Jones have tactically utilized the creation and sale of merchandise to extend their brands, building additional awareness while increasing revenue.

MAKING A NAME FOR THEMSELVES

Sports marketers were quick to point out that each of Jones' proposals were brand-building opportunities designed to enhance the Cowboys brand name. Analysts noted that if organizations don't continue to reinforce and extend their brands, they will wake up someday and another company will have overtaken them. This concept applies throughout sports, where sports teams and leagues must not become defensive about brand management. The players will come and go, but it's the brand—for better or worse—that will live on.

Recall from Chapter 9 that the Cowboys' brand value, as determined by FutureBrand, a global consultant on corporate brands, was worth $300 million and ranked second in sports behind only the Yankees.

FutureBrand determined the value of each brand by calculating the revenue and profit stream generated by the brand and the strength or degree of risk of the brand in its market in relation to competitors.

The Cowboys have historically—and successfully—positioned themselves as the "Spirit of Texas" even though they are not located in the largest city in Texas. The team has also either won consistently or been perceived as attempting to make the necessary moves to achieve success on the field.

Although boasting a strong and committed fan base certainly adds to brand value, so does management's ability to market a team's popularity. In fact, by allocating the necessary time and resources to building (or repositioning) a brand, sports franchises like the Cowboys—like any organization—can protect important customer relationships and ensure that there is healthy cash flow even during losing seasons.

Few companies enjoy the notoriety and television exposure provided the Cowboys every Sunday afternoon in the fall, but there are creative ways to gain exposure for a company, allowing it to stand out from its competitors.

National companies that have large advertising budgets don't limit their high-profile sports marketing activities to buying a 30-second ad during the Super Bowl or a half-inning virtual advertisement behind home plate during the World Series.

Many large companies have put a slightly different spin on the Cowboys strategy of subtle, almost subliminal, marketing. Rather than selling merchandise directly to avid fans who, in turn, market the team, companies have utilized product placement in television shows or in movies to associate their products with popular entertainment brands. Reese's Pieces experienced 65 percent short-term growth after being featured in the blockbuster movie *E.T.*, and companies hoping to reach sports fans, including Nextel, were provided broad exposure in the sports-themed movie *Driven*, an auto-racing movie starring Sylvester Stallone.

Small companies must similarly be creative when attempting to extend their brand by doing so on a local or regional level. This can be accomplished by sponsoring a local Little League team or by having its products strategically placed in community theaters where local actors tacitly promote the company's products during a play.

Brands, regardless of their size or stature, that successfully reposition themselves leverage their customer base by creatively and effectively communicating their product attributes through strategic marketing campaigns.

The Cowboys have demonstrated their understanding of this concept as evidenced by the team's extending its sellout streak at Texas Stadium beyond 100 games, a streak that dates back to 1991 and includes both regular and postseason games.

Sports business analysts assessed the team's ability to do so during a time in which the Cowboys fielded less competitive teams than its fans were accustomed to. These analysts were quick to point out that the Cowboys, unlike most franchises, were nimble and able to respond quickly to changing market conditions.

However, these same analysts indicated the importance of the Cowboys brand name in the process by suggesting that the Cowboys are fortunate they've got a top brand because it is easier to be agile and astute when you have a premier global brand.

CHAMPIONSHIP POINTS

Jerry Jones not only understands FutureBrand's perspective on brand building and the shareholder (fan) value it creates, he has taken it to a level not previously found in the sports world. Love 'em or hate 'em, Jones' Cowboys continue to define and then redefine how businesses are run and, when necessary, repositioned.

Jones and his Cowboys have provided vivid examples of what it takes to turn a business around. Business people that seek to revitalize their businesses must do the following:

- Realize that all industries are cyclical and that it's merely a matter of when—not if—a business will incur a down cycle. How far into the business season was it before you realized your company was further behind the competition than you thought? The Cowboys slipped to 3-13; how far below .500 might you fall? Failing to properly delegate authority undermines management's relationships.

- Thoroughly craft or revise a comprehensive strategy. It is necessary to revisit all internal and external aspects of the business, including senior management. When conducting this analysis and making changes, it is critical to include employees in the process, appreciating the role they play.

- Redouble their efforts to secure visionary leadership. Making the tough calls will not be easy but strong and credible stewardship will go a long way to assuaging employee and shareholder concerns.
- Recognize that not all elements of the business or organization need an overhaul. Know who your "Wendy's" are and make sure you keep them; don't throw the baby (Snapple) out with the bath water.
- Identify—and invest in—their "franchise" players like the Cowboys did with Troy Aikman. Conversely, companies must not underestimate the harm serious personnel problems can cause to the organization.
- Understand that the more successful the company has been, the quicker results (i.e., the turnaround) will be expected.
- Recognize the critical role of savvy media and public relations. The media filters any and all messages and can position a company as it sees fit. A failure to allocate sufficient resources to ensure a positive relationship with the media leaves a company vulnerable during periods of change.
- Leverage the brand's positives. Whether this involves acquiring or extending a brand, keen attention must be paid to all elements of the marketing process whenever a significant brand opportunity presents itself.
- Invest in and protect the business. If you consistently refine your business you might not be faced with having to totally reposition it.

Once a business has been established, customers have been reached and adequately serviced, attention is turned to branding, as well as dealing with employees, business allies, and the inevitable crisis.

Throughout it all, one consistent theme emerges: Without proper leadership, businesses and organizations of all types, including those operating throughout the sports world, cannot succeed in the long run.

11 LEADERSHIP

The Point: It is not possible to achieve and extend success in any of the business tenets highlighted throughout On the Ball *without the presence of leadership. The approaches to, and styles of, leadership laced throughout earlier chapters might vary, but the primary point is the same: Tremendous business acumen might move the ball down the field but, without leadership, it will be nearly impossible to punch it over the goal line.*

When most of us think about America's greatest sports leaders, prominent coaches, and Hall-of-Fame ballplayers who redefined their game or fundamentally changed the way the sport was perceived, a few names quickly come to mind: John Wooden, Vince Lombardi, Red Auerbach, Bear Bryant, Tommy Lasorda, and Pat Summit are all top of mind. So too are Jerry West, Roger Staubach, Michael Jordan, Billie Jean King, and Wayne Gretzky.

Each of these coaches and players—in his or her own way and with his or her own style—demonstrated power and influence. Each had a vision, and each was innovative.

The same has held true over the years on the business side of sports, where noteworthy leadership has resulted in sports fans' ability to follow and, in many cases, live vicariously through the exploits of the coaches and players just mentioned.

For example, NFL Commissioner Pete Rozelle, who led the league from 1960 through 1989, increased the 12-team league to 28 teams and, in the process, increased the NFL's revenue by billions of dollars by crafting lucrative TV deals and maintaining an unparalleled degree of labor stability.

Roone Arledge, like Rozelle, redefined his business—in this case televised sports. Arledge is credited with creating both of ABC's most prolific sports programs—the anthology show *Wide World of Sports*, which debuted in 1961, and *Monday Night Football*, which hit the airwaves in 1970. It was Arledge's leadership and vision that provided "the thrill of victory and the agony of defeat" to generations of sports fans.

Former MLB Commissioner Peter Ueberroth who, in 1984, led the Los Angeles Olympic Organizing Committee, ushered in the era in which sports truly became a business. It was under Ueberroth's leadership that, for the first time, the Olympic Games were privately funded, financed in large part through a relatively underutilized sports marketing concept—corporate sponsorship. The 1984 Los Angeles Games posted a profit of $215 million and resulted in Ueberroth's being named *Time* magazine's "Man of the Year."

University of Maryland athletics director Debbie Yow has blazed trails for women administrators who one day hope to lead other powerhouse universities. Hired in 1994, Yow, who was the president of the National Association of Collegiate Directors of Athletics, has not only seen her Terrapins win nine national championships, including the men's basketball championship in the 2001-02 season, but she has also measurably improved the department's financial standing. Among her most impressive accomplishments: The defending NCAA basketball champs now play at the Comcast Center, a new arena that was financed and constructed under her leadership.

It is not just executives who have become sports business pioneers and leaders. Great athletes who have championed causes have also become sports business leaders. Chief among these are Jackie Robinson and, indirectly, Curt Flood. After signing with the Brooklyn Dodgers in 1945, Robinson, who realized the importance of having an impact on the lives of others, forever changed sport's landscape by breaking baseball's color barrier two years later.

A quarter-century later, baseball's new player leader was the St. Louis Cardinals' Curt Flood, who refused to be traded to the Philadelphia Phillies in 1969. Although not as vocal or passionate a leader as Robinson, Flood's refusal to change teams triggered one of the sports industry's most important events. Despite the fact that Flood eventually lost his legal battle to become a "free agent," his actions set the stage for free agency, a development that subsequently and significantly increased player salaries in baseball.

Although they demonstrated them quite differently on occasion, each of these leaders, whether "mere" coaches or athletes, league executives, or media moguls shared many leadership traits. Each understood, whether they knew it or not, the essence of leadership.

THE ESSENCE OF LEADERSHIP

Attempting to define leadership is a lot like trying to hit a moving target. As business and society change, so do the expectations and traits of its leaders. Although the process of providing leadership is a dynamic and ever-changing one, its basic definition varies little: Leadership is the process of influencing others to accomplish an established mission by providing purpose, direction, and motivation.

What makes a great leader—either on the field or in the board-room? Distinguished leaders tend to possess and demonstrate a confluence of personal and professional attributes. Effective leaders tend to do things addressed in the following sections.[1]

BE PASSIONATE

Without passion for the game of business and its purpose, it's easy to become complacent. When passion is lacking in leadership, it limits the motivation of others.

Few doubt that Yankees owner George Steinbrenner is extraordinarily passionate about the game. Sure, with a large local television contract and three million fans packing Yankee Stadium each year, he has the sport's greatest means in the nation's largest media market. Even with these advantages that make the Yankees a perennial World Series contender, Steinbrenner continues to spend millions each year in an attempt to acquire that last free agent—that final piece of the puzzle—before the team's final playoff push.

Steinbrenner's passion to make the Yankees the best at everything the team undertakes translates into a standard of excellence

---

1. Reprinted with permission: True Leaders, by Bette Price and George Ritcheske. © 2001, by Dearborn Financial Publishing, Inc. Chicago, IL. All rights reserved. For more information call toll free: 1-800-245-BOOK.

that exists even when Steinbrenner isn't around. His passion extends to manager Joe Torre, who instills the same passion with his team. Passionate leadership is not only embraced by those within an organization, but it can also be contagious, leading others to demonstrate important leadership skills.

BE INTUITIVE

Prominent leaders never underestimate the important role played by intuition. Years of management experience can make "going with your gut" an invaluable leadership trait.

Joe Montana, the 49ers quarterback who won all four Super Bowls he played in, also led his team to 32 fourth-quarter comebacks throughout his Hall of Fame career. He wasn't able to win these games by simply relying on the same plays over and over again. He won many of these games because, under intense pressure to perform, he was able to draw from his vast experiences to successfully improvise. Montana's improvisation would not have been nearly as successful had he or his teammates lacked confidence in his ability to achieve where others had fallen short.

Once Montana determined a course of action—scrambling, throwing the ball out of bounds, or taking a rare sack—he didn't second-guess himself. This contributed to his ability, under extreme duress, to deliver the perfect spiral that eventually moved the chains and allowed the team to emerge victorious.

LISTEN CAREFULLY

By listening, renowned leaders facilitate dialogue and provide a forum for sharing ideas. Listening provides the opportunity to exchange meaningful feedback, making everyone in the process feel as if they are part of it.

Gavin and Joe Maloof, owners of the NBA's Sacramento Kings, go out of their way to be good listeners. Similar to Mark Cuban, owner of the Mavericks, the Maloofs appreciate that they alone cannot recognize or uncover every little detail that might be missing from their customers, the fans, total experience. They repeatedly make themselves available and ask the fans what they want and need to become and remain long-term customers. The Maloofs are so interested in learning what they need to improve that they are among the only owners who give out business cards to fans with their office and, on occasion, their cell phone numbers on it.

The Maloofs roam Arco Arena with an open-door attitude. Great leaders in the office don't go out of their way to sit far away from where the action in the office occurs. They make sure their door is open not only to the employees, but also find ways to have direct interaction with customers, whether it's through one-on-one interaction at shareholder meetings or simply reading occasional e-mail feedback. Thanks in part to their dedication to listening to the fans, both the Maloofs and the Kings, who fell one game short of advancing to the 2002 NBA Finals, have become industry leaders.

HAVE INTEGRITY

Notable leaders continually demonstrate the ability to make just and right decisions, and do so courageously and truthfully.

Legendary UCLA basketball coach John Wooden will be remembered in the record books for winning 10 NCAA men's championships in 12 years and concluding a 40-year coaching career with an .813 winning percentage. Equally—if not more—important, Wooden will also be remembered for his commitment to being a consummate teacher and mentor to his players, athletes who he not only treated as students, but as extended family as well.

Wooden realized that he was a role model and made sure to conduct himself in a manner he would want his players to emulate. He became famous for his Pyramid of Success, a framework that helps demonstrate what Wooden believes to be the optimal balance to achieve success in life. The pyramid, elements of which include friendship, self-control, and competitive greatness, continues to serve as a framework subscribed to by sports and business leaders at all levels of their respective games.

BE CARING

Great leaders show that they care about those around them by identifying, embracing, and capitalizing on their strengths. Leaders not only uncover each individual's uniqueness, but also acknowledge and reward it, as well as seek to maximize it.

African-American track star Jesse Owens will always be remembered for taking home four gold medals in the 1936 Berlin Olympics, stunning Nazi leader Adolf Hitler in the process. However, Owens should also be remembered for what he did following the Olympics as a playground director in Cleveland and director of the Chicago Boys Club. Owens devoted his post-Olympic career to helping poor children living in downtrodden areas by helping them appreciate that sports could serve as a valuable outlet in their lives. Owens worked individually with these kids, encouraging and convincing them to become keenly interested in the sport that they most enjoyed or were good at playing.

Like Owens, great business leaders spend time observing what "sport" (i.e., business interest or skill) their associates are most adept at and enjoy playing the most. Like Owens, who demonstrated to children that participating in sports held great rewards, including being an alternative to mischief and potentially a way out of a troubled community, successful business leaders make clear to associates the rewards of doing the work they are assigned.

THINK STRATEGICALLY

Absent a strategic approach to the game, leaders compromise their ability to identify meaningful information and to spot important trends that help them see the entire playing field.

Amos Alonzo Stagg, the legendary football coach at the University of Chicago for 41 years (1892-1932), revolutionized the sport by recognizing the role strategy played in fielding a winning team. Stagg not only invented the huddle, the T-formation, the onside kick, and the lateral pass—all of which helped his teams dominate the opposition—but he also is credited with numbering plays and having his players wear different numbered jerseys. Such ingenuity made it quite difficult on his competition because each time the opposition played Stagg's Maroons they were trying to comprehend and adapt to his ever-changing innovations and strategies.

Because Stagg, from a strategic perspective, was constantly on the offensive, his opponents were routinely relegated to playing defense—an exhausting and often losing proposition for many organizations.

DEVELOP TRUST

Successful leaders understand the importance of fostering trust throughout the organization. Not only does trust enhance commitment throughout the organization, it enables people to deal more realistically and effectively with winning and losing.

Duke basketball coach Mike Krzyzewski isn't just a great recruiter. He also teaches his talented players to play through difficult situations. While many coaches call timeouts during every tough stretch, "Coach K"—much like Lakers coach Phil Jackson—often lets his players figure out how to get out of the situation themselves. Not only does this say to his players "I have faith in you," but it can also foster a measure of trust between the players and between the players and their coach. When the players lose in a system like this, there's less finger-pointing. When players emerge victorious, there are enough accolades for everyone.

Krzyzewski might have a talented team every year, but he also deserves credit for the system of trust he has established and passed along to generations of student-athletes.

TAKE CHANCES

Knowing how and when to take chances—and the impact doing so will have on the organization and its people—is an important skill shared by strong leaders. By providing support and encouragement along the way, the leader will gain buy-in when taking measured risk.

Brooklyn Dodgers president and GM Branch Rickey wasn't all that great of a player, but as a general manager with the St. Louis Cardinals, he invented the modern-day farm system, a concept that helped earn the team nine pennants and six World Series titles. However, the reason Rickey was named the fourth most influential person in 20th-century sports history by ESPN (behind Rozelle, baseball's first Commissioner, Kenesaw Mountain Landis, and Arledge), was because he had the self-confidence and the courage to sign the first African-American player, Jackie Robinson, in 1945.

At a time when desegregation was still 20 years away, not only did Rickey want to sign the best players possible in an effort to be competitive, but he admittedly wanted to make a statement with Robinson's signing, never fearing being ridiculed or scorned by others. Robinson, of course, became one of the top 50 players of all time and helped the Dodgers compete for the championship year after year.

KEEP LEARNING

Eminent leaders realize they don't know it all. They recognize the talents of the people around them and appreciate that these individuals often have important perspectives on how to address critical situations.

Look at the sidelines during a Florida State Seminole football game and you will notice that head coach Bobby Bowden does very little active coaching or play calling. The septuagenarian legend is neither tired nor lazy. Nor is he so cocky about his team's ability that he believes he can simply strut the sidelines, occasionally giving live interviews to the press while plays are being run.

Rather, Bowden has mastered the art of surrounding himself with other great leaders, secure in his ability to delegate authority and create an environment in which decisions made by those under him are thoroughly supported by the team. He and his staff teach— and learn from—one another in extraordinarily public and pressure-packed settings. It is, therefore, not much of a surprise that Bowden's assistant coaches are also highly coveted each season by other teams who are looking to replace their head coaches.

FIND BALANCE

When a leader fails to encourage a semblance of balance in the workplace, the organization often suffers greatly by incurring hidden costs, not the least of which is a demoralized team.

NFL referees perform some of the greatest balancing acts seen in the workplace. Unlike referees and umpires in the other three major sports, whose officiating duties constitute a full-time occupation, NFL officials work only part time due to the limited number of games in the season. However, this doesn't diminish their value or impact on the field. They spend most of the week at regular day jobs (as school principals, lawyers, doctors, golf pros, etc.) and part of each week studying film, reviewing their prior week's performance, and officiating games.

Former NFL referee Jerry Markbreit, who worked for 23 seasons and a record four Super Bowls, is one of the most recognizable officials in sports history. Markbreit, who served as the league's head of officials, sold and bartered advertising time for 3M during the week, but was always prepared to make the important calls on the weekends.

The leadership demonstrated by NFL referees doesn't suggest that one needs to have two real jobs. In essence, we all have at least two "jobs" that we need to balance, whether it's work and work, work and play, work and family, or work and rest. Influential leaders know how to best allocate their time to each of these professional and personal needs, and do so while inspiring others in the process.

THE HOME STRETCH

Stellar leadership has not been limited to the exploits of players, coaches, administrators, or team owners. It has become increasingly apparent in all areas of sports business, enabling executives to lead their employees and organizations, while navigating the business tenets described throughout this book. In some cases, it has been a lack of leadership or vision that has provided important business lessons.

PASSION MATTERS WHEN BUILDING A BUSINESS

It is important never to forget the value in doing the little things that may, at first blush, seem mundane or "beneath" you. Just because companies succeed in growing and evolving to become global brands like NASCAR, it doesn't mean that they should shy away from doing the little things that helped them secure their lofty position in the first place. Brett Yormark, vice president of corporate marketing for NASCAR, knows that doing so can pay big dividends.

Yormark walks the floors at trade shows searching for new corporate sponsors and since he's one of the only sports executives that does, it pays off.

NASCAR has signed at least six new sponsors over the last several years as a result of this press-the-flesh strategy: Nikon, Arctic Cat, Just Born, M/I Homes, and numerous Sara Lee brands, including Ballpark Franks. This highly personalized and one-on-one approach to relationship building is all too rare among companies the size of NASCAR.

It must be noted that Yormark doesn't simply wander aimlessly from trade show to trade show picking up goodie bags while weaving from booth to booth. Rather, he and NASCAR choose the shows based on numerous criteria, including sponsor categories it seeks to fill, extend, or better service. Beyond these criteria, NASCAR culls through exhibitor lists for specific companies whose customer demographic matches that of NASCAR's.

It is precisely this attitude and approach that has enabled NASCAR to grow from a small, family-owned business into a big-league operation while enjoying an industrywide leadership position in the process. When it's all said and done, those that continue to lead NASCAR, including Yormark, are passionate about their business and its purpose.

RELY ON INTUITION WHEN SEGMENTING MARKETS

Even inadvertently and without any expectation of return on investment, companies must remember that although coveted markets can be easily identified and accessed, exploiting them might still carry a high price, especially in an era of skepticism.

Consider the ShopRite of Brooklawn Gymnasium. That's right, an elementary school gym planned for the small New Jersey town has sold the naming rights to the facility to a corporate sponsor. The owner of the local supermarket, part of a major New Jersey-based chain, pledged $100,000 over 20 years for the naming rights. Suddenly, Alice Costello Elementary School, with 230 students in kindergarten through eighth grade, has gone "big league."

Sports Illustrated cited the deal in is segment entitled, "This Week's Sign of the Apocalypse." ESPN Radio held a call-in debate about whether nothing is sacred. A sports radio talk show host in Philadelphia suggested calling the gym by its acronym, the SOB Gymnasium, and asked if there were plans for a Bud Light Library.

ShopRite owner Jeffrey Brown could not understand all the media attention. As a prominent local benefactor, Brown has helped out a transportation business assisting senior citizens and paid for repairs at a local skating rink. He said he made the $5,000-a-year pledge before the mayor told him he would name the gym ShopRite. Brown conceded that he wasn't likely to see a big increase in business from having the ShopRite name on a gym at a school with 230 students; in fact, this was not among his primary considerations. Due to his track record of philanthropy and community support, he didn't believe such a deal would be the beginning of a new trend in naming rights as critics feared.

Nonetheless, and because many believed Brown's well-intentioned maneuver was a sign of corporate excess, ShopRite's good name was tarnished by those not familiar enough with the situation to see that the payment had more to do with charity than market segmentation. Had Brown exercised a bit more intuition along the way—the sort that enabled him to build ShopRite into a household name—some of the highly public debate might have been muted.

Many of business and industry's great leaders might have the instincts to successfully run their own organizations, but they often lose that advantage when attempting to apply the same type of business acumen, including intuition, to the world of sports.

LISTEN INTENTLY WHEN DEALING WITH CUSTOMER SERVICE ISSUES

Organizations would do well to remember that they are built one customer at a time and that providing them a compelling "takeaway" from their interaction with your business will differentiate it from the competition. Further, knowing your customers wants and needs—whether those customers are other corporations or the end user—has gained unparalleled importance in today's business world.

Throughout professional sports, marketing has focused as much on stemming potential erosions in the corporate and everyday fan bases as it has on developing the next generation of customers.

The Dodgers not only understand the need to replenish customers; they are unceremoniously perfecting it by embracing the changing face of Southern California. Recently released census figures revealed that the Latino population grew 35 percent during the 1990s, resulting in one-third of the nation's Latinos calling California home. The same Census Bureau report indicated that unincorporated East Los Angeles, Santa Ana, El Monte, and Oxnard were among the nation's 10 largest Latino hubs. All totaled, 46.5 percent of Angelenos are Latino.

This extraordinary increase in the Latino population and, by extension, its spending power, has not been lost on the Dodgers or its corporate partners. For the 17th year, the team drew more than 3 million fans to Chavez Ravine, nearly one-third of whom were Latino.

Building and maintaining a loyal Latino fan base is critical, as research shows these fans to be the Dodgers most avid supporters, a fact not lost on either the team or its sponsors; each of which seeks to build a better relationship with this important demographic group. To ensure that this occurs, the Dodgers, in addition to having numerous Latino players on their roster, undertake several marketing initiatives designed to both service and increase this fan base.

For example, the team's "Dia de los Niños" promotion was an event that celebrated the Mexican tradition and combined family entertainment with a special ticket offer, autograph sessions, and interactive games. The Dodgers were able to reinforce their appreciation of, and connection to, Latino fans—while attracting 12,000 additional fans.

The Dodgers followed this event by hosting their annual "Viva Los Dodgers" event. Featuring concerts, player appearances, and exhibitors, this event was strongly supported by major team sponsors such as Coca-Cola, Anheuser-Busch, and Toyota. These corporate partners eagerly participate in these promotions as they too recognize the importance of embracing the Latino community and its growing economic clout.

Working together, the team and its sponsors seek to continually reinforce and communicate their commitment to the next generation of Dodger fans. By listening, the team has endeared itself to both fans and sponsors, simultaneously demonstrating and reinforcing its leadership position in professional sports.

INTEGRITY MATTERS WHEN ESTABLISHING, MAINTAINING, AND EXTENDING A PERSONAL BRAND

Business people would be wise to take seriously what so many athletes seem to brush off—that their personal brand needs to be managed and extended daily, particularly for those occupying high-profile positions. A failure to micromanage this part of one's career can be detrimental in the long run.

During the 2001 French Open, Serena Williams, admitting she had bought everything from flowers to handbags online, was concerned about her rapidly emerging spending habits. In an apparent effort to save energy and time, and to avoid crowds, Williams feared that she had become a "shopaholic," addicted to making online purchases. Once the situation became public, the matter gained importance and, along with it, broad media attention and dialog about the compulsion.

Had Williams and her management team not confronted the problem it could have led potential sponsors to wonder whether she had other, potentially more destructive compulsions. By demonstrating the ability to make just the right decisions, and by doing so courageously and truthfully, this shopping addiction has had little impact on her ability to establish and extend her personal brand.

Today, there's plenty of extending to do. Serena, who for so long played second fiddle to her sister, Venus, both on the court and in endorsement appeal, first took over the number one ranking in July 2002. In 2002, she won three out of the four grand slams—the French Open, Wimbledon, and the U.S. Open—beating her sister in the championship match in all three.

BE CARING WHEN ISSUES OF EMPLOYEE RELATIONS ARISE

Both employers and employees must prepare themselves to deal with change, while acting in the best interests of both parties when addressing "hot-button" issues.

Over nearly a four-year period between 1997 and 2001, these employee relations dynamics were on full display between the PGA Tour and golfer Casey Martin. Martin filed a lawsuit in federal court in November of 1997 against the PGA Tour in an attempt to earn the right to use a cart during competition. Martin, who suffers from a disorder in his right leg called Klippel-Trenaunay-Weber Syndrome, has a condition that not only prevents him from walking long distances, but may even eventually force his leg to be amputated.

Following years of various court rulings, the U.S. Supreme Court ruled in Martin's favor in May 2001. Throughout the process PGA Tour Commissioner Tim Finchem held the belief that allowing Martin to use a cart afforded him an unfair competitive advantage.

This position was echoed by many of the sport's icons, including Jack Nicklaus, who emphatically believes that walking the golf course is part of the sport. Nicklaus suggested that the members of the Supreme Court who voted in favor of the use of carts should be taken out to play a round of golf and, in doing so, they would no doubt recognize that walking the course is fundamental to the sport.

Once the final ruling was handed down, Finchem was quick to acknowledge Martin's victory by crediting how well Martin had handled the situation. Finchem even went so far as to say that Martin is the kind of young man Finchem wants playing on his tour.

Although it can be debated whether Martin's circumstances were rooted in medicine, law, or in a sympathetic figure's ability to overcome adversity, what cannot be denied is that a strong undercurrent of employee relations was present throughout the ordeal.

Had Finchem not handled this employee issue with care by measuring his response to both Martin's claim and the ensuing Supreme Court decision, major constituents, including the sport's TV partners, sponsors, equipment manufacturers, and even players, would have jeopardized the emerging success of the PGA Tour brought about by Martin's college roommate at Stanford, Tiger Woods. Although Martin ultimately didn't have an enormous impact on the links (he made just 6 of his first 20 cuts in the Buy.com—now called the Nationwide Tour—tournaments after the ruling), the PGA Tour's approach to reconciling such a hotly debated matter was applauded.

THINK STRATEGICALLY WHEN CONTEMPLATING THE MERITS OF AN ALLIANCE

It is critical to remember that the value of an alliance lies in its ability to create opportunities for positioning a company and its allies in a stronger position to conduct business. By joining forces and know-how, the organizations can leverage their core strengths, allowing the whole to be greater than the individual parts.

Such was the thinking behind AOL and the NBA when they announced a strategic marketing alliance to promote NBA.com and WNBA.com, as well as AOL's Internet service and Web sites.

By partnering a global sports brand like the NBA with AOL's 22 million members, both entities find themselves uniquely positioned to extend their reach to coveted target markets. In the deal AOL receives extensive promotion on TNT cable TV channels during their coverage of NBA games. Further, AOL was granted access to NBA trademarks, player names, and logos for use on its site and throughout its fantasy basketball section.

For its part, the NBA exploited the marketing alliance by promoting its content through AOL's Internet properties, including AOL's main Web site, CompuServe, and Netscape. Additionally, information, highlights, and stats from the NBA and WNBA will be directly integrated into the various AOL channels that cover basketball, such as "AOL Sport" and "Kids Only."

This alliance, which seems to be a match made in heaven for Web-surfing hoops fans, should help increase the asset value of both the NBA and AOL, a development not lost on either partner. Those responsible for crafting this alliance were both imaginative and strategic, which enabled each to capitalize on important and emerging business opportunities.

DEVELOP TRUST WHEN DEALING WITH CRISES

Organizations must be prepared to confront the challenge head on, and do so at a time of heightened media attention.

When Danny Almonte threw a no-hitter for the "Baby Bombers" of the Rolando Paulino Little League in the Bronx, New York, on national TV, it enabled the team to make it to the Little League World Series (LLWS). Almonte then followed this amazing feat by throwing the first no-hitter in 44 years in his team's opening game at the LLWS against a team from Apopka, Florida.

As it turned out, after the Baby Bombers finished third in the LLWS, the primary reason for Almonte's dominance was that he was much older than the other kids—too old, in fact, to be a member of the team. During the LLWS, Almonte, along with his manager, Alberto Gonzalez and league founder, Rolando Paulino, repeatedly denied that Almonte was too old to play in the tournament, which only allows players who are 12 or younger. When the three were questioned, they produced documents, including a birth certificate and a passport, that indicated Almonte was indeed 12.

However, the day after the Bronx team placed third in the LLWS, a reporter for *Sports Illustrated* in the Dominican Republic found another birth certificate showing that Almonte was 14 years old, and its authenticity was verified by the Dominican government. Making matters worse, further investigation showed Almonte had not been in the United States until shortly before the international tournament began, meaning that he could not have met Little League's residency requirements. For the short time Almonte was in the country, another piece of news broke: He had never attended school.

Yes, the Baby Bombers were stripped of their third-place finish. Yes, Almonte's remarkable performances were expunged from the record. Yes, Paulino and Almonte's father, Felipe de Jesus Almonte, were banned for life from Little League. And yes, Stephen D. Keener, President and CEO of Little League Baseball Inc., announced changes in the way Little League verifies player eligibility.

However, none of this mattered to the media—or many of the other stakeholders in this crisis including LLWS sponsors, who were dismayed that such a breach in integrity could have happened to such an American institution. The media found this story too good to pass up, covering impromptu news conferences on live TV and stating that this instance signaled the end of integrity in sports as we knew it.

Because a significant lack of trust emerged between and among the leaders in this crisis, and by not finding a way to nip this crisis in the bud, the Almonte story became one of the leading sports stories in 2001.

KNOW WHEN TO TAKE CHANCES WHEN ATTEMPTING TO PENETRATE A NEW MARKET

You must remember to carefully navigate the cultural and political differences, as well as differences in consumer tastes and preferences.

Over the last couple of seasons, officials of the Montreal Expos have flirted with the notion of relocating to Washington, D.C. The franchise's desire to leave Canada for the U.S stemmed from, among other issues, the team's poor fan base and comparably weak Canadian dollar. On the one hand, the team, which is now controlled by MLB following a series of league changes, finds itself in a more favorable position to penetrate this market given the collective influence of the league instead of a single, individual owner. However, the league's attempt to enter the nation's capitol also poses major challenges dealing with potential customers, political forces, and litigation.

Not only does no one live in this commuter town, but Washington, D.C. is known for its pork, whether attached to political bills or the NFL's Redskins, whose notorious fans, the "hogs," are among the most ravenous in sports. Whenever a sports franchise threatens to move, local politicians routinely weigh in on the issue, hoping to demonstrate to voters their keen understanding of sports' proper place in the community. It's one thing when such an occurrence happens in Peoria, and quite another when it happens in the political capitol of the world. Although MLB might want to move the Expos to avoid further monetary losses and to make money by selling the team to a Washington, D.C.-based group, MLB might find relocating to Washington D.C. at a time when baseball's antitrust exemption is a hot political potato as challenging a circumstance to overcome as an uncertain fan base.

The market for professional sports entertainment differs greatly between Montreal and Washington, D.C. The Redskins, along with the NBA's Wizards and the NHL's Capitals, contribute mightily to the competition for the entertainment dollar. Moreover, the Expos would lack the long-standing connection to the region enjoyed by the Redskins and their loyal fans.

In short, penetrating a "foreign" market, such as Washington, D.C. might be a tough task. At the very least, it requires MLB to closely scrutinize market conditions before attempting to change addresses. If it chooses to take this chance, it will be required to measure the impact doing so will have on the organization and its people.

KEEP LEARNING WHEN SETTING OUT TO BUILD A CORPORATE BRAND

Organizations must retain a brand management visionary who not only identifies internal and external opportunities for, and influences on, the brand, but also commits to providing stellar customer service.

The great world-spanning Harlem Globetrotters, whose rich heritage has included all-time greats Wilt Chamberlain and Meadowlark Lemon, were going bankrupt in the early 1990s when former Globetrotter turned successful businessman Mannie Jackson bought them for $5.5 million with the intention of returning the team to prominence.

Jackson was perfect to lead the renaissance because as a former Globetrotter he knew what the brand was all about and what made it great in its heyday. Jackson paid his players very well, more than any basketball league in the U.S., with the exception of the NBA. He made sure they understood what the brand stood for and made sure the team once again became synonymous with good, clean, affordable family fun. Once accomplished, he went to sponsors and raised more than $50 million.

To gain respect among hard-core basketball fans, Jackson arranged for the Globetrotters to play collegiate teams, doing so in 1997 for the first time in 35 years. By 2000, the team was beating the likes of University of Iowa, St. John's, and Minnesota, and received great accolades for having the guts to take on the defending national champs, the Michigan State Spartans, despite the fact that their loss meant an end to their well-chronicled 1,270-game winning streak.

Fan surveys conducted in 2001 indicated that 71 percent of the audience in attendance to see the kings of comedy on the court and listen to Sweet Georgia Brown was with a family member. With the median ticket price of $12.50 and the team's attendance increasing every year, average annual revenue growth has been about 17 percent since 1993. The Globetrotters 2002 schedule had two teams playing in 300 cities worldwide with 100 games overseas in 25 countries.

Per-capita spending on souvenirs from Globetrotters events is now among the highest of any professional sports team. This is a testament to the fact that Jackson has revived the Globetrotters brand to a point where it is once again sought after, even though their greatest fans, unlike those of any other professional sports franchise, likely only see the team play once a year.

By constantly learning more about his customers and their likes, dislikes, and spending habits, Jackson was able to rescue a great American sports brand.

In September 2002, the Globetrotters were inducted into the Basketball Hall of Fame in the same class as Lakers great Magic Johnson.

Seek balance when it comes time to turning a business around

Organizations must, among other things, redouble their efforts to secure visionary leadership, recognize the critical role of savvy media and pubic relations, and invest in and protect their brand.

This is precisely what occurred at the University of Notre Dame, when the school—after the O'Leary bio debacle—selected Stanford head coach Tyrone Willingham to lead its football program. The Fighting Irish hired Willingham as their first African-American head coach in any sport in the school's history after he proved he could win at an institution with high academic standards, even higher than those of Notre Dame's. Willingham's Stanford teams reached four bowl games in seven years, including the 1999 Rose Bowl.

Not only was it anticipated that Willingham would turn Notre Dame around in its first season, 2002, but it was all but expected by legions of Irish faithful. There was little room for error at the only university boasting its own contract with a television network—NBC will reportedly pay Notre Dame $9.2 million a year through 2005 to air at least five Fighting Irish games per season. Even despite its recent foibles, Notre Dame remains the most popular football team in the country in terms of avid fan base.

And Willingham didn't disappoint. He communicated to his team and to the media that he would make no excuses from day one, and accepted that any learning curve had to be abbreviated—if it were to exist at all. The day he was named coach, a media member asked Willingham what he thought of the tough schedule against Maryland, Purdue, and Michigan. Instead of being vague, as many coaches are inclined to be in such circumstances, Willingham set the bar high, saying that Notre Dame must prevail, it must win, it must go out and get the job done. With a roster containing many of the players that led the team to a woeful 5-6 record in 2001, Willingham's team opened the season strong. By winning its first eight games, including victories over nationally ranked Maryland, Michigan, and Florida State, the team was consistently ranked in the top 10.

With his trademark index finger near his mouth or his arms sternly crossed on the sidelines, Willingham's nonverbal communication skills exude intensity and confidence to his players, the school, and, perhaps even more importantly, to opposing teams. His demeanor, presence, and well-spoken ways off the field have enabled Willingham to become quickly one of college football's most revered leaders.

Businesses that seek to revitalize themselves must have a leader like Willingham who can quickly and easily garner consensus about not only senior management's ability and vision, but do so while masterfully handling important stakeholders, including (prospective) employees (i.e., recruits), board members (university trustees), sharcholders (alumni), and the media.

Because Willingham has constantly delivered an acceptable balance to his constituents, especially his players, he has been better able than most to establish and extend a winning atmosphere.

By now it should be abundantly clear that the sports business has become an extremely involved industry that includes the same elements and applies the same business principles seen throughout the rest of big business.

On the Ball has chronicled many of the sports industry's most important, if not outrageous developments, hoping to provide specific lessons that can be learned from the actions and, in all too many cases, inaction, of industry leaders.

There is much that can be applied to "regular businesses" from the teachings of sports business leaders, many of whom have done well as others have stumbled, damaging both their organization's brand and their own. *On the Ball* has attempted to provide relevant and important takeaways courtesy of those running (ruining?) sports that readers can immediately and readily apply to their own business environment.

INDEX

8 reasons why you should read the Financial Times for 4 weeks RISK-FREE!

To help you stay current with significant
developments in the world economy ...
and to assist you to make informed business
decisions — the Financial Times brings you:

 Fast, meaningful overviews of international affairs ... plus daily briefings on major world news.

 Perceptive coverage of economic, business, financial and political developments with special focus on emerging markets.

 More international business news than any other publication.

 Sophisticated financial analysis and commentary on world market activity plus stock quotes from over 30 countries.

 Reports on international companies and a section on global investing.

 Specialized pages on management, marketing, advertising and technological innovations from all parts of the world.

 Highly valued single-topic special reports (over 200 annually) on countries, industries, investment opportunities, technology and more.

Ⓐ The Saturday Weekend FT section — a globetrotter's guide to leisure-time activities around the world: the arts, fine dining, travel, sports and more.

FT FINANCIAL TIMES
World business newspaper

The *Financial Times* delivers a world of business news.

Use the Risk-Free Trial Voucher below!

To stay ahead in today's business world you need to be well-informed on a daily basis. And not just on the national level. You need a news source that closely monitors the entire world of business, and then delivers it in a concise, quick-read format.

With the *Financial Times* you get the major stories from every region of the world. Reports found nowhere else. You get business, management, politics, economics, technology and more.

Now you can try the *Financial Times* for 4 weeks, absolutely risk free. And better yet, if you wish to continue receiving the *Financial Times* you'll get great savings off the regular subscription rate. Just use the voucher below.

---

4 Week Risk-Free Trial Voucher

Yes! Please send me the *Financial Times* for 4 weeks (Monday through Saturday) Risk-Free, and details of special subscription rates in my country.

Name _____

Company _____

Address _____ ❏ Business or ❏ Home Address

Apt./Suite/Floor _____ City _____ State/Province_____

Zip/Postal Code_____ Country _____

Phone (optional) _____ E-mail (optional)_____

Limited time offer good for new subscribers in FT delivery areas only.

To order contact Financial Times Customer Service in your area (mention offer SAB01A).

The Americas: Tel 800-628-8088 Fax 845-566-8220 E-mail: uscirculation@ft.com

Europe: Tel 44 20 7873 4200 Fax 44 20 7873 3428 E-mail: fte.subs@ft.com

Japan: Tel 0120 341-468 Fax 0120 593-146 E-mail: circulation.fttokyo@ft.com

Korea: E-mail: sungho.yang@ft.com

S.E. Asia: Tel 852 2905 5555 Fax 852 2905 5590 E-mail: subseasia@ft.com

www.ft.com

FT FINANCIAL TIMES
World business newspaper

Where to find tomorrow's best business and technology ideas. TODAY.

- Ideas for defining tomorrow's competitive strategies — and executing them.

- Ideas that reflect a profound understanding of today's global business realities.

- Ideas that will help you achieve unprecedented customer and enterprise value.

- Ideas that illuminate the powerful new connections between business and technology.

ONE PUBLISHER.
Financial Times Prentice Hall.

FT Prentice Hall
FINANCIAL TIMES

WORLD BUSINESS PUBLISHER

AND 3 GREAT WEB SITES:

Business-minds.com

Where the thought leaders of the business world gather to share key ideas, techniques, resources — and inspiration.

InformIt.com

Your link to today's top business and technology experts: new content, practical solutions, and the world's best online training.

ft-ph.com

Fast access to all Financial Times Prentice Hall business books currently available.